ABCTE
Professional
Teaching Knowledge

SECRETS

Study Guide
Your Key to Exam Success

**ABCTE Test Review for the
American Board for Certification of
Teacher Excellence Exam**

Dear Future Exam Success Story:

First of all, **THANK YOU** for purchasing Mometrix study materials!

Second, congratulations! You are one of the few determined test-takers who are committed to doing whatever it takes to excel on your exam. **You have come to the right place.** We developed these study materials with one goal in mind: to deliver you the information you need in a format that's concise and easy to use.

In addition to optimizing your guide for the content of the test, we've outlined our recommended steps for breaking down the preparation process into small, attainable goals so you can make sure you stay on track.

We've also analyzed the entire test-taking process, identifying the most common pitfalls and showing how you can overcome them and be ready for any curveball the test throws you.

Standardized testing is one of the biggest obstacles on your road to success, which only increases the importance of doing well in the high-pressure, high-stakes environment of test day. Your results on this test could have a significant impact on your future, and this guide provides the information and practical advice to help you achieve your full potential on test day.

Your success is our success

We would love to hear from you! If you would like to share the story of your exam success or if you have any questions or comments in regard to our products, please contact us at **800-673-8175** or **support@mometrix.com**.

Thanks again for your business and we wish you continued success!

Sincerely,
The Mometrix Test Preparation Team

Need more help? Check out our flashcards at: http://MometrixFlashcards.com/ABCTE

TABLE OF CONTENTS

Introduction

Thank you for purchasing this resource! You have made the choice to prepare yourself for a test that could have a huge impact on your future, and this guide is designed to help you be fully ready for test day. Obviously, it's important to have a solid understanding of the test material, but you also need to be prepared for the unique environment and stressors of the test, so that you can perform to the best of your abilities.

For this purpose, the first section that appears in this guide is the **Secret Keys**. We've devoted countless hours to meticulously researching what works and what doesn't, and we've boiled down our findings to the five most impactful steps you can take to improve your performance on the test. We start at the beginning with study planning and move through the preparation process, all the way to the testing strategies that will help you get the most out of what you know when you're finally sitting in front of the test.

We recommend that you start preparing for your test as far in advance as possible. However, if you've bought this guide as a last-minute study resource and only have a few days before your test, we recommend that you skip over the first two Secret Keys since they address a long-term study plan.

If you struggle with **test anxiety**, we strongly encourage you to check out our recommendations for how you can overcome it. Test anxiety is a formidable foe, but it can be beaten, and we want to make sure you have the tools you need to defeat it.

Secret Key #1 – Plan Big, Study Small

There's a lot riding on your performance. If you want to ace this test, you're going to need to keep your skills sharp and the material fresh in your mind. You need a plan that lets you review everything you need to know while still fitting in your schedule. We'll break this strategy down into three categories.

Information Organization

Start with the information you already have: the official test outline. From this, you can make a complete list of all the concepts you need to cover before the test. Organize these concepts into groups that can be studied together, and create a list of any related vocabulary you need to learn so you can brush up on any difficult terms. You'll want to keep this vocabulary list handy once you actually start studying since you may need to add to it along the way.

Time Management

Once you have your set of study concepts, decide how to spread them out over the time you have left before the test. Break your study plan into small, clear goals so you have a manageable task for each day and know exactly what you're doing. Then just focus on one small step at a time. When you manage your time this way, you don't need to spend hours at a time studying. Studying a small block of content for a short period each day helps you retain information better and avoid stressing over how much you have left to do. You can relax knowing that you have a plan to cover everything in time. In order for this strategy to be effective though, you have to start studying early and stick to your schedule. Avoid the exhaustion and futility that comes from last-minute cramming!

Study Environment

The environment you study in has a big impact on your learning. Studying in a coffee shop, while probably more enjoyable, is not likely to be as fruitful as studying in a quiet room. It's important to keep distractions to a minimum. You're only planning to study for a short block of time, so make the most of it. Don't pause to check your phone or get up to find a snack. It's also important to **avoid multitasking**. Research has consistently shown that multitasking will make your studying dramatically less effective. Your study area should also be comfortable and well-lit so you don't have the distraction of straining your eyes or sitting on an uncomfortable chair.

The time of day you study is also important. You want to be rested and alert. Don't wait until just before bedtime. Study when you'll be most likely to comprehend and remember. Even better, if you know what time of day your test will be, set that time aside for study. That way your brain will be used to working on that subject at that specific time and you'll have a better chance of recalling information.

Finally, it can be helpful to team up with others who are studying for the same test. Your actual studying should be done in as isolated an environment as possible, but the work of organizing the information and setting up the study plan can be divided up. In between study sessions, you can discuss with your teammates the concepts that you're all studying and quiz each other on the details. Just be sure that your teammates are as serious about the test as you are. If you find that your study time is being replaced with social time, you might need to find a new team.

Secret Key #2 – Make Your Studying Count

You're devoting a lot of time and effort to preparing for this test, so you want to be absolutely certain it will pay off. This means doing more than just reading the content and hoping you can remember it on test day. It's important to make every minute of study count. There are two main areas you can focus on to make your studying count:

Retention

It doesn't matter how much time you study if you can't remember the material. You need to make sure you are retaining the concepts. To check your retention of the information you're learning, try recalling it at later times with minimal prompting. Try carrying around flashcards and glance at one or two from time to time or ask a friend who's also studying for the test to quiz you.

To enhance your retention, look for ways to put the information into practice so that you can apply it rather than simply recalling it. If you're using the information in practical ways, it will be much easier to remember. Similarly, it helps to solidify a concept in your mind if you're not only reading it to yourself but also explaining it to someone else. Ask a friend to let you teach them about a concept you're a little shaky on (or speak aloud to an imaginary audience if necessary). As you try to summarize, define, give examples, and answer your friend's questions, you'll understand the concepts better and they will stay with you longer. Finally, step back for a big picture view and ask yourself how each piece of information fits with the whole subject. When you link the different concepts together and see them working together as a whole, it's easier to remember the individual components.

Finally, practice showing your work on any multi-step problems, even if you're just studying. Writing out each step you take to solve a problem will help solidify the process in your mind, and you'll be more likely to remember it during the test.

Modality

Modality simply refers to the means or method by which you study. Choosing a study modality that fits your own individual learning style is crucial. No two people learn best in exactly the same way, so it's important to know your strengths and use them to your advantage.

For example, if you learn best by visualization, focus on visualizing a concept in your mind and draw an image or a diagram. Try color-coding your notes, illustrating them, or creating symbols that will trigger your mind to recall a learned concept. If you learn best by hearing or discussing information, find a study partner who learns the same way or read aloud to yourself. Think about how to put the information in your own words. Imagine that you are giving a lecture on the topic and record yourself so you can listen to it later.

For any learning style, flashcards can be helpful. Organize the information so you can take advantage of spare moments to review. Underline key words or phrases. Use different colors for different categories. Mnemonic devices (such as creating a short list in which every item starts with the same letter) can also help with retention. Find what works best for you and use it to store the information in your mind most effectively and easily.

Secret Key #3 – Practice the Right Way

Your success on test day depends not only on how many hours you put into preparing, but also on whether you prepared the right way. It's good to check along the way to see if your studying is paying off. One of the most effective ways to do this is by taking practice tests to evaluate your progress. Practice tests are useful because they show exactly where you need to improve. Every time you take a practice test, pay special attention to these three groups of questions:

- The questions you got wrong
- The questions you had to guess on, even if you guessed right
- The questions you found difficult or slow to work through

This will show you exactly what your weak areas are, and where you need to devote more study time. Ask yourself why each of these questions gave you trouble. Was it because you didn't understand the material? Was it because you didn't remember the vocabulary? Do you need more repetitions on this type of question to build speed and confidence? Dig into those questions and figure out how you can strengthen your weak areas as you go back to review the material.

Additionally, many practice tests have a section explaining the answer choices. It can be tempting to read the explanation and think that you now have a good understanding of the concept. However, an explanation likely only covers part of the question's broader context. Even if the explanation makes sense, **go back and investigate** every concept related to the question until you're positive you have a thorough understanding.

As you go along, keep in mind that the practice test is just that: practice. Memorizing these questions and answers will not be very helpful on the actual test because it is unlikely to have any of the same exact questions. If you only know the right answers to the sample questions, you won't be prepared for the real thing. **Study the concepts** until you understand them fully, and then you'll be able to answer any question that shows up on the test.

It's important to wait on the practice tests until you're ready. If you take a test on your first day of study, you may be overwhelmed by the amount of material covered and how much you need to learn. Work up to it gradually.

On test day, you'll need to be prepared for answering questions, managing your time, and using the test-taking strategies you've learned. It's a lot to balance, like a mental marathon that will have a big impact on your future. Like training for a marathon, you'll need to start slowly and work your way up. When test day arrives, you'll be ready.

Start with the strategies you've read in the first two Secret Keys—plan your course and study in the way that works best for you. If you have time, consider using multiple study resources to get different approaches to the same concepts. It can be helpful to see difficult concepts from more than one angle. Then find a good source for practice tests. Many times, the test website will suggest potential study resources or provide sample tests.

Practice Test Strategy

If you're able to find at least three practice tests, we recommend this strategy:

Untimed and Open-Book Practice

Take the first test with no time constraints and with your notes and study guide handy. Take your time and focus on applying the strategies you've learned.

Timed and Open-Book Practice

Take the second practice test open-book as well, but set a timer and practice pacing yourself to finish in time.

Timed and Closed-Book Practice

Take any other practice tests as if it were test day. Set a timer and put away your study materials. Sit at a table or desk in a quiet room, imagine yourself at the testing center, and answer questions as quickly and accurately as possible.

Keep repeating timed and closed-book tests on a regular basis until you run out of practice tests or it's time for the actual test. Your mind will be ready for the schedule and stress of test day, and you'll be able to focus on recalling the material you've learned.

Secret Key #4 – Pace Yourself

Once you're fully prepared for the material on the test, your biggest challenge on test day will be managing your time. Just knowing that the clock is ticking can make you panic even if you have plenty of time left. Work on pacing yourself so you can build confidence against the time constraints of the exam. Pacing is a difficult skill to master, especially in a high-pressure environment, so **practice is vital**.

Set time expectations for your pace based on how much time is available. For example, if a section has 60 questions and the time limit is 30 minutes, you know you have to average 30 seconds or less per question in order to answer them all. Although 30 seconds is the hard limit, set 25 seconds per question as your goal, so you reserve extra time to spend on harder questions. When you budget extra time for the harder questions, you no longer have any reason to stress when those questions take longer to answer.

Don't let this time expectation distract you from working through the test at a calm, steady pace, but keep it in mind so you don't spend too much time on any one question. Recognize that taking extra time on one question you don't understand may keep you from answering two that you do understand later in the test. If your time limit for a question is up and you're still not sure of the answer, mark it and move on, and come back to it later if the time and the test format allow. If the testing format doesn't allow you to return to earlier questions, just make an educated guess; then put it out of your mind and move on.

On the easier questions, be careful not to rush. It may seem wise to hurry through them so you have more time for the challenging ones, but it's not worth missing one if you know the concept and just didn't take the time to read the question fully. Work efficiently but make sure you understand the question and have looked at all of the answer choices, since more than one may seem right at first.

Even if you're paying attention to the time, you may find yourself a little behind at some point. You should speed up to get back on track, but do so wisely. Don't panic; just take a few seconds less on each question until you're caught up. Don't guess without thinking, but do look through the answer choices and eliminate any you know are wrong. If you can get down to two choices, it is often worthwhile to guess from those. Once you've chosen an answer, move on and don't dwell on any that you skipped or had to hurry through. If a question was taking too long, chances are it was one of the harder ones, so you weren't as likely to get it right anyway.

On the other hand, if you find yourself getting ahead of schedule, it may be beneficial to slow down a little. The more quickly you work, the more likely you are to make a careless mistake that will affect your score. You've budgeted time for each question, so don't be afraid to spend that time. Practice an efficient but careful pace to get the most out of the time you have.

Secret Key #5 – Have a Plan for Guessing

When you're taking the test, you may find yourself stuck on a question. Some of the answer choices seem better than others, but you don't see the one answer choice that is obviously correct. What do you do?

The scenario described above is very common, yet most test takers have not effectively prepared for it. Developing and practicing a plan for guessing may be one of the single most effective uses of your time as you get ready for the exam.

In developing your plan for guessing, there are three questions to address:

- When should you start the guessing process?
- How should you narrow down the choices?
- Which answer should you choose?

When to Start the Guessing Process

Unless your plan for guessing is to select C every time (which, despite its merits, is not what we recommend), you need to leave yourself enough time to apply your answer elimination strategies. Since you have a limited amount of time for each question, that means that if you're going to give yourself the best shot at guessing correctly, you have to decide quickly whether or not you will guess.

Of course, the best-case scenario is that you don't have to guess at all, so first, see if you can answer the question based on your knowledge of the subject and basic reasoning skills. Focus on the key words in the question and try to jog your memory of related topics. Give yourself a chance to bring the knowledge to mind, but once you realize that you don't have (or you can't access) the knowledge you need to answer the question, it's time to start the guessing process.

It's almost always better to start the guessing process too early than too late. It only takes a few seconds to remember something and answer the question from knowledge. Carefully eliminating wrong answer choices takes longer. Plus, going through the process of eliminating answer choices can actually help jog your memory.

Summary: Start the guessing process as soon as you decide that you can't answer the question based on your knowledge.

How to Narrow Down the Choices

The next chapter in this book (**Test-Taking Strategies**) includes a wide range of strategies for how to approach questions and how to look for answer choices to eliminate. You will definitely want to read those carefully, practice them, and figure out which ones work best for you. Here though, we're going to address a mindset rather than a particular strategy.

Your chances of guessing an answer correctly depend on how many options you are choosing from.

How many choices you have	How likely you are to guess correctly
5	20%
4	25%
3	33%
2	50%
1	100%

You can see from this chart just how valuable it is to be able to eliminate incorrect answers and make an educated guess, but there are two things that many test takers do that cause them to miss out on the benefits of guessing:

- Accidentally eliminating the correct answer
- Selecting an answer based on an impression

We'll look at the first one here, and the second one in the next section.

To avoid accidentally eliminating the correct answer, we recommend a thought exercise called **the $5 challenge**. In this challenge, you only eliminate an answer choice from contention if you are willing to bet $5 on it being wrong. Why $5? Five dollars is a small but not insignificant amount of money. It's an amount you could afford to lose but wouldn't want to throw away. And while losing $5 once might not hurt too much, doing it twenty times will set you back $100. In the same way, each small decision you make—eliminating a choice here, guessing on a question there—won't by itself impact your score very much, but when you put them all together, they can make a big difference. By holding each answer choice elimination decision to a higher standard, you can reduce the risk of accidentally eliminating the correct answer.

The $5 challenge can also be applied in a positive sense: If you are willing to bet $5 that an answer choice *is* correct, go ahead and mark it as correct.

Summary: Only eliminate an answer choice if you are willing to bet $5 that it is wrong.

Which Answer to Choose

You're taking the test. You've run into a hard question and decided you'll have to guess. You've eliminated all the answer choices you're willing to bet $5 on. Now you have to pick an answer. Why do we even need to talk about this? Why can't you just pick whichever one you feel like when the time comes?

The answer to these questions is that if you don't come into the test with a plan, you'll rely on your impression to select an answer choice, and if you do that, you risk falling into a trap. The test writers know that everyone who takes their test will be guessing on some of the questions, so they intentionally write wrong answer choices to seem plausible. You still have to pick an answer though, and if the wrong answer choices are designed to look right, how can you ever be sure that you're not falling for their trap? The best solution we've found to this dilemma is to take the decision out of your hands entirely. Here is the process we recommend:

Once you've eliminated any choices that you are confident (willing to bet $5) are wrong, select the first remaining choice as your answer.

Whether you choose to select the first remaining choice, the second, or the last, the important thing is that you use some preselected standard. Using this approach guarantees that you will not be enticed into selecting an answer choice that looks right, because you are not basing your decision on how the answer choices look.

This is not meant to make you question your knowledge. Instead, it is to help you recognize the difference between your knowledge and your impressions. There's a huge difference between thinking an answer is right because of what you know, and thinking an answer is right because it looks or sounds like it should be right.

Summary: To ensure that your selection is appropriately random, make a predetermined selection from among all answer choices you have not eliminated.

Test-Taking Strategies

This section contains a list of test-taking strategies that you may find helpful as you work through the test. By taking what you know and applying logical thought, you can maximize your chances of answering any question correctly!

It is very important to realize that every question is different and every person is different: no single strategy will work on every question, and no single strategy will work for every person. That's why we've included all of them here, so you can try them out and determine which ones work best for different types of questions and which ones work best for you.

Question Strategies

Read Carefully

Read the question and answer choices carefully. Don't miss the question because you misread the terms. You have plenty of time to read each question thoroughly and make sure you understand what is being asked. Yet a happy medium must be attained, so don't waste too much time. You must read carefully, but efficiently.

Contextual Clues

Look for contextual clues. If the question includes a word you are not familiar with, look at the immediate context for some indication of what the word might mean. Contextual clues can often give you all the information you need to decipher the meaning of an unfamiliar word. Even if you can't determine the meaning, you may be able to narrow down the possibilities enough to make a solid guess at the answer to the question.

Prefixes

If you're having trouble with a word in the question or answer choices, try dissecting it. Take advantage of every clue that the word might include. Prefixes and suffixes can be a huge help. Usually they allow you to determine a basic meaning. Pre- means before, post- means after, pro - is positive, de- is negative. From prefixes and suffixes, you can get an idea of the general meaning of the word and try to put it into context.

Hedge Words

Watch out for critical hedge words, such as *likely, may, can, sometimes, often, almost, mostly, usually, generally, rarely,* and *sometimes.* Question writers insert these hedge phrases to cover every possibility. Often an answer choice will be wrong simply because it leaves no room for exception. Be on guard for answer choices that have definitive words such as *exactly* and *always.*

Switchback Words

Stay alert for *switchbacks.* These are the words and phrases frequently used to alert you to shifts in thought. The most common switchback words are *but, although,* and *however.* Others include *nevertheless, on the other hand, even though, while, in spite of, despite, regardless of.* Switchback words are important to catch because they can change the direction of the question or an answer choice.

Face Value

When in doubt, use common sense. Accept the situation in the problem at face value. Don't read too much into it. These problems will not require you to make wild assumptions. If you have to go beyond creativity and warp time or space in order to have an answer choice fit the question, then you should move on and consider the other answer choices. These are normal problems rooted in reality. The applicable relationship or explanation may not be readily apparent, but it is there for you to figure out. Use your common sense to interpret anything that isn't clear.

Answer Choice Strategies

Answer Selection

The most thorough way to pick an answer choice is to identify and eliminate wrong answers until only one is left, then confirm it is the correct answer. Sometimes an answer choice may immediately seem right, but be careful. The test writers will usually put more than one reasonable answer choice on each question, so take a second to read all of them and make sure that the other choices are not equally obvious. As long as you have time left, it is better to read every answer choice than to pick the first one that looks right without checking the others.

Answer Choice Families

An answer choice family consists of two (in rare cases, three) answer choices that are very similar in construction and cannot all be true at the same time. If you see two answer choices that are direct opposites or parallels, one of them is usually the correct answer. For instance, if one answer choice says that quantity x increases and another either says that quantity x decreases (opposite) or says that quantity y increases (parallel), then those answer choices would fall into the same family. An answer choice that doesn't match the construction of the answer choice family is more likely to be incorrect. Most questions will not have answer choice families, but when they do appear, you should be prepared to recognize them.

Eliminate Answers

Eliminate answer choices as soon as you realize they are wrong, but make sure you consider all possibilities. If you are eliminating answer choices and realize that the last one you are left with is also wrong, don't panic. Start over and consider each choice again. There may be something you missed the first time that you will realize on the second pass.

Avoid Fact Traps

Don't be distracted by an answer choice that is factually true but doesn't answer the question. You are looking for the choice that answers the question. Stay focused on what the question is asking for so you don't accidentally pick an answer that is true but incorrect. Always go back to the question and make sure the answer choice you've selected actually answers the question and is not merely a true statement.

Extreme Statements

In general, you should avoid answers that put forth extreme actions as standard practice or proclaim controversial ideas as established fact. An answer choice that states the "process should be used in certain situations, if..." is much more likely to be correct than one that states the "process should be discontinued completely." The first is a calm rational statement and doesn't even make a definitive, uncompromising stance, using a hedge word *if* to provide wiggle room, whereas the second choice is a radical idea and far more extreme.

Benchmark

As you read through the answer choices and you come across one that seems to answer the question well, mentally select that answer choice. This is not your final answer, but it's the one that will help you evaluate the other answer choices. The one that you selected is your benchmark or standard for judging each of the other answer choices. Every other answer choice must be compared to your benchmark. That choice is correct until proven otherwise by another answer choice beating it. If you find a better answer, then that one becomes your new benchmark. Once you've decided that no other choice answers the question as well as your benchmark, you have your final answer.

Predict the Answer

Before you even start looking at the answer choices, it is often best to try to predict the answer. When you come up with the answer on your own, it is easier to avoid distractions and traps because you will know exactly what to look for. The right answer choice is unlikely to be word-for-word what you came up with, but it should be a close match. Even if you are confident that you have the right answer, you should still take the time to read each option before moving on.

General Strategies

Tough Questions

If you are stumped on a problem or it appears too hard or too difficult, don't waste time. Move on! Remember though, if you can quickly check for obviously incorrect answer choices, your chances of guessing correctly are greatly improved. Before you completely give up, at least try to knock out a couple of possible answers. Eliminate what you can and then guess at the remaining answer choices before moving on.

Check Your Work

Since you will probably not know every term listed and the answer to every question, it is important that you get credit for the ones that you do know. Don't miss any questions through careless mistakes. If at all possible, try to take a second to look back over your answer selection and make sure you've selected the correct answer choice and haven't made a costly careless mistake (such as marking an answer choice that you didn't mean to mark). This quick double check should more than pay for itself in caught mistakes for the time it costs.

Pace Yourself

It's easy to be overwhelmed when you're looking at a page full of questions; your mind is confused and full of random thoughts, and the clock is ticking down faster than you would like. Calm down and maintain the pace that you have set for yourself. Especially as you get down to the last few minutes of the test, don't let the small numbers on the clock make you panic. As long as you are on track by monitoring your pace, you are guaranteed to have time for each question.

Don't Rush

It is very easy to make errors when you are in a hurry. Maintaining a fast pace in answering questions is pointless if it makes you miss questions that you would have gotten right otherwise. Test writers like to include distracting information and wrong answers that seem right. Taking a little extra time to avoid careless mistakes can make all the difference in your test score. Find a pace that allows you to be confident in the answers that you select.

Keep Moving

Panicking will not help you pass the test, so do your best to stay calm and keep moving. Taking deep breaths and going through the answer elimination steps you practiced can help to break through a stress barrier and keep your pace.

Final Notes

The combination of a solid foundation of content knowledge and the confidence that comes from practicing your plan for applying that knowledge is the key to maximizing your performance on test day. As your foundation of content knowledge is built up and strengthened, you'll find that the strategies included in this chapter become more and more effective in helping you quickly sift through the distractions and traps of the test to isolate the correct answer.

Now it's time to move on to the test content chapters of this book, but be sure to keep your goal in mind. As you read, think about how you will be able to apply this information on the test. If you've already seen sample questions for the test and you have an idea of the question format and style, try to come up with questions of your own that you can answer based on what you're reading. This will give you valuable practice applying your knowledge in the same ways you can expect to on test day.

Good luck and good studying!

Instructional Design

Student diversity

Many people think of visible racial differences—African-American, Caucasian, Asian, Asian Indian, Hispanic, Native American, Pacific Islander, etc.—when they think of diversity. However, diversity also includes socioeconomic, from the highest wealthy tiers to the impoverished and everything in between; homelessness; living in transitional housing; all manners of disabilities, both obvious and "hidden"; intellectual and creative giftedness; urban, suburban, exurban, and rural living; different home cultures; learning English as a new language; illiterate families, parents with advanced degrees, and everything in between; younger and older ages than classmates; and many more. General principles include: treat students as individuals with unique, complex identities; ask open-ended questions, inviting reports of experiences and observations. Do not ask students to speak for their minority group. Pronounce every student's name correctly. Be aware of influences on student responses by making eye contact with everybody. Extend wait time to include more reflective and less assertive students. Ask questions challenging dominant students by drawing out quieter students in small groups; talk with and encourage students outside class. Vary teaching methods to address various learning styles and expand student strategy repertoires. Establish egalitarian norms and rules, promoting respect. Be cognizant of potential student performance anxiety in competitive settings, but not overprotective. Empathetically and tactfully give clear, straightforward standards, assessment criteria, and early feedback.

Native English speakers, including teachers, may take for granted the many idiomatic expressions we use, e.g., "between a rock and a hard place," "once in a blue moon," etc. But because they do not convey literal meanings, these sayings confuse students whose first language is not English, causing them to miss important concepts. Teachers should avoid using idioms. If they do, they should translate and/or explain them. All students benefit from linguistic redundancy, e.g., seeing print or writing while hearing speech; ELLs especially benefit. Teachers reinforce information by presenting it in multiple forms. They should also examine whether the examples they give assume or favor certain experiences or backgrounds, e.g., hobbies or activities preferred by one gender; examples based on regional, cultural, historical, or political knowledge unfamiliar to students from other countries, regions, or cultures. Teachers should provide diverse examples. They can learn some of these from their students. Teachers should not assume students who do not speak up do not know class material: Asian and other cultures find silence respectful and frown on attracting attention, while some students have learned responses to aversive consequences for participating. Teachers should also examine classroom humor to ensure jokes do not disparage any groups or differences, which occurs surprisingly often.

Cognitive disabilities

(1) Intellectual disability (ID): students function intellectually two standard deviations or more lower than average age peers. Adaptive functioning may be equal, higher, or lower than intellectual functioning depending on strengths, background experience, and training. Students often learn the same ways as others, but at slower rates. Developmental milestones occur at later ages; learning accomplishments take longer periods to acquire. Emotional and social maturity often correspond to mental age, but also frequently advance beyond it with experience. Students have difficulty understanding abstract concepts, interpreting things literally and concretely. (2) Autism spectrum disorders (ASD): considered an emotional as well as cognitive disability, the spectrum ranges from profound to negligible impairment in activities of daily living and behavior. Intelligence ranges from profound ID to gifted. ASDs often impair social understanding and interaction, e.g., observing,

interpreting, and producing nonverbal signals indicating emotions, attitudes, etc. Students have difficulty recognizing sarcasm, figurative language, humor; starting conversations; and conversational give-and-take. Behavioral characteristics include repetitive actions, restricted interests, rigid routines or schedules, focusing on one activity for long times, and difficulty transitioning among activities. (3) <u>Specific learning disabilities</u>: students are not intellectually impaired, but have deficits processing linguistic and/or numeric information. Typically their school achievement is far behind their intellectual ability.

Auditory disabilities

(1) One auditory disability not involving the hearing mechanism is central auditory processing disorder, a neurological deficit in interpreting the structure and meanings of speech sounds. Other auditory disabilities involve hearing loss. (2) Totally deaf students cannot hear any sound, often not even with hearing aids. (3) Hard of hearing students have hearing loss but some residual hearing. Hearing loss can be sensorineural, i.e., the cochlea, cochlear hair cells, and acoustic or auditory nerves do not function; or conductive, i.e., something in the outer or middle ear prevents conduction of sound waves, e.g., outer-ear wax buildup, middle-ear pus, fluid from otitis media infection, fused or immobilized middle-ear ossicles from otosclerosis, etc. Sensorineural hearing loss is irreversible, but cochlear implants enable hearing for some. Conductive hearing loss is most often treatable with surgery, medication, hearing aids, etc. Slight hearing loss, i.e., inability to hear whispering, is measured at 25-40 dB; mild hearing loss, i.e., understanding conversation with normal loudness up to 3-5 feet, 41-54 dB; moderate hearing loss, i.e., only understanding loud speech nearby, 55-69 dB; severe hearing loss, i.e., hearing only loud voices a foot away, 70-89 dB; profound hearing loss, i.e., feeling vibrations but not hearing tones, 90 dB or more. Noise-induced hearing loss is only at middle frequency (c. 4000 Hz).

Visual impairments

The definition of 20/20 vision is reading at 20 feet from a Snellen eye chart what one normally should see. Comparably, 20/200 vision is reading at 20 feet what one should see at 200 feet. Legal blindness is defined as 20/200 after correction in the better eye. Low vision is described as anywhere from 20/200 to 20/70 after correction in the better eye and a visual field of 30 degrees or less. A visual field of 20 degrees or less is tunnel vision. Travel vision ranges from 5/200 to 10/200. Motion perception is 3/200 to 5/200, typically for moving objects. Seeing bright light from 3 feet away but not movement, i.e., below 3/200 vision, is light perception. Not seeing strong light directly in the eyes is total blindness. Students may be born blind or become blind adventitiously. Some children are born with congenital cataracts, causing opacity clouding the lenses and blindness unless surgically removed with a replacement lens implanted. Students with diabetes can develop diabetic retinopathy, i.e., vascular changes causing retinal hemorrhaging and blindness. Some students inherit glaucoma, wherein inner-eye fluid buildup creates pressure which causes visual impairment and blindness when untreated. Genetically, students may inherit total or red-green color-blindness; lack of pigment in albinism causes photosensitivity and vision problems. Accidents or injuries include retinopathy of prematurity from insufficiently regulated incubator oxygen, eyeball punctures, and retinal dislocation or detachment.

Motor or physical disabilities

Physical or motor disabilities impair mobility and may also affect coordination, balance, strength, and/or flexibility. Some students are missing one or more limbs, congenitally or through accident, injury, or amputation. They may use prostheses and/or wheelchairs, walkers, canes, crutches or other mobility aids. Students with cerebral palsy have neurological deficits in control and

- 16 -

coordination of muscular movements. Impairments range from a slight limp to being in a wheelchair or bed-bound. Cerebral palsy (CP) patients often have dyspraxia or apraxia, i.e., impaired development of their motor coordination. This can affect any body parts, e.g., speech muscles, hand grasp, fine motor skills, walking, etc. with varying degrees of severity. CP also causes spasticity, i.e., excessive muscle tension or rigidity; athetosis, i.e., excessive involuntary body movements; or both combined. Students born with spina bifida may have foot, ankle, or lower-limb weakness to below-waist paralysis, depending on the spinal level of incomplete neural tube closure. Students with severe type 1 diabetes may require amputations when the disease impairs blood circulation, especially in their lower extremities. In addition to assistive and adaptive devices and prostheses, treatments include physical therapy for large muscles, occupational therapy for small muscles, recreational therapy for adapted activities, etc.

Speech or language disorders

Speech or language disorders may involve speech only, language only, or both. Speech-only disorders include articulation disorders, the most common of which makes children distort, substitute, or omit certain speech sounds—typically consonants—at ages above typical norms for correct pronunciation. Typical remediation is speech therapy, which can include exercising articulatory muscles, audio feedback, targeting correct articulatory positions, tools (tongue depressors and bite plates), etc. Voice disorders include hypernasality, often secondary to cleft palate; hoarseness secondary to vocal polyps, nodules, or dysarthria (a neurological muscular control disorder); too-high, too-low, or unstable pitch; volume control problems, etc. Treatment depends on causes: nodules and polyps are surgically removed, clefts are repaired, and therapeutic techniques address other problems. Another speech disorder is stuttering, or rate and rhythm disorders. A variety of therapies exists, such as breathing methods, delayed auditory feedback, etc. Some stutterers actually outgrow the condition regardless of therapy. Some become "fluent stutterers." Some benefit greatly from some therapies, some little or none. Language disorders include delayed language development, secondary to intellectual disability or environmental deprivation; aphasia, secondary to neurological damage or deficits, e.g., traumatic brain injury or cerebral palsy, impairing expressive and/or receptive language processing; and language-related learning disabilities, like dyslexia (reading) or dysgraphia (writing). Language disorder therapies include stimulation and practice.

Impacts sensory impairments have on learning

Students with visual impairments miss a lot of input in our highly visually-oriented society. Orientation and mobility specialists can help them navigate school and other public environments more independently. Blind students may have canes or service dogs to aid mobility; teachers must plan for these and classmate interactions with them. In classrooms, blind and visually impaired students benefit from magnifiers, large-print texts, seating close to the board and teacher, audiobooks, and text-to-speech computer software for adapting texts; speech-to-text software for dictating written compositions; Braille materials or OptaCons for reading; and modified lighting, brighter and/or with less glare depending on the type and degree of impairment. Teachers can also provide materials with bright, solid colors and bold black outlines. Students with hearing impairments are safer in environments that accompany sound-based fire alarms with strobe lights. Teachers and classmates must remember to face or touch them to get their attention; speak face-to-face with students who read lips; include American Sign Language (ASL) interpreters in conversations or lessons for students who have them; and accompany spoken instruction and discussion with supplementary visual information. Speech-to-text software enables deaf and hearing-impaired students to read spoken language. Educators must also respect and teach classmates the importance and strength of deaf culture for students identifying with it.

Behavioral disorders

Attention deficit hyperactivity disorder (ADHD) is familiar to many: student attention spans are deficiently short; students are too easily distracted; self-regulation deficits cause impulsive behaviors; students display excessive physical activity and have difficulty sitting still, focusing attention, and persisting in the same activity for extended durations. Medication like Ritalin, Cylert, other stimulants—even caffeine—enable better focusing, but must be accompanied by behavioral therapy. Some students are identified with oppositional defiant disorder (ODD), symptomatized by irritability, aggression, hostility, negativity, and defiance. They frequently lose their tempers, argue with adults, purposely irritate others, blame others for their behaviors and mistakes, express or demonstrate anger and resentment, and act vindictively and spitefully. Roughly half of preschoolers with ODD outgrow it by age 8, a few develop ADHD instead, and some develop comorbid disorders (anxiety, depression). Some develop conduct disorder (CD) in a few years. ODD students tend to have better school performance but worse social skills than CD patients. CD is the severest childhood psychiatric disorder, involving physical aggression to people and animals, bullying, cruelty, property destruction, lying, theft, and serious rule or legal violations. Nearly 20 percent of teens with ODD or CD have antisocial personality disorder (APD)—an extension of CD—in adulthood. Multisystem therapy is most effective; many improve, but few completely recover.

Different disorders can cause similar classroom behaviors. For example, students with intellectual disabilities (ID), autism spectrum disorders (ASD), communication disorders, attention deficit hyperactivity disorder (ADHD), and others can all display disruptive behaviors. The reasons may differ, but the net results are the same. Some inappropriate behaviors are caused by lack of maturity or understanding, as with IDs. Students with ASDs, communication disorders, or ADHD may explode out of frustration over not having their needs met. Students with communication deficits may scream, hit, or throw things in lieu of having the language or speech skills to express what they feel, need, or want. ADHD students unable to sit still or concentrate often disrupt classes with out-of-seat behavior, excessive movements, vocal interruptions, etc. ASD students can have "meltdowns" or tantrums at sensory overload, having to switch activities, etc. Students with IDs or emotional or behavioral disorders often have immature or deficient self-regulation abilities. Attention-seeking behaviors are frequently inadvertently reinforced by the attention of adults trying to address them. While it requires planning and consistent, systematic implementation, behavior modification techniques can successfully resolve many behavioral dilemmas by teaching more acceptable replacement behaviors for communicating, meeting needs, making adjustments, and establishing and reinforcing self-control and social interaction skills.

Learning style, gender, culture, socioeconomic status, and prior knowledge and experience

Learning style: student A is nonplused by verbal teacher explanation of a new physics concept, but lights up immediately when shown a drawing of it (visual learning style). Student B does not understand the drawing, but "gets" it exactly when guided by the teacher to act it out physically (kinesthetic learning style). Gender: boys are physically aggressive; girls engage in relational aggression (hurting feelings, undermining self-esteem and reputations). Boys respond positively when educators redirect their aggression to athletic competition; girls when educators redirect their energy to performing services helping others. Culture: students from Asian, Latin, and Native American cultures prefer cooperative over competitive activities; helping others and being part of the group is more important to them than standing out individually. They volunteer to speak in class less not for lack of preparation but to show respect. Socioeconomic status: students in poverty miss school from lacking proper clothing and shoes. Malnutrition impairs ability to concentrate, remember, and perform. Affluent parents can afford private tutoring if their children struggle with academic subjects; poor ones cannot. Prior knowledge and experience: students with marginal

- 18 -

literacy cannot write stories but excel at oral storytelling, a strong and familiar tradition in their cultures and families.

Motivation, self-confidence, self-esteem, cognitive development, maturity, and language

Motivation: the best-designed and implemented instruction will fail if students are not first motivated. Research finds internal locus of control, wherein students attribute their success or failure to causes within themselves (ability, effort, interest, or ambition, for instance), more motivating for achievement than external locus of control, wherein students attribute their success or failure to outside causes (unfair tests, poor teachers, distracting classmates, classroom conditions). Teachers engage student interest by selecting subjects students want to know about, and offering choices of learning activities and specific subtopics to investigate. Self-confidence: students lacking overall self-confidence hesitate to try anything, anticipating failure. They need encouragement and approval of themselves as persons, plus ample reinforcement of every initial small success. Others only lack self-confidence for specific tasks or subjects; Bandura calls this self-efficacy. Providing alternative learning methods and enabling successful experiences improve self-efficacy. Self-esteem: largely determines self-confidence. Teachers can raise self-esteem by showing and communicating that they value and care about students, entrusting them with responsibilities, and recognizing their accomplishments. Cognitive development: students cognitively ahead of or behind classmates need differentiated instruction appropriate to their cognitive levels for engagement and achievement. Maturity: teachers must consider whether emotional or social maturity differs from physical and/or cognitive maturity and interact appropriately. Language: many teachers mistake ELL deficits for learning disabilities, causing overrepresentation in special education.

Americans with Disabilities Act (ADA)

Signed into law in 1990, the ADA granted the same civil rights protections based on disabilities as previously accorded by the 1964 Civil Rights Act based on race, color, religion, gender, or national origin. The ADA was thus modeled on the Civil Rights Act, and also on the 1973 Rehabilitation Act requiring federally funded programs and activities to provide equal access to persons having disabilities. The terms of the ADA include public buildings, facilities, programs, and activities, which include all public school buildings, facilities, programs, and activities. Hence this law makes it illegal for public schools to prevent students with disabilities from accessing them because of architectural and other barriers. Titles II and III of the ADA include enforceable standards for accessible design and construction of buildings and facilities, barrier removal, alterations, and accessibility. Predating the Individuals with Disabilities Education Act (IDEA), which would more extensively address the rights of children with disabilities to education, the ADA also requires equal opportunities, participation, and benefits from public facilities for individuals with disabilities, "in the most integrated setting appropriate to the needs of the individual." This foreshadowed the IDEA's later emphasis on inclusion. The ADA prohibits discrimination based on disability.

Individuals with Disabilities Education Act (IDEA)

Passed in 1975 and reauthorized a number of times since, IDEA guarantees the right of children with disabilities to a free, appropriate, public education (FAPE) in the least restrictive environment (LRE) possible that meets their educational needs. The right to education of school-aged children is covered in IDEA Part B; Part C, added subsequently, addresses the right to early intervention and early childhood education of babies and toddlers with disabilities. The LRE clause has dual purposes: (1) to prevent segregation of children with disabilities to special schools or classes, and (2) to be interpreted differently according to the needs of every individual student. An important provision of IDEA is that every student to receive special education and related services for an identified, eligible disability must have an Individual Education Plan (IEP). An IEP team including students, teachers, parents, special educators, therapists, and others involved develops the student's IEP, identifying goals the student needs and is able to achieve; related, specific learning objectives; timeframes; and numerical criteria for determining success. The IEP includes any assistive and adaptive devices and equipment and other supports the student requires to achieve identified educational goals.

Section 504 of the Rehabilitation Act of 1973

Section 504 protects the rights of people with disabilities in activities and programs receiving federal funds by prohibiting discrimination against them based on disability. When the US Department of Education (ED) provides financial assistance to public school districts and other local or state education agencies, activities, or programs, it enforces Section 504. ED also has an Office for Civil Rights (OCR), headquartered in Washington, D.C. with 12 enforcement offices, to ensure civil rights laws including Section 504 are followed. Section 504 requires school districts to provide "free, appropriate public education" (FAPE) to each of their qualifying students with disabilities. This law defines an appropriate education as designed to meet disabled students' individual educational needs as well as ensuring that non-disabled students' needs are met; provided together with non-disabled students as much as meets the needs of the student with disabilities; having established evaluation and placement procedures to prevent inappropriate placement or misclassification, and periodic reevaluations; affording due process for parents to receive mandated notices, review their children's records, and challenge identification, evaluation, and placement choices.

Elementary and Secondary Education Act's (ESEA)

The Every Student Succeeds Act (ESSA), replacing the ESEA and NCLB acts, demands fair, rigorous accountability for all school performance levels; meeting diverse learner needs; and more equitable provision of fair opportunities for student success; to ensure opportunity and equity for every student. The reauthorization of ESEA into ESSA requires its programs to offer a wide range of supports and resources enabling students to graduate, attend college, and establish careers. ESSA includes programs for meeting the special educational needs of ELL students, students with disabilities, homeless students, Native American students, migrant workers' children, and delinquent and neglected students. It states the federal government's responsibility for giving assistance to rural school districts, districts sustaining impacts of federal activities and properties, and other high-need areas and regions. The 2010 ESEA reauthorization also proposed to increase support for inclusion and better outcomes for students with disabilities as a supplement to funding for the Individuals with Disabilities Education Act (IDEA). This support includes more appropriate, accurate assessment measures of students with disabilities; better teacher and administrator preparation for meeting diverse learner needs; and better locally and state-determined curricula, incorporating universal design principles, implemented by more districts and schools.

The ESEA's 2010 reauthorization continues formula grants to states and school districts for ELL programs, allowing a variety of program types and ELL teacher professional development. The 2010 reauthorization requires new state criteria for consistent eligibility determination, placement, and program or service duration based on valid, reliable state ELP assessments; and system implementation for evaluating ELL program effectiveness and garnering data on ELL subgroup achievement for driving better district program improvement decisions and effective program selection. This reauthorization also proposed new, competitive grants to states, districts, and nonprofits for innovative program development; best-practice knowledge base building; ELL

- 20 -

instructional practice improvement; and funding research, leadership, and partnerships for effective teacher development. Another provision requires states to adopt and implement statewide ELP standards by grade, aligned with state academic content standards for college and career readiness. Strengthening formula grants for meeting migrant student educational needs included updating the funding formula for timelier, accurate data incorporation; and facilitating and reinforcing interstate endeavors for supporting migrant student transitions into local communities and schools. Funds for homeless students were changed from Title I allocation shares to allocations based on student numbers. The administration proposed to remove service obstacles, clarify statutory ambiguities causing service delays, and require grantees to report academic outcomes.

Characteristics of ELL students as a population

The ELL student population is widely heterogeneous. Some families speak no English at home, only English, or several languages. They may identify only with American culture, strongly with several cultures, or deeply with one non-American culture. They have been stigmatized for not speaking English, speaking English, or how they speak English. They live in communities sharing common culture, without other ELLs, or have lived in America for generations. They struggle or excel in school—some in specific subjects. They may feel competent or disaffected in school. ELL immigration status, birthplace, socioeconomic status, academic knowledge, language proficiency levels, and expectations of school all vary. ELL student prevalence has extended from a few to all US states. This diversity within and among ELLs requires multiple responses for meeting educational needs. Disabilities are not more prevalent among ELLs: research shows assessments not distinguishing ELL status from disability cause misdiagnoses. Educators should not assume ELL students learn English easily or readily. Also, English oral fluency does not equal mastery: systematic academic assessments are necessary. Differing L1s, previous education, socioeconomic and immigration status mean not all ELLs learn English the same way. Accommodations benefit not only ELLs, but others. Vocabulary is not the sole focus of ELL instruction: structures and meanings are equally important, even with limited ELP.

Instructing ELL students effectively

Teachers should give ELLs challenging, meaningful curriculum content, text choices, and authentic reading and writing activities. Placement by academic achievement, not ELP, with high-quality instruction in challenging classes enables greater learning and performance. Technology supports ELL motivation, writing and editing skills development, and class blog and website collaboration. Teacher awareness of ELLs' previous literacy experiences, backgrounds, and L2 learning benefits and challenges enables more effective instruction. ELLs are challenged to understand implicit cultural norms and knowledge; learn to translate and code-switch; develop metalinguistic awareness; negotiate differences between school literacy practices and home or community; and address the social, cultural, and political dimensions of linguistic status issues. Studies show ELL reading comprehension, writer identity development, and peer collaboration are developed through extracurricular composition. Teachers can use these methods to promote ELL investment in school learning, decrease home-school distance, and help students view their home languages and cultures not as obstacles or discards, but educational resources and contributors. Teachers should teach K-12 ELLs academic literacy basics and help them connect school content to their own knowledge.

Classrooms where all students participate and have their educational needs met

Establish a classroom climate where students feel safe, secure, and engaged in learning rather than unchallenged or threatened. Discuss how students want the classroom to work and how to maintain the best climate. Promote cooperation, involvement, and a stimulating, inviting, productive, learner-friendly environment with functional, appealing arrangements and displays through a classroom plan, including students in decision-making processes. Organize the classroom to allow movement, stations for long-term involvement and learning, and easy technology and information access. Engage students in the processes of developing, comprehending, and maintaining procedures and routines, with a limited number of positively stated, specific, clear rules; practice and reinforce these throughout the school year. Assign and manage meaningful assignments with purposes, in real-life settings with audiences. Prepare for teaching: active student involvement in planning, preparing, implementing, and assessing learning units reduces behavior and discipline issues. Consider having students create and submit actual proposals to organizations, corporations, or city councils needing new ideas. Consistently communicate and reinforce class procedures and routines. Discuss behavior in class. Discuss adding, removing, or changing procedures. Have students enforce rules. Students' having a voice enables superior classroom functioning. Consistently celebrate success. Evaluate and reflect daily or weekly throughout the year.

Inclusive practices in regular education classrooms with special education students

According to expert Peter Westwood (2003), research into effective instruction finds that effective teachers keep the focus on academics; give students maximal opportunities for learning; demonstrate good classroom management; use work-oriented, business-like styles; express enthusiasm; communicate high expectations to students of what they can achieve; apply strategies for keeping students motivated, on-task, and productive; introduce new material step-by-step; use explicit and direct instruction techniques; structure all content; give clear explanations and instructions; closely monitor student activities; demonstrate appropriate strategies for approaching tasks; utilize varied resources; adjust instruction to individual student needs; reteach as needed; give students frequent feedback; and spend considerable amounts of time doing whole-class, interactive teaching. In classes including special education students, teachers include: descriptive praise and encouragement, ample guided practice, fast-paced lessons, high engagement and participation levels of all students, careful curriculum content sequencing and control, positive peer assistance and interactions, many practice and application opportunities, modeling of effective school task completion methods, interactive group teaching, and teaching students how best to attempt new learning tasks.

Creating supportive, positive classroom environments for student diversity

(1) Teachers can intentionally teach responsible behaviors. To afford a multidimensional approach for every student, particularly those requiring more intensive intervention, teachers can collaborate with parents, school psychologists, and counselors. General behaviors to teach include communication skills, social skills, character development, anger management, self-control skills, conflict resolution, decision-making skills, taking responsibility for one's actions, and developing emotional intelligence (EQ). (2) Teachers can establish classroom harmony through creating warm, supportive atmospheres wherein every student feels s/he is an important class member. Class meetings, class-building and team-building activities engender senses of a learning community and class ownership. Experts use the acronym "VIABLE": students develop self-respect and respect for authority figures when they feel they are *valued* by teachers and classmates, *included* in classroom activities, *accepted* in their classrooms and schools, have senses of *belonging* to cooperative learning groups, and adults who *listen* to and *encourage* them. (3) Teachers can empower students and promote their sense of class ownership by involving them actively in disciplinary processes. Instead of being part of the problem, students become part of the solution. Activities include

arranging study and homework buddies; peer tutors, mediators, and counselors; peer recognition; assigning classroom responsibilities; and student-led conferences.

Invite or involve parents to meet student needs together. The "crucial Cs of parental support" are parent-teacher Communication, Connection, and Collaboration. Invite other teachers and staff—administrators; school psychologists, counselors, social workers, nurses; speech language pathologists (SLPs), occupational therapists (OTs), physical education (PE) teachers, special education teachers, music teachers; ELL or bilingual teachers, etc.—to collaborate in solving learning and discipline problems. Encourage and praise students' positive steps, efforts, strengths, progress, and improvement, not just finished products. Encouragement helps students self-validate and reflect on their own responses to their strengths and accomplishments. Effective praise is informative and appreciative, not evaluative or controlling. Build senses of accomplishment and capability in all students, and particularly in those lacking the following: focus on improvement, not perfection; turn mistakes into learning opportunities; let students struggle and succeed within ability levels; build upon student strengths; analyze past successes, then focus on the present; acknowledge task difficulty; use task analysis; teach positive self-talk; celebrate all students' successes and achievements. Develop positive teacher-student relationships to receive and give respect. Listen to students. Communicate positive expectations. Involve students in class decision-making: use a suggestion box; provide "voice and choice." Show enthusiasm for teaching and learning. Show interest in student interests. Keep communication open. Accept and value diversity and individual differences. Model positive, helpful, and kind behaviors.

Curriculum scope and sequence

In curriculum design, curriculum scope is the breadth and depth in which it covers content in each subject; clearly identified learning objectives reflecting local, state, and national standards; or how coherent curriculum is made through instructing basic concepts across several years of content coverage. Scope includes both how much material teachers must cover on any specified topic, and how much teachers should expect students to accomplish resulting from instruction. Sequence is the order in which scope is taught. If educators fail to structure curriculum scope and sequence deliberately, they risk having students miss significant learning when instruction is delivered without adequate planning. As examples, elementary school teachers might use a curriculum organizer table or chart where they enter titles and descriptions of each learning unit by time period, and the subject focus of each unit (e.g., arranged horizontally in columns). In the first column, before the series of units per time period, they can label cells vertically to enter main ideas, i.e., core student understandings; key concepts and questions to focus learning; teacher focus, i.e., unit goals like language development, group work, a culminating activity, etc.; fundamental content; subject foci, e.g., literacy, math, and respective programs, tasks, texts, and resources to use.

Whereas scope represents breadth and depth of content coverage and learning objectives, sequence represents presenting material in logical order. Sequencing reflects the philosophy that students should be instructed starting with concrete concepts, becoming progressively more abstract throughout successive grade levels. After establishing scope, educators must determine when to teach it. This is important when certain learning is often dependent on previous other knowledge, e.g., understanding certain science or geography concepts requires certain numeracy skills. Even when some learning experiences are not reliant on mastering prerequisite knowledge, curricula may be sequenced instead according to increasing complexity, e.g., in science subjects; logical progression, e.g., from the local environment to the global environment in social studies; or psychological valence, e.g., from immediate to more distant interests in vocational education. Teachers must carefully sequence instruction, both within and across key learning areas (KLAs). For example, "reading effectively" would precede "writing effectively" in a curriculum sequence

- 23 -

represented by a curriculum map showing English Language Arts (ELAs) taught by KLA because receptive language like listening and reading develops before expressive language like speaking and writing. Critical text interpretation follows reading and writing. Similarly, understanding and applying numbers precedes selecting and utilizing measures.

The scope of a curriculum refers to all of the content it will include within a specified length of time. The curriculum sequence refers to at which points during the time range specific parts of the scope of learning will occur. In other words, educators must decide which content should be taught during certain grade levels, or to certain classes or student groups. Teachers must also determine sequencing within work units, courses, and school years. Hence scope and sequence support maximal student learning, as well as providing continual opportunities for students to learn. By coordinating the scope of curriculum content and the sequence of curriculum instruction, educators give order to their delivery of curricular content. For teaching and learning to be effective, the important parts of all subjects must be included in scope, and must be delivered in the right order for students to benefit. By mapping curriculum scope, teachers can ensure they integrate the state and district learning standards guiding their curriculum. By mapping sequence, they can ensure they address curricular principles as well as matching knowledge prerequisites, increasing complexity, logical progression, psychological preferences, or other factors influencing temporal order.

Curriculum scope and sequence work together to furnish instruction with an organized structure which enables students to receive the maximum numbers of opportunities to learn and to take advantage of these to learn the most that they can. For educators to overlook important parts of subject content instruction is entirely too easy without the organizing structure of curriculum scope and sequence. It is also much more difficult to deliver instruction depending on previous learning, and avoid repeating material over grade levels, without planning sequence in advance. Most states develop scope and sequence directly from state-level standards. Some school districts design curriculum frameworks, which provide the scope of content and sequence in which to teach it. It is also popular for state education departments and district curriculum departments to divide learning sequences into developmental strands or bands. A common method of organizing a curriculum scope is to divide it into key learning areas (KLAs) or integrated themes used as curriculum organizers. Depending on their size, structure, and sector, different schools approach curriculum scope and sequence development through different processes. Some states define scope and sequence in certain subjects, but leave this to individual districts in others.

Standards-based learning

In standards-based education, all grade levels and subjects have clear learning goals; all instruction and assessment are aligned to these because the strongest school-level influence on student achievement is opportunity to learn: students are unlikely to learn specific content without opportunity. Students are given multiple opportunities to demonstrate achievement because reading, math, social studies, and science should be treated like PE and music: poor initial performances do not receive low grades, but rather require repeated practice until students master the skills. Formative assessments, giving feedback and promoting growth, are emphasized because research shows effective feedback is the strongest single classroom instructional change increasing learning and achievement. Rubrics and scoring guides are consistently employed because they enable teachers to give students better, criterion-referenced feedback about specific skill and knowledge levels, not merely norm-referenced feedback via percentage scores. This helps teachers evaluate their learning objectives as well as advance student achievement. Teachers regularly report student progress toward learning goals because specific, formative, more frequent feedback than annual standardized tests critically affects teacher conscientiousness and effectiveness with

- 24 -

initiatives developing new reporting practices and forms; with instructing, assessing, and encouraging students; and student success. Instructional activities represent the "how," standards the "what" and "why" of school programs.

The US Department of Education (ED) funds and supports high curriculum standards in public schools, but does not itself develop them; individual state education departments do. ED has given over $350 million in funds to a consortium of the Council of Chief State School Officers and National Governors Association for developing the Common Core State Standards (CCSS). Most US states have voluntarily chosen to adopt these standards. The CCSS has a website with information. Additional sites with information on federal support of other state educational initiatives include a site on the Every Student Succeeds Act (ESSA, replacing No Child Left Behind, or NCLB) flexibility, whereby ED enables states to develop their own accountability systems; sites about the federal Race to the Top initiative and its assessment; and a webpage with US Secretary of Education Arne Duncan's speech about high standards. CCSS are concepts students should know and understand; school districts develop specific curricula, and teachers plan specific lessons, to help students master standards. Districts and schools have traditionally had printed copies of their state standards; today, these are typically also published online, the easiest way for teachers to access them—including any updates, which can be posted electronically more easily and frequently than printed.

While the abundance of federal-level and state-level curriculum standards might seem to facilitate teachers' preparing relevant classroom curricula, it can overwhelm educators trying to design standards-based learning units. However, teachers discover that standards enable more curricular focus, refinement of their previous work, clearer communication of expectations to students, and enhanced learning—provided some model and processes for classroom standards application, many of which are available today. Standards articulate clear expectations for what all students should know and be able to do—regardless of gender, minority status, socioeconomic status, history of academic success (or failure), and previous access or lack thereof to any kinds of educational opportunities—while addressing school constituencies' varying needs. Standards give states common referents for assuring coordinated functioning of educational system components across schools and districts; offer parents, businesses, and community stakeholders a common language for discussing educational processes and communicate shared learning expectations, enabling more effective partnering in education; provide impetus and focus for new school programs and innovations in organizing content, delivering instruction, and planning assessment; make teachers design more intentional, purposeful learning of important content; and for all students, clearly identify performance expectations and means for meeting them; promote more equitable, challenging, and rewarding experiences; and improve performance.

Cognitive, affective, and psychomotor domains

The cognitive domain represents mental skills, i.e., facts, information, ideas, and concepts that one can learn, understand, and apply. Among knowledge, skills, and attitudes that a learner can acquire, the cognitive domain corresponds most to *knowledge*. The affective domain represents emotional *attitudes* that one can develop and apply, with respect to the self and others. The psychomotor domain represents physical *skills* that one can learn and apply. For example, when a student reads some information about physical exercise, understands it, analyzes it, compares it with other information sources, judges it according to established criteria, and writes a paper about it, these activities are in the cognitive domain. When this student finds value in exercise knowledge, demonstrates this by voluntarily participating in athletic events, and becomes an accomplished athlete in a certain sport, these activities are in the affective domain. When this student watches, copies, practices, and perfects the specific physical skills required for his or her preferred sport, these activities are in the psychomotor domain.

Bloom's taxonomy

Bloom's 1950s taxonomy originally included levels or categories of knowledge, i.e., recalling learned information; comprehension, i.e., grasping, restating, and explaining meaning; application of knowledge to new and different situations; analysis, i.e., separating components of material and showing relationships among components; synthesis, i.e., bringing separate concepts and ideas together to create new wholes and relationships; and evaluation, i.e., judging the value or worth of information according to established criteria. Anderson and Krathwohl's 2001 revision changed these nouns to verbs: remember, understand, apply, analyze, evaluate, and create—also switching the order of evaluate from after synthesis to before create. Instructional objectives should include learning activities that address each of these categories, sequenced correspondingly from remembering to creating to reflect the hierarchy's progressively increasing difficulty. Krathwohl and Bloom's taxonomy in the affective domain covers receiving, or attending to something; responding, or showing new behaviors influenced by experience; valuing, or showing definitive commitment or involvement; organization, or integrating new values into priorities; characterization by value, or behaving consistently with new values. Dave (1970), Simpson (1972), and Harrow (1972)'s psychomotor taxonomies include observing a physical action or event; imitating another's action; practicing repeatedly; and adapting, i.e., fine-tuning performance. In all three domains, these taxonomies progress sequentially from basic to higher levels, as corresponding instructional objectives should.

Observable behavior

Educational interest in observable behaviors was influenced by behaviorist learning theory, which proposed that because internal mental or emotional states could not be externally observed or measured, the study and modification of behavior should be confined to observable behaviors, i.e., actions or states of being that others could outwardly observe an individual producing. However, because only observable behaviors could be accurately measured, these were the only kind that could be changed through behavior modification techniques based on operant conditioning principles. In applying Bloom's taxonomy to cognitive learning objectives, the same proposition is embraced in that only action verbs are appropriate. For example, under the second category of Understanding, the verb *understand* itself is not found because it is internal, hence impossible to quantify; action verbs under Understand include *describe, differentiate, discuss, cite examples of, demonstrate use of, identify, select, tell*, etc. Thus a good instructional objective would not require a student simply to know or remember something, which requires assuming the student knows or remembers, but rather to *recall, name, list*, or *repeat* it because these demonstrate the student's knowledge and memory in ways that others can observe.

Measurable outcomes

Learning objectives must be not only observable, meaning teachers and others can see, hear, or otherwise observe evidence a student has learned something; but also measurable, meaning there is some way to quantify the behavior demonstrating learning. Behaviorist learning theory pointed out only observable behaviors can be measured, therefore changed. As a corollary, it has demonstrated that by nature, observable behaviors can nearly always be measured because if people can observe another's behavior, they can also find a way of measuring it. To be measurable, outcomes or results must be specific. For example, "The student will use correct grammar" is not measurable because it is too vague, not specifying what or whether all or some percentage of grammar must be correct, etc. But the objective "The student, given a sentence written in the present or past tense, will be able to rewrite it in future tense with no contradictions (e.g., 'I will see them yesterday') or errors in tense" is a measurable objective, specifying the condition (given a sentence written in present or past tense) and behavior (rewrite it in future tense). These are elements of the ABCD method—*audience, behavior, conditions, degree of mastery* required (e.g. 100 percent, 95 percent, 90 percent, etc.).

Evaluating technological and other instructional resources

State education departments typically publish guidelines for their districts to evaluate instructional materials according to state criteria, aligned with state content standards and curriculum frameworks for each subject. In some instances, educators tasked with evaluating new instructional materials for certain subject domains (e.g., mathematics or science) and/or grade levels (e.g., preschool, elementary, middle, or high school), after studying various sets of evaluation criteria, found them all inadequate and decided to develop their own criteria instead. Some examples of elements found important to address and overlooked by existing criteria include: need for more authentic assessment practices within the materials evaluated; evaluation criteria focusing on technology's overall role in a specific instructional unit, rather than only criteria for evaluating individual pieces of technology; and criteria for evaluating whether an instructional unit is practical, e.g., whether teachers in schools with typical insufficient funding, overloaded classrooms, long hours, etc. can effectively implement the materials. Educators have consulted resources like standards published by national organizations for their discipline, e.g., the National Council of Teachers of Mathematics, National Council of Teachers of English; research articles and books on subject-specific assessment; local districts; and teacher and researcher experiences.

Learning resources vs. learning materials

Teaching resources include locations and means for finding teaching materials, e.g., websites, libraries, stores, etc.; intangibles, e.g., theories of learning or education, published research articles and books, or support from colleagues; and materials. Teaching materials most often mean concrete objects, e.g., worksheets, workbooks, or manipulatives including tools and games that students can physically handle and interact with to learn new concepts and skills. For example, younger students can use blocks to learn counting. Teaching materials should ideally be customized to the subject content, students in the class, and teacher using them. Students achieve more when their learning is supported by materials. For example, students learning a new skill in class have significant opportunities to practice it using a worksheet. This not only affords necessary repetition, but also enables independent student exploration of knowledge. Learning materials help structure lesson planning and delivery, especially in earlier grades, by guiding teachers and students through regular routines, e.g., having a weekly vocabulary game relieves teachers of pressure while giving students needed practice with new words taught weekly, as well as fun. Materials also facilitate differentiating instruction for individual students. Some teachers make their own; many more are available online, most free.

Thematic instruction

Thematic instruction reflects a holistic belief that learning is best in the context of a coherent whole, and connected to real life. Teaching thematically organizes curriculum around overarching themes—teaching around experiences, not isolated disciplines. For example, a teacher might design a unit wherein students explore a broad environmental theme including river basins, rain forests, communities, energy use, etc., simultaneously integrating reading, math, science, and social studies into each lesson. Thematic instruction's goal is teaching these cognitive skills within the context of real-world topics, combining both enough broadness to enable creative exploration and enough specificity for practical application. Teachers and students first choose a theme, typically around a broad concept—weather, democracy, etc.; or a large, integrated system such as an ecosystem, city, etc. They then organize their core curriculum's content knowledge and process skills learning objectives around the theme, e.g., with river basins, literature could include Mark Twain or other authors' books involving rivers; science could include floods, weather, etc.; social studies, the characteristics of river communities; math, calculating water volume and flow. Designing instruction includes combining subject hours, adjusting class schedules, inviting outside experts, planning field trips, team-teaching, etc. Teachers also encourage and assign student projects, which are naturally compatible with thematic units.

Interdisciplinary instruction

Interdisciplinary or cross-curricular instruction applies knowledge, principles, and values to multiple school disciplines and subjects concurrently. Disciplines and subjects are often related through central themes—thematic units have been identified as interdisciplinary teaching's organizational structure—or experiences, processes, topics, problems, and issues. Schools first integrated listening, speaking, reading, writing, and thinking as language arts components, thereafter trending to more widely integrating all curriculum subjects through unifying themes. Cross-curricular instruction is often a remedy to recurring educational problems like instruction in isolated skills and fragmentary learning; and a means of supporting goals like giving students more relevant curricula, teaching reasoning and thinking, and facilitating skills transfer to other contexts. It enables students to apply and integrate knowledge across subjects, which isolated skills instruction does not; raises student motivation and engagement when, through participation, students realize the value of the knowledge; and supplies conditions for effective learning. Subject teachers collaborate, for example, a PE and math teacher may combine math skills of counting and graphing with PE skills of throwing, catching, hitting, and kicking balls, including student practice and teacher assessment of both physical and numerical techniques. Elementary classroom teachers may combine multiple subjects in one thematic unit, e.g., using a bean-growing project to teach science via botany, the life cycle, research questions, and observation; mathematics via counting and measuring; and English-writing reports.

Teachers of different subjects collaborate to plan interdisciplinary instructional units, generating topics, and developing instruction and assessment. For example, math and PE teachers have students count the number of times they can hit paddleballs consecutively, practice graphing them, and practice paddleball skills. Teachers might assess counting skills observationally, assess paddleball skills by observing student demonstrations, and assess graphing skills by reviewing handmade or computer graphing assignments. Elementary-grade teachers integrate English, math, and science, connecting classroom plant study to forest field trips, having students write about these connections. Vocational or technical high school students restored a historic landmark, integrating what they learned in math, journalism, and shop classes—applying learning to a real-life experience. Students also transferred learning, using creative, original thinking: after successfully completing the restoration project, they generated ideas for additional school and community service projects integrating various school subjects, presenting their ideas to teachers. A social sciences and math teacher co-taught students using ancient Egyptian computation techniques, comparing them to modern-day math. Students discussed ancient math in historical context, reflecting on past and present and what "modern" meant. Teachers find students gain more complex understandings of disciplines and their relationships through interdisciplinary instruction.

Lesson plan that builds on prior student knowledge

One model (Cunningham, ASCD, 2009) contains eight steps. (1) Introduction: state overall lesson reason or purpose. Introduce main idea, topic, and key concepts. "Hook" student attention with a challenge or a quirky or amazing fact, etc. Explain lesson relevance for extending prior knowledge and promoting future learning. (2) Foundation: confirm prior student knowledge, either by clarifying or double-checking. Connect the lesson to standards. Tell students precisely what they will know and be able to do from the lesson. Include additional information, preparing the main lesson. Introduce essential vocabulary visually, aloud, in reading, and in writing. (3) Brain activation: clarify concepts; add information through probing questions, engaging students and building background. Brainstorm concepts, ideas, and possibilities, enabling students to clarify and expand thinking. Plan activities revealing misconceptions; correct or clarify these. (4) Body of new information: present the main lesson via whole-class lecture, teacher-supervised small-group, or partner activity, including teacher input of new and key points, reading, problem-solving, and active student participation with specific goals. (5) Clarification: check for understanding with sample questions, problems, or situations; guide learning; give practice. (6) Practice and review: supervise practice; work with students. (7) Independent practice: supervise, selecting further strategies for small groups needing them; others work independently. (8) Closure: connect lesson steps and information; summarize; discuss lesson in larger learning context; have students write or explain learning, ideas, questions, and problems.

Eight step lesson plan

Introduction – 5 minutes: teacher writes Lincoln's quotation of the Declaration of Independence's "All men are created equal"; students discuss potential 1860s meaning. Foundation - 5-10 minutes: brief discussion about slavery, men and women, educated and uneducated white men; the goal is explaining the significance of the Gettysburg Address to American history and today's voting rights. Key vocabulary words and phrases include *conceived in liberty; dedicated; proposition; equal*. Brain activation – 5 minutes: ask what the words mean, why Lincoln phrased it thus, what would happen today with this speech, what the speech informs us about 1860s America, how the phrase connects to the American history then and now, and how the first paragraph leads to the ideas in the second and third paragraphs. Body of new information - 10-15 minutes: referring to specified textbook pages and illustrations, discuss the Battle of Gettysburg. Teacher writes key ideas or notes on overhead; students add to history notes. Clarification - 5-10 minutes: students write reflections on text. Practice and review - 5-10 minutes: small-group discussions of the battle's and speech's significance, Lincoln's speaking on the battlefield, and its turning point in the Civil War. Independent practice - 10 minutes: students select and write brief summaries of two or three other key phrases from the speech. Closure - 5 minutes: students share phrases with partners, write favorites with short explanations on "exit passes," and the teacher collects these to assess understanding and inform tomorrow's lesson.

Technology applications whereby teachers can more efficiently complete tasks

Today, mobile applications abound to save teachers time, effort, and space on administrative tasks, freeing more of their attention for teaching and helping students learn. One example is an app for the iPad called Paperless Teacher (Evon Technologies). It automates and customizes processes of taking attendance, planning lessons, creating rubrics, and entering grades in grade books. It weighs each gradable element, e.g., attendance, participation, assignments, tests, and homework, according to teacher specifications, and then automatically calculates grades. It enables teachers to email these results directly to students and parents. This eliminates the repetition of entering names, calculating numbers, and entering them manually one at a time. Users can easily share common data using this app; hence teachers can exchange student profiles or lesson plans anytime, remotely and effortlessly. The app features an integrated Dropbox framework, preventing data loss and enabling users with various other devices to access data. Its Message User Interface enables exporting and emailing data sharing in format allowing other users to open data directly in their apps. This facilitates notifying students of tests, assignments, schedules, etc. Semester planning and grade setting are customizable for multiple semester plans or grading systems. A protection feature keeps data safe for separate users.

Roles that special education teachers can contribute to collaborative teaching activities

Special education teachers have great expertise in how to adapt curriculum and instruction and provide classroom modifications and accommodations for students with various disabilities who receive special education and related services. They can share knowledge with classroom teachers about instructional considerations for each category of disability, individual special education students, and their needs. Since the Individuals with Disabilities Education Act (IDEA) legislation first mandated education in the least restrictive environment possible for students with disabilities, inclusive education has increased and mainstreaming is more prevalent today. This presents challenges to regular classroom teachers, and advantages to collaborating with special education teachers, who can help integrate Individualized Education Program (IEP) goals into daily classroom instruction. In addition to knowing more techniques and strategies for teaching students with special needs, they also are likely familiar with individual special education students at their school to inform classroom teachers from experience about particularly effective and ineffective specific techniques. They can show new teachers how task analysis, chaining, and shaping enable intellectually disabled students to learn complex behaviors; advise newly mainstreaming teachers on practical matters like classroom logistics with wheelchairs and assistive devices, teaching other students device and disability etiquette; and help teachers coordinate varied adaptations, modifications, or accommodations to prevent their interference with each other.

Collaboration between library media specialists and classroom teachers

Library media specialists are experts at locating information and resources, among other things. As information specialists, they contribute skills for accessing and evaluating information resources in different formats for both students and teachers. They function as models for students, showing them strategies for finding, accessing, and evaluating information that is available in their school library media centers and outside them. Due to the impact of technology development on library media center environments, library media specialists also keep up with mastering the newest, continually evolving electronic resources, and pay ongoing attention to the quality, character, and ethical use of information in traditional and electronic formats. They are instructional partners collaborating with teachers, other educators, and administrators. They identify connections among school expectations for student learning, student achievement, school curriculum content, student information needs, and available information resources. They work closely and cooperatively with teachers in designing authentic learning activities and assessments. Collaborating with teachers, they help integrate information and communication skills to meet content standards. They have knowledge of current research literature in teaching and learning, and expertise for its application. They help students find information from multiple sources, evaluate it critically, and use it to support learning, problem-solving, and critical thinking.

Gifted and Talented Teachers

Teachers of the gifted and talented have specialized training in instructing this population. Considering mainstreaming requirements, increasing demographic diversity, school underfunding, staff shortages, and oversized classes, classroom teachers are challenged to meet all student needs in one class. They may have to spend large portions of time on differentiated instruction to students with disabilities, in addition to satisfying whole-class accountability requirements to cover enough required curriculum content and enable every student to perform to standards on high-stakes, large-scale tests to meet Adequate Yearly Progress (AYP). Some teachers having limited or no experience with gifted students may assume they can work more independently and need less teacher attention due to their high IQs and/or special talents. However, advanced students are frequently bored or impatient with the pace of instruction for average student abilities. They can demand more material to learn, at faster rates; more in-depth, extended, or enriched content; answers to their pressing questions; and advice, guidance, and feedback even as they work independently on projects. Teachers specializing in giftedness and creativity can help take some pressure off classroom teachers, by both working directly with these students, and giving teachers ideas for enrichment activities and coordinating these with classroom units and lessons.

Collaboration between paraprofessionals and classroom teachers

Teachers today not only must differentiate instruction for individual students with a diverse range of needs, they frequently must also do this with excessive class sizes. Teachers' aides and other paraprofessionals provide vital help with these demands. Their collaboration with teachers includes not only concrete assistance like taking attendance; physically setting up activities; helping with adaptive devices, distributing materials, snacks, etc.; but also scoring tests, grading papers; participating in training they receive from teachers, specialists, therapists, etc.; and then working one-on-one with individual students to deliver differentiated instruction and help students needing individual supervision for classroom tasks. They may be trained by school psychologists to observe students and collect behavioral data, relieving teachers of these additional duties. In mainstreamed classes, teachers cannot always work with all individual students enough. Paraprofessionals are invaluable in making it possible for more students to receive more individualized attention, supervision, and instruction more regularly, for longer time periods, and more often. They can enable more students to achieve their individual educational goals.

Individualized Education Program (IEP) team members

Student IEP team members can include any or all the following and more: parents; special education teachers; classroom teachers; audiologists; occupational, physical, speech-language, activity, and/or other therapists; American Sign Language (ASL) interpreters; orientation and mobility specialists; school social workers; school nurses; school psychologists; counselors; advocates, etc. Parents collaborate with teachers, sharing their experience with their children, children's histories, personal preferences, effective behavioral and learning techniques; and may volunteer to help in the classroom and/or at school functions. By advocating, they help teachers meet children's special needs. Special education teachers help address IEP goals by incorporating related instruction and activities into daily classroom lessons and routines; and offer expertise in differentiated instruction, teaching, and behavior management strategies. Audiologists contribute knowledge of hearing loss, hearing aids, classroom accommodations, and modifications. Therapists add expertise in their respective disciplines—physical therapists (PTs) make or adapt devices, provide targeted postural and large-muscle exercises; occupational therapists (OTs), fine-motor, ADL development; speech language pathologists (SLPs) incorporate language development into instruction; ASL interpreters translate between hearing and deaf or hearing-impaired students and families; orientation and mobility (O&M) specialists help blind and visually impaired students navigate classrooms, schools, and communities. Social workers provide student and family histories, coordinate special services, and help families locate and access resources. School nurses help with medications, monitoring diabetic diets and blood checks; school seizures, accidents, and emergencies, etc. Psychologists administer, score, and interpret IQ tests; provide behavior management plans and training; data collection and analysis, etc.

Resources whereby teachers and schools can provide enrichment for students

The Stanford Mobile Inquiry Learning Environment (SMILE) uses technology innovatively for educational enrichment. This interactive learning model includes mobile software for learning management, plus its own server, which can run on a battery and functions as a Wi-Fi connection, router, and storage device. At schools adopting SMILE, students can exchange questions and ideas with other students worldwide; and teachers can instantaneously collect summaries of learning data analytics. Another American enrichment resource is Students for the Advancement of Global Entrepreneurship (SAGE), a program emphasizing civic responsibility and duty for high school students, who form teams and develop social enterprise businesses (SEBs) or socially responsible businesses (SRBs), which compete in the annual SAGE World Cup. An American remediation resource is Teach for All, a model teaching lifetime educational advocacy and leadership foundations at both local and policy levels, training and developing effective leaders to change education for the most disadvantaged students; and promoting innovation by encouraging best practice sharing. PenPal Schools teach six-week courses about world issues, giving students global partners to share multicultural understandings. Its Pay-What-You-Want policy enables low-income student participation. Many other resources are available in other countries or are shared among the US and other nations.

Vertical alignment and horizontal alignment

Vertical alignment is the process through which courses are sequenced across a curriculum. What a student learns in a 4th grade math course will prepare him or her for what he or she will learn in a vertically aligned 5th grade math course. Horizontal alignment is the process through which different sections of the same course are standardized such that what one student learns in a section of Biology with Ms. Smith is similar (though not exactly the same) as the material learned by a student in a section of Biology with Mr. Johnson. Typically horizontal alignment is addressed locally, perhaps through professional learning communities in coordination with district guidelines for course content. Vertical alignment is often developed on a state or even national level. School districts develop their course outlines in coordination with standards adopted from either the state or national level. Educators at the state level decide the general scope of the schools' curricula and choose yearly statewide assessments for students. Educators at the district level adapt the state course guidelines to fit local communities and teachers implement those curricula in their classrooms. The success of the entire system is dependent on educators at all levels working collaboratively in the best interests of the students.

Cognitive theory

In cognitive theories, e.g., Piaget's theory of cognitive development, the individual seeks to establish and maintain equilibrium or balance to keep things the same, i.e., homeostasis. When unexpected events occur and/or the individual encounters novel environmental stimuli, these disrupt equilibrium. To restore balance, the individual must adapt. The process of adaptation consists of assimilation and accommodation. In learning to understand the world, Piaget said children form schemata. A scheme is a mental construct about some aspect of the environment—people, things, events, and/or categories of these. A baby might form schemata for "things I can suck on," "things I can shake that make noise," and "people I know," for example. When a child encounters a new stimulus, s/he either assimilates it—fitting it into his/her existing schema for similar things; or accommodates to it—modifying an existing schema to accommodate some different characteristics

- 32 -

of the new stimulus; or forming a new schema for it. Thus the process of learning, especially for children, involves frequently forming new schemata and changing existing schemata by adding to, subtracting from, or modifying the characteristics they include as experience and interaction with the environment progress.

Cognitive information processing theory

As computers were developed to function analogously to the human brain in many aspects of receiving, encoding, storing, and retrieving information, so in turn computers were used as concrete models for information processing theory to describe how humans execute and sequence cognitive activities. Information processing theories characterize how people attend to environmental events, encode new information and relate it to existing knowledge, store new information in memory, and retrieve information as needed from storage. According to the computer metaphor, people receive sensory input in the sensory register or sensory memory; attend to it through the process of attention; "chunk" and rehearse it temporarily via working memory in short-term memory; encode it for transferring to long-term memory, where it may be stored indefinitely; and then retrieve it as needed, transferring selected data via working memory from long-term to short-term memory. Encoding includes grouping data into categories, outlining, establishing hierarchies, and developing concept trees as organizational mechanisms. It also uses imagery and mnemonics. Retrieval includes recalling information from memory independently, and recognizing provided information matching remembered information. Cognitive mapping (Tolman, 1948) mentally represents the literal physical and metaphorical environment according to relative importance of features for the individual, enhancing navigation, learning, and recall.

Social learning theory

According to Albert Bandura, who originated social learning theory, students need not experience everything directly and personally to learn. Bandura found that children could observe other children engaging in certain behaviors and receiving desirable rewards (reinforcers) for doing so; they would then imitate the other children's behaviors in the hope of receiving similar rewards. Children not only imitate the actions of peers, but also the actions of adults, as all parents have observed. Bandura referred to these examples of behaviors provided by adults as modeling. He thus extended the behaviorist concept that an individual will emit a behavior to get a reward; once it is rewarded, the individual will repeat the behavior to obtain repeated rewards, by showing that because learners also emit behaviors they have observed others emitting, they can learn to produce behaviors based on their observation of others being rewarded for those behaviors. Bandura refers to this process as observational learning or vicarious learning.

Reciprocal determinism

Albert Bandura concurred with many concepts found in behaviorist learning theory, e.g., that individuals emit responses to environmental stimuli; that desirable consequences immediately following a behavior reinforce or strengthen the probability that an individual will repeat the behavior; and the deterministic nature of behaviorism in its attribution of behaviors to environmental causes. However, whereas behaviorism is sometimes called "learning theory," Bandura calls his theory "*social* learning theory." This name emphasizes a key difference in his theory: his orientation to the social contexts wherein learning occurs. Unlike behaviorists, Bandura finds social interactions vital to learning. This relates to Bandura's concept of reciprocal determinism. By this he means learning is a process involving the individual, the environment, and the behavior. The environment includes other people as well as physical surroundings and stimuli. The individual includes personality; cognitive factors; past experiences with reinforced behaviors;

and psychological processes like beliefs, thoughts, expectations, etc. The environment and behavior mutually influence one another. Individual, personal characteristics and social factors reciprocally influence and are influenced by individual behaviors. Bandura identified the conditions of attention (observation), retention (remembering), reproduction (imitating or copying), and motivation (a good reason—past, promised, and/or vicarious rewards) for an individual to learn from a model's behavior.

Constructivism

Constructivist philosophy and psychology view learning as a process whereby the learner actively constructs or builds his/her own knowledge and understanding of the world. Cognitive developmental theorist Jean Piaget was a constructivist. He proposed that children learned by interacting with and acting upon their environments. He likened them to "little scientists" who gathered information about the world, experimented with aspects of the environment by interacting with it, and drew progressively more informed conclusions about the world from observing their results. On the basis of this approach, children need experiences interacting with the environment to learn. Consistently with Piaget's characterization of young learners as scientists, problem-based learning is important to constructivist approaches: like scientists who conduct experiments to answer questions and solve problems, children develop higher cognitive capacities and learn more when they experiment with the environment and learn better trying to solve problems than only for obtaining external rewards or avoiding external punishments. Inquiry and discovery learning involves such active student questioning and inquiry and discovering answers or solutions. Vygotsky's zone of proximal development is the area between where a learner can accomplish something independently vs. with assistance, guidance, or encouragement, illustrating how more knowledgeable others (MKOs) enhance learning. Scaffolding is temporary needed support, gradually withdrawn as learners gain proficiency.

Classical and operant conditioning

Pavlov discovered and described classical conditioning when he found he could condition dogs to respond reflexively to a secondary, previously unrelated stimulus by repeatedly pairing it with the stimulus originally producing the reflex. Ringing a bell every time he gave them meat powder, causing them to salivate, eventually enabled the bell alone to stimulate salivation without the meat. Skinner later described what he named operant conditioning. Based on Thorndike's law of effect that a desirable consequence increased the probability of repeating a behavior while an undesirable one decreased that probability, Skinner found through experiments that new behaviors could be established, existing behaviors made much more frequent, and other behaviors made less frequent or extinguished through controlling the antecedents (events or stimuli immediately before) and consequences (events or stimuli immediately after) each behavior. The key difference between classical and operant conditioning is that classical conditioning manipulates reflexive or involuntary behaviors, whereas operant conditioning manipulates conscious or voluntary behaviors. Both contribute to the behaviorist proposition that behaviors can be established, increased, decreased, eliminated, connected, and shaped through manipulating related environmental stimuli. Skinner called classical conditioning "respondent" to differentiate it from operant conditioning, which involves choice.

Internal and external rewards

According to behaviorist theories of learning, rewarding specific behaviors reinforces or strengthens the probability of their repetition. Rewards can be internal or external. Internal or intrinsic rewards originate within the individual, e.g., feeling gratification at learning or knowing

- 34 -

something for the sake of additional knowledge, feeling self-efficacy for being able perform a given task successfully, feeling general competence or self-esteem for acquiring more knowledge or skills, engaging in behaviors congruent with one's self-image, etc. Both traditional and radical behaviorism ignored internal states as not outwardly observable or measurable, but many related theories, e.g., social learning theory, cognitive-behavioral theory, etc. incorporate sources of motivation and loci of control. External or extrinsic rewards are provided by other people or the environment. Research finds internal rewards more powerful for increasing and especially maintaining behaviors than external rewards. Behaviorism defines reinforcement as any consequence strengthening the probability of repeating a behavior. This can be positive reinforcement, i.e., introducing something desirable; or negative reinforcement, i.e. removing something undesirable. Positive punishment, conversely, is introducing something undesirable or aversive consequently to a behavior, making that behavior less likely to recur. Negative punishment is removing something desirable or removing a reinforcer, also decreasing the probability of behavior repetition.

Howard Gardner's theory of multiple intelligences

Gardner outlines eight distinct intelligences that people use in problem solving: namely, linguistic, musical, logical-mathematical, spatial, bodily-kinesthetic, naturalistic, interpersonal and intrapersonal, with a possible ninth: existential. Schools traditionally emphasize linguistic and logical-mathematical. Gardner placed emphasis upon learning skills in context, such as apprenticeships, rather than solely by textbooks. Traditional subjects, like English and math, should be taught in ways that appeal to all the multiple intelligences. History, for example, could be taught through dramatic reenactments, biographies, and architecture. He also thought that assessments should be tailored to different abilities and that student choice with assessments would ensure that the students were completing the task to the best of their abilities and utilizing the intelligence in which they were most skilled.

Constructing knowledge

Knowledge is constructed via a dynamic process wherein learners assimilate new information into existing mental schemes or concepts; modify existing schemes to accommodate radically different or new ideas; reorganize ideas to connect them into coherent patterns; and draw on existing knowledge to make sense of new information, actively interpreting it based on established insights, attitudes, and beliefs. Four iterative learning processes (Timperley et al, 2007), one or more of which are involved in cycles for developing new skills and understandings, are: (1) cueing or retrieving previous knowledge; the outcome is an examination and/or consolidation of existing knowledge. (2) Integrating new skills and information into current belief and value systems; the outcome is an adoption or adaptation of new knowledge. (3) Creating cognitive dissonance with an existing belief, value, or position; the outcome is the rejection or acceptance resolving dissonance; reconstruction or repositioning of current belief and value system. (4) Developing self-regulated learning related to testing instructional effectiveness; the outcome is the monitoring of student proficiency; adjustment of teaching practices to maximize efficacy. Cycle (1) prepares the way for cycles (2) and (3).

Acquiring skills

In early childhood, children acquire motor, cognitive, language, emotional, social and other skills through playing. Learners of all ages acquire skills through direct instruction from educators. Students in public schools learn academic content in required courses, and may also enroll in elective or outside courses to learn other desired specific skills. Students also learn by doing. Many skills, e.g., riding a bicycle, driving a car, dancing, all PE skills, art skills, etc. require hands-on learning and practice. Students may read books about a specific skill or skill set—not only required class textbooks, but on their own; not only to learn in more depth, breadth, and specificity about a school subject, but also learn other subjects. For example, a high school student interested in becoming a photographer might find his/her school offers art classes in drawing, painting, and sculpture but nothing in photography; and then enrolls in an outside course, and/or reads books on photography. Today, students have access to a plethora of YouTube video tutorials covering a diverse range of subjects. They can search a topic to find videos teaching specific skills. Internet searches also yield more information to read about skills. Apprenticeships and internships combine instruction, observation, imitation, and hands-on experience and practice.

Metacognition, schema, transfer, self-efficacy, self-regulation, and ZPD

Metacognition: thinking about thinking and understanding one's thought processes. Example: a student observes, "I learn better from a picture of something than words about it." Schema: coined by Piaget; a mental construct or representation of a concept. Example: a toddler has a schema for cows. Seeing a large, brown dog, she says "moo"—it fits her cow schema. Told this is a dog, she forms a new "dog" schema. Transfer: applying a learned skill to another activity or setting. Example: a child learns to make a clay pot in art class, then makes clay pots at home. Self-efficacy: coined by Bandura; a sense of competence for specific tasks. Example: based on experience, a student has high self-efficacy for getting an A grade in AP English, but low self-efficacy for passing calculus. Self-regulation: the ability to monitor, control, and adjust one's behaviors. Example: a high school student's grades are not high enough for his preferred college admissions; he watches less TV nightly and studies more. ZPD: coined by Vygotsky; the difference between what one can do unassisted vs. with what s/he can do with help or guidance. Example: a 4-year-old who can read a few words acquires more phonics rules and vocabulary from reading with her 6-year-old brother.

Classical conditioning and operant conditioning

Ivan Pavlov discovered and described classical conditioning. Experimenting with dogs, he placed meat powder on their tongues, causing them to salivate. At the same time he rang a bell. After repeatedly pairing the bell and meat powder, Pavlov found he could ring the bell alone without meat powder and the dogs still salivated by association. Classical conditioning involves evoking a reflexive response to a stimulus that did not originally evoke it through associating it with another stimulus that does trigger the response. Applying this to humans, if someone shines a bright light in your eyes, your pupils will reflexively contract. If someone says the word "contract" along with the light, after enough repetitions the person can say "contract" without shining the light and your pupils will contract. Based on Thorndike's Law of Effect, B. F. Skinner coined the term operant conditioning, differentiating it as "operant behaviors" from classical conditioning, which he called "respondent behaviors" (i.e., reflexive). Operant conditioning involves choice. Thorndike's law says actions followed by desirable consequences are likely to be repeated, while those followed by undesirable consequences are less likely to be repeated. Skinner found behaviors could be increased, decreased, or otherwise shaped through manipulating rewards and punishments.

Developing skills and making sense of the world through play

Children and all humans learn through adaptation to the environment, as Piaget described it. Humans and other beings or organisms naturally seek to establish and maintain equilibrium, or balance. Adaptation seeks equilibrium, encompassing processes of assimilation and accommodation. If a young child can fit a new concept or experience into an existing schema—e.g., things I can eat, throw, or stack; people I know and trust, etc.—s/he assimilates it. If new

- 36 -

information is radically different from any existing schema, the child accommodates to it by either altering the existing scheme or creating a new one—e.g., gum is something I chew but do not eat or swallow. Piaget also said children learn by interacting with and acting upon their environments. In play, children interact with the world at much earlier ages than academic activities. They learn physical concepts through their visual, auditory, tactile, olfactory, and gustatory senses. They learn and develop concepts—spatial, like under, over, through, etc.; temporal, like before and after, etc.; numerical and serial; sharing, taking turns, compromising, negotiating, and leading others, developing social skills; gross and fine motor skills through movement; language and literacy skills, including phonological awareness and conversation skills; self-esteem through demonstrating skills, accomplishments, and peer comparisons; and thinking, decision-making, independence, and cooperation and collaboration, including with diverse others, to prepare for adulthood and master life.

Human development vis-à-vis behaviorist and social learning theories

Because psychoanalytic theories of human development, e.g., Freud's psychosexual and Erikson's psychosocial theories, made claims about internal processes that could not always be substantiated by empirical evidence, behaviorist learning theorists sought in response to restrict their examinations to outwardly demonstrated behaviors they could observe, quantify, and measure. As an example, a child who falls and feels some pain will initially cry as a natural reaction. However, when adults respond to the fall by rushing to help the child and expressing concern, this attention reinforces the crying behavior—not the fall, because the child associates the consequence immediately following with the most recent preceding event. The reinforcement of attention increases the probability the child will cry again next time s/he falls, whether it hurts or not, to reduplicate the attention. This is an example of what Skinner termed operant conditioning. In a related example illustrating Bandura's social learning theory, we have all witnessed a child falling, not feeling significant pain, and looking around at adults to gauge whether to cry or not. Bandura found children can learn by observing others' actions and their consequences (rewards and punishments), and can imitate others' behaviors that they observe.

The behaviorist approach to learning theory is justified in limiting its principles and practices to observable, measurable behaviors in that change cannot be proven nor accurately quantified unless existing behaviors can first be observed and measured to establish baseline rates; and subsequent behaviors following intervention can be measured again for comparison to assess changes from baselines. However, a primary limitation of this approach is that it fails to account for or explain maturational, hormonal, and other changes occurring throughout the human lifespan. For example, puberty, the major experience during adolescence, typically has many outward physical, social, and behavioral manifestations as well as many inward physical, cognitive, and emotional changes. These changes are primarily driven by hormones (though of course societal roles and expectations interact). This internal biological mechanism is not addressed by theories that behaviors are responses to external environmental stimuli. Hence human development has impact on learning theory: finding this theory incomplete, development demands explanation informed by additional biological, psychological, and sociological knowledge about how hormonal maturation, emotions, thinking, and social interactions are interrelated and interdependent, and how they ultimately combine to affect human behavior.

Student transitions from elementary to middle school

Middle school students contend not only with pubertal changes in their bodies and feelings, but also changes from elementary to middle school, e.g., differences in location, learning environments, scheduling, activities, classmates, etc. While early teens become preoccupied and anxious about

- 37 -

their appearances, behaviors, and peers' perceptions, they also become more independent, expressing more of their own personalities and interests and making more autonomous choices in friends, school, studying, sports, appearance, etc. Adults must realize this independence prompts greater privacy needs, as well as withdrawing from parents, seeking friends and other adults as role models, identifying their own peer groups, finding groups and friends more important, and experiencing peer pressure. Students' emotional and social development changes their self-perceptions, and educators should adjust instruction accordingly. The adolescent's "imaginary audience" causes self-centered hypersensitivity to others' perceptions; the "personal fable" is the belief their experiences and feelings are unique, and that nobody understands (Elkind). Educators should avoid overreactive discipline interfering with student self-regulation, overwhelming teens; establish safe classroom environments, discussing issues and emotions. Teachers can issue each student a (counterfeit-detecting designed) "leave me alone" pass—not applicable on test or quiz days—to excuse active participation or interaction during class on some days, promoting student empowerment, control, and stress management.

Student growth model

A number of states use student growth models to track student progress. These models are statistical methods to gauge student progress on standardized tests, typically from the end of one school year to the end of the next school year. Statistical models allow students to be evaluated more appropriately, based on a dynamic growth measure instead of a static placement measure. A number of background factors (e.g., ELL status, learning differences, or student exceptionalities) may have contributed to low-achieving scores. Growth models incentivize BOTH progress toward proficiency in underachieving students and continued improvement in proficient students. Teachers and schools can be graded based, in part, upon success in facilitating student improvement and are not penalized for having students who begin an assessment cycle with low-achieving scores.

Response to Intervention (RtI) model

The RtI model is a framework for providing high-quality instruction for all K-12 learners. RtI's three tiers are: 1) research-based **core** classroom instruction, 2) **targeted** instruction for students in need of additional challenge or support, and 3) **intensive** instruction for students whose needs are not accommodated by the first two tiers. The needs of all learners are addressed through the RtI framework with research-based instructional practices, curriculum adaptations responsive to students' individual backgrounds, and appropriate interventions including the extension of the standard curriculum toward greater rigor. The RtI model is data driven. Analysis of student data guides instructional decisions. RtI instructional decisions are made via collaborations of teachers and administrators. No one individual teacher or administrator is capable of implementing RtI. The best interests of the students are served by teachers and administrators teaming to interpret data and decide whether students are in need of additional tiers of (targeted or intensive) instruction.

Universal Design for Learning (UDL)

The Universal Design for Learning is a curriculum implementation/development framework for guiding educational practice that specifically addresses the "what," "how," and "why" of learning. The framework moves away from the "one-size-fits-all" nature of traditional curricula that teaches to the "average" student while overlooking exceptional students. The three principles of UDL are: 1) provide multiple means of representation ("what"), 2) provide multiple means of action and expression ("how"), and 3) provide multiple means of engagement ("why"). UDL embraces learner variability through flexibility in its methods and goals. Learners do not have to start from some predefined point. Rather, teachers are able to differentiate their curriculum implementations, maximize learning opportunities for each student, and empower all students to aim for the most appropriate levels of success.

Facilitating young children's learning through play activities

Adults often observe young children talking about what to play. They should assist this planning by discussing with children who they will be, what will happen, etc.; and encourage children to plan together. If play breaks down, e.g., children wrangle over a toy or object, adults can intervene, pretending to knock on a door, asking if this is a good time to visit—redirecting their attention from distractions, refocusing and extending play time. To engage children in establishing safe environments for play, adults can do more than simply providing them with age-appropriate play materials by involving children in actively developing play rules to help them avoid sustaining or causing injuries and keep them safer. Young children have strong capacities for imitation, imagination, and creativity. Adults should encourage the latter, replacing the former. When children imitate violent or foolish behaviors they have observed, adults can refocus their play on other skills, problem solutions, and roles for accomplishing equal results than derivative actions with narrower scope. Storytelling and painting for younger children, and writing for older elementary-age children, are more controllable ways to work through issues impeding creativity and imagination to access and exercise them.

Processes whereby adolescent students acquire and integrate new knowledge

Younger children have had less time to generate a limited repertoire of schemata about the world and either fit new experiences into these or create new ones. However, older students, having had more time and life experiences, have accumulated more schemata and made more modifications in them to construct more extensive, detailed, and sophisticated knowledge. The first learning process they engage in when encountering new information or experiences is activating their existing knowledge, examining what they already know and believe. When new information or skills are congruent with prior knowledge and extend or supplement without significantly redefining it, older students integrate these into their present belief and value systems. This second process represents assimilation, i.e., acquiring additional knowledge without disequilibrium. When new information and experiences challenge adolescents' fundamental understandings, beliefs, or values, this creates cognitive dissonance, hence disequilibrium. Students then accept or reject the new input, reconstructing or repositioning existing beliefs if needed and resolving dissonance. This third process represents accommodation, i.e., acquiring new knowledge through encountering and resolving disequilibrium, and restoring a new equilibrium informed by new positions or beliefs. Teachers can facilitate ELL access to meaningful learning by relating new concepts taught in English to student L1s, activating their prior or existing knowledge. When teachers pair unfamiliar with familiar language and experience, this facilitates concept understanding and acquisition.

Sources of academic difficulty for ELL students

Some school difficulties for ELL students are directly attributable to teaching and learning environment deficits. These include lack of student access to effective ESL or bilingual instruction, mismatches between middle-class-oriented instruction and low socioeconomic student backgrounds, cultural and linguistic differences that create communication gaps between learners and teachers, etc. Other ELL students may additionally have specific learning disabilities, which require specialized instructional methods to enable successful learning. Experts believe many educators lack expertise to differentiate limited English-language proficiency from true learning disabilities as sources of school failure, evidenced by overrepresentation of ELL students in special education classes. Additional problems include shortages of both assessment instruments and trained assessors that are appropriate and linguistically and culturally relevant, and in special educators trained in concurrently addressing linguistically related as well as disability-related student needs. Factors necessary to ELL success include recognizing the importance of student L1s, collaborative community and school relationships, shared educator knowledge bases of effective instructional methods for ELLs, effective teaching, and academically rich programs that integrate instruction in basic and higher-order cognitive skills in both L1s and English.

Developmentally appropriate practices for kindergarten environments

According to early childhood education experts, developmentally appropriate practice (DAP) must ensure that classrooms, instructional techniques, and assessment methods for young children consider three main aspects: age, individual growth patterns, and cultural influences. Educators can try various strategies, observing which are effective for different situations and learning goals: acknowledge children's actions and words by commenting, giving positive attention, or sometimes simply observing nearby. Encourage effort and perseverance, not only products and accomplishments. Make feedback specific, e.g., "That didn't reach the basket; try throwing it harder." Model—show, not just tell, approaches to problems and interpersonal behaviors—e.g., saying you must think about why something didn't work or admitting you missed part of a child's message, requesting repetition. Demonstrate correct physical procedures. Add challenge slightly beyond current skills, e.g., once children count objects after subtracting some, hide subtracted ones, requiring strategies other than counting. Decrease challenge as needed, e.g., guide children to touch objects while counting. Ask questions stimulating thought, e.g., "If you couldn't talk, how would you tell classmates what to do?" Give children hints or cues furthering progress, e.g., supply a word rhyming with a child's name, or ask the child for additional words. Directly provide verbal labels, names, facts, and other information. Accompany demonstrations and modeling with clear verbal directions for behaviors and actions.

Teacher expectations, teacher behaviors with students, and student performance

In an experiment, Harvard psychologist Robert Rosenthal (1964) told teachers a standardized IQ test was a "special" test predicting dramatic IQ growth, identifying randomly selected students as about to make significant intellectual gains. In the following two years, teacher expectations became self-fulfilling prophecies: those students' IQs actually did increase. Rosenthal's additional research identified myriad, nearly imperceptible ways teacher expectations influence interactions with students. They consistently smile, nod at, and touch; give more approval; offer more specific feedback; and allow more time for answering questions to students they expect to succeed. Exemplary teachers strive to motivate all of their students to achieve more than they thought they could through high expectations. Dean of University of Virginia's Curry School of Education and researcher Robert Pianta (c. 2012) compared two approaches to changing teacher expectations: talking to convince teachers via information that their beliefs are incorrect, vs. intensive training in new teacher behaviors. The latter shifted teacher beliefs more than the former. For example, a teacher believing boys are disruptive quashes a boy's loud, effusive response, emotionally disengaging and frustrating the student. Contrastingly, a teacher without that belief encourages the student to continue, but while sitting quietly. Different beliefs prompt different interpretations of the same behavior.

Interacting with students who display problematic behavior

Experts observe we must change our own behavior to change others' behavior. Educational researchers have found teacher expectations and resulting behaviors subtly yet powerfully influence student behavior. There are several suggestions for teacher behaviors to influence student behaviors. For instance, observe how every student engages, interacts, and what s/he likes doing to comprehend their capabilities. Listen to students, try to understand their goals and motivations, and note their perceptions of classmates, yourself, and assignments you give. Engage with students: ask about and listen to their individual interests without offering opinions or advice. Experiment with different responses to challenging behaviors. Instead of your first impulse, stop and consider the behavior's motivation or function, which could be to connect with you. If or when time permits, interact with students in nonacademic games or activities of their choice; observe student strengths and interests. Assign projects wherein students use preferred media to express, individually and in groups, their extracurricular interests. Consider school through students' eyes. Reflect on your own worst and best teachers, supervisors, and bosses. List five words describing how you felt when interacting with them, and what they did or said specifically to evoke those feelings. List how your students might describe you. Consider parallels between your beliefs and their responses, and how your expectations shape their perceptions of you.

Robert Marzano's strategies for improving teaching quality and student achievement

According to expert Robert Marzano, instructional strategies for effective teaching and learning include: (1) identifying similarities and differences. Students more easily understand, and frequently solve, complex problems through analyzing them more simply by breaking concepts into similar and different characteristics. Teachers may identify these directly and then guide student inquiry and discussion, or have students identify them independently. Research finds the former helps identify specific items, while the latter promotes broader understanding and variation. Venn diagrams and charts are useful visual graphics for showing similarities and dissimilarities. Teachers should also engage student classifications, comparisons, analogies, and metaphors. (2) Summarizing and note-taking. Students comprehend better through analyzing subjects, revealing essential content, and restating it in their own words. Studies find students must be aware of the information's basic structure and delete, retain, and replace some components. Teachers should give students summarizing rules; prepare notes; use consistent note formats, allowing student refinements as needed; have students question, clarify, and predict coming occurrences in texts; and provide time to review and revise notes, often the best test study guides. (3) Reinforcing effort, giving recognition. Connect effort and achievement through success stories and student log-keeping and analysis. Personalize or individualize symbolic, not tangible rewards.

Marzano's strategies include: (1) homework and practice. Students extend learning beyond classrooms. Studies find homework amounts should vary by grade levels, parents should be minimally involved, students should adapt skills as they learn them, and the primary indices of practice effectiveness are speed and accuracy. Teachers should explain homework purposes to students and parents; try to give students feedback on every assignment; vary feedback delivery to maximize effectiveness; inform students whether homework is practice or to prepare for coming units; establish homework policies, advising students to maintain consistent settings, time limits, and schedules; assign timed quiz homework, having students report speed and accuracy; allocate practice time, focusing on difficult concepts. (2) Visual or nonlinguistic representations: studies show knowledge is stored in linguistic and visual forms, and students achieve more using both. Visual representation both stimulates and increases brain activity. Represent information with physical models and movements, relationships with symbolic images and words. (3) Cooperative learning: applied consistently and systematically—not overused—with small groups, cooperative activities enhance learning. Group students by multiple criteria, e.g., common interests or experiences; vary objectives and group sizes; and design projects around core components of individual and group accountability, face-to-face interaction, group processing, appropriate social skills, and positive interdependence.

(1) Objectives and feedback: give student learning direction through setting goals—not overly specific, readily compatible with students' personal goals. Setting each unit's core goal, inviting student personalization identifying areas where they want to know more, helps students consider their own interests and engage actively in goal-setting processes. Define specific student goals and grades they will receive for achieving them through writing contracts. Feedback should be corrective (comparing student achievement to specific knowledge levels as with rubrics), specific, and timely. Invite students to lead feedback sessions. (2) Hypothesis formulation and testing: studies show deductive reasoning—from general principles to specific predictions—most effective. Students must explain hypotheses and conclusions, whether deductive or inductive (from specific observations to generalizations). Ask students to predict what might occur if some aspect of government, transportation, or some other familiar system changed. Have students build things using limited resources, generating inquiries and hypotheses about what might or might not work. (3) Help students apply pre-existing knowledge for additional learning using questions, cues, and advance organizers. Studies find these must focus on important content, be highly analytical, and presented before lessons or activities. Pausing briefly after questions increases students' answer depth. Vary advance organizer styles—graphic images, skimming text, telling stories, etc.—for pre-"learning" exposure.

Learning activities that promote both critical thinking skills and ownership of learning

In *Democracy and Education* (1916), John Dewey wrote that true student involvement is stimulated by activities that "give pupils something to do, not something to learn; and the doing is of such a nature as to demand thinking, or the intentional noting of connections; learning naturally results." Thus the same learning activities that promote higher-order thinking, including critical thinking and organizational and time-management skills, also promote student ownership of learning. While interests in community issues fluctuate, students regularly find school-based issues important. Issues—curricular, extracurricular, or leadership-related—must also be relevant, reflecting student identities, interests, and passions; and student roles meaningful, enabling their design, implementation, and evaluative participation for improving student learning and schools. Schools can involve students as planners in designing new buildings, developing classroom behavior guidelines, selecting textbooks, researching careers and planning coursework accordingly, participating in principal or administrator hiring, etc. Students as teachers learn about all curriculum subjects in exchange for instructing teachers how to use technology, enhancing ownership and meaningful involvement. Students as professional development partners collect and analyze data and participate in team development as learning community members. Students as decision-makers in student government influence school climate, policy, and curriculum.

Age-appropriate study skills

Research finds when students must analyze information to identify its most important aspects and then express it in their own terms, they need to know how the information is basically organized, and be able to remove, replace, and preserve elements of it. Thereby they understand it better. These learning processes are included in note-taking and summarizing. Teachers can provide students with rules for summarizing; prepare their own notes for students; and adhere to regular note-taking formats, including necessary student refinements. When teachers prepare their lecture or lesson notes in outline form, students can more easily take notes in outline form. Having students question text, clarify as needed, and make predictions improves their summarizing skills. Allotting time and encouraging students to review and revise their notes frequently enables them to study for tests at their highest potential. Advance organizers help students activate and build on their prior knowledge to learn further. Teachers should introduce analytical advance organizers concentrating on essential subject matter before learning experiences and vary their style, e.g., skim text, tell stories, produce graphic images, etc.

Steps students need to do in school and libraries in order to write research papers

(1) Topic: appeal to student curiosity; possible yet somewhat challenging for student skill and learning levels; support grade-level standards so library research matches classwork. Triangulate data, confirming topics in three kinds of available, readable sources; cross-check encyclopedias to broaden or narrow as needed. (2) Subtopics: informed by what students want to know; provide blueprints or outlines for examining topics. Brainstorm for general subtopics, e.g., physical characteristics, habitats, diets, enemies, offspring of specific animal species. "Pre-search" specific subtopics in topic-specific book tables of contents and encyclopedia subheadings. Research time management depends on controlling subtopic number (minimum three) and difficulty. (3) Sources: three kinds minimum, print or non-print; text, images, ideas. Consider student age, ability, topic for primary and secondary sources. Require MLA, APA, Turabian, or other accepted styles to prevent plagiarism and cite sources or use Creative Commons. Teach fair use and copyright regulations. Source evaluation offers lifelong skills. (4) Read, think, select: model, discuss, practice critical reading strategies—scanning, skimming, visual clues, chunking; asking what is important; identifying information supporting subtopics. (5) Note-taking: using subtopics as titles, pre-sort notes; beginners copy facts, phrases, and keywords, citing sources; experienced researchers summarize or paraphrase. (6) Sort notes by subtopic, then into paragraphs. Advanced is logical plan-based, e.g., concepts, timeline, etc. Rereading all notes per section, rearranging into logical order consolidates new information, cementing learning. Number notes consecutively. Write from notes, inserting previous knowledge.

Roles played by teachers and students in different instructional models

In traditional teacher-centered instructional models, the teacher plays the most active role, delivering instruction through lectures and lessons; assigning homework; and creating, administering and grading tests while the students play more passive roles of attending to, absorbing, retaining, and repeating information. In more progressive student-centered instructional models, if the model espouses inquiry and discovery learning, for example, students play more active roles as teachers encourage and guide them to ask their own questions, form their own hypotheses, investigate and test these, and draw their own conclusions. When teachers differentiate instruction for students with diverse needs, teachers may play varying roles of part-time individual tutor; part-time whole-class instructor; and, when teachers include small-group cooperative learning, part-time group facilitator and guide. Teachers providing one-on-one intensive training to students with profound disabilities play highly directive, active roles. At the other end of the spectrum, when students conduct independent projects, teachers may serve only as consultants or occasional advisors until they grade the projects. While some students need explicit instruction, research also finds that while rote memorization works with factual information, active student participation and teaching learning or thinking *skills*, not just information, produces more original thinkers and lifelong learners.

Community, home, and school factors with regard to teaching and learning

Community: socioeconomic factors affect learning. For example, students living in more affluent communities have more educational resources and supports like after-school activities, learning and tutoring centers, and educational product stores. Affluent neighborhoods are also populated

- 43 -

with more highly educated residents: students are expected to pursue post-secondary educations. In low-income neighborhoods, economic survival often takes precedence over education, or high school diplomas are primarily for obtaining after-graduation employment. <u>Home</u>: parents with higher incomes can access more educational resources. Frequently more educated, they regard education more highly, have higher educational expectations and goals for children, serve as their role models, and either directly or indirectly educate them. Doctors, lawyers, educators, etc. are more likely have children pursuing similar educations and careers. Conversely, some children with less-educated parents have been motivated to become first in their families to attend college. <u>School</u>: urban schools where riots occur make school unsafe. Students cannot concentrate, so they stop attending. Less dramatic but equally important is classroom environment. Consider true stories of a speech language pathologist (SLP) required to conduct therapy between library shelf "stacks," and a teacher's aide instructing ELL students in school hallways. Such uncomfortable, distracting, and/or noisy settings interfere with teaching and learning.

Characteristics shared by effective learning groups

Experts find all kinds of effective learning groups share certain common characteristics. For example, their teachers are always involved actively as guides, coaches, questioners, evaluators, and resource people in student group learning processes. Groups are given work to do that is meaningful to students and challenges them. Teachers ensure students clearly understand learning objectives and schedules, and teachers monitor these. Cooperating is more important than competing. All students in each group are actively involved; groups are heterogeneous. Learning group processes enable students to feel comfortable with asking questions and discussing topics and issues. Students in learning groups experience the sense that they are able to achieve more by learning with each other than they could by learning individually. Although learning groups demand adequate social skills and interpersonal interactions, grouping is not primarily for social purposes. Group time is not considered "free time" for either students or teachers. With effective learning groups, teachers can evaluate individual student members, whole groups, or a combination of both. Teachers are able to assess group work through multiple instruments, e.g., presentations, interviews, portfolios, rubrics, quizzes, etc.

Incorporating different learning modalities to optimize individual student learning

Students need not have sensory or cognitive processing disabilities to learn better through one sensory modality than another. All students have learning styles. Teachers can optimize classroom learning by including multiple and alternative modalities in lessons. For example, some students are auditory learners: they have greater sensitivity, attention, comprehension, and retention for what they hear than what they see or touch. Teachers can provide audiobooks and earphones along with books during reading times. This strategy also benefits students who do have visual impairments. Other students are visual learners: they attend, understand, and remember what they see better than what they hear or touch. Pairing visuals with sounds enhances their learning and other experiences. For example, Walt Disney's classic film *Fantasia* provides visually rich animated sequences accompanying classical music by Tchaikovsky, Grieg, Mussorgsky, etc. Students with haptic learning styles respond to tactile stimuli. Teachers can give younger students materials with varied textures to accompany story reading, assigning older students projects to interpret literature, science lessons, etc. by constructing collages, models, or displays with different textures. Students with kinesthetic styles learn through physical movement. Teachers can let them dance to music and apply exercise and sports movements to physics, mathematical, and other principles, etc.

Benefits of learning theory to education

Behaviorism, or learning theory, has given educators a wealth of tools because it is practical, not only theoretical; applies to all organisms including humans, regardless of cognitive or intellectual level; gives clear procedures and steps to follow; deals only with observable, measurable behaviors, eliminating much ambiguity; follows logical sequences; can change behaviors much faster than other methods; and has undergone much research, yielding specific information about reinforcement schedules and corresponding response rates, effective and ineffective techniques, etc. For example, for students with cognitive or intellectual disabilities (ID) who have difficulty understanding or remembering complex tasks with multiple steps, task analysis derives from behaviorism in its principle of breaking tasks down into smaller, more manageable steps, teaching them separately until mastered, and then connecting them one more at a time. Students with autistic spectrum disorders (ASD) as well as IDs can have horrible trouble making transitions between activities. Behaviorist shaping, via reinforcing successive approximations toward an ultimate target behavior; and chaining, similar to the step-connecting portion of task analysis; are both highly valuable. Students with communication deficits might scream in class to get teacher attention; differential reinforcement of another behavior (DRO) or differential reinforcement of an incompatible behavior (DRI), e.g., raising a hand, waving, touching the teacher's arm, or operating a signal button or switch teaches more acceptable replacement behaviors.

Sigmund Freud's theory of human development

Freud proposed each psychosexual development stage revolves around the erogenous zone where pleasure focuses at the time. Freud divided the personality into three structures: the id, ego, and superego. During toddlerhood's (c. 1-3 years) anal stage, the ego emerges, providing a sense of self and reality, regulating id impulses unmediated during infancy's oral stage. Toilet-training is an important life event. If parents reward toilet use excessively, children may become possessive of bowel movements, deriving excessive pleasure from them. Overly strict toilet-training can cause anal fixation, manifested as either an anal-retentive (compulsively neat, overly structured, rigid, righteous, and stubborn) or anal-expulsive (sloppy, defiant of authority, and irresponsible) personality. Preschoolers (c. 3-5 years) are in Freud's phallic stage. The superego or conscience emerges, providing a moral compass, further governing the ego and id. Children discover their genitals, which become this stage's erogenous zone. In Freud's Oedipus complex during this stage, boys unconsciously desire their mothers, wishing to destroy their fathers as rivals. They fear paternal retribution, i.e., castration anxiety. They resolve the conflict through identification with the aggressor—emulating fathers. Freud saw elementary years as the latency period, wherein sexual impulses are suppressed in favor of developing social skills and relationships.

Sigmund Freud's developmental theory relative to the adolescent years

After a latency period wherein school-age children suppress sexual id impulses to focus on developing social relationships and learning academic content, Freud termed his fifth and final stage of psychosexual development the genital stage, which begins with puberty and continues throughout life. Freud considered this stage as a kind of reprise of the phallic stage in early childhood, when children first discovered their genitals. Both stages are periods involving *exploration*. A physician by training and background, Freud accorded primary importance to the physical areas and processes of the body. Each of his stages is organized around an erogenous zone: oral in infancy, around nursing; anal in toddlerhood, around toilet-training; phallic and genital in preschool and teen years respectively, around sexual drives, with a calm latency period in between when such urges are buried in favor of the outward focus on friendships and school. The powerful physical changes and events of *puberty* are Freud's focus for the genital stage. Unlike his follower

- 45 -

Erikson, Freud felt the personality was basically formed by adolescence and did not essentially change much thereafter; so this was his final stage, which he believed applied to adults as well.

Erik Erikson's theory of human development

Early childhood years

Erikson took major influences from Freud's theory in also viewing major life events, e.g., nursing during infancy; toilet-training during toddlerhood; exploration during preschool years; and school during school years as central to each developmental stage. But his orientation was psychosocial, not psychosexual: rather than Freud's focus on physical erogenous zones and parent-child relationships, Erikson focused on personal self-images and social interactions. In each of Erikson's stages, a nuclear conflict must be resolved. Toddlers (c. two to three years) confronting toilet-training experience autonomy vs. shame and doubt. In learning physical control, successful children develop independence; failing children develop self-doubt and shame. According to Erikson, preschoolers (c. three to five years) encounter the nuclear conflict of initiative vs. guilt. At these ages, they are exploring their environments and need to experiment with exercising personal control over their surroundings. Children who succeed in interacting with and manipulating their environments develop a sense of purpose. Children who fail in this endeavor by exerting excessive power, and/or by receiving disapproval from their parents for their efforts, develop guilt feelings. School-age (c. 6-11 years) children face industry vs. inferiority. Successful coping with new social and academic requirements develops feelings of competence; failure develops feelings of inadequacy.

Adolescence and early adulthood

Unlike his predecessor and strong influence, Sigmund Freud, Erikson believed people continue to develop throughout life. Hence he proposed stages for each life period until death. He identified the nuclear conflict characteristic of every stage as being identity vs. role confusion in adolescence (c. 12-18 years). Teenagers begin developing their individual personal identities. *Social relationships* are the focus of this stage. Teens that are successful in defining their personal roles and identities develop feelings of being *true to themselves.* Teens who fail in this endeavor develop *confusion about their roles* in life and *weak and/or poorly defined self-images.* Young adults (c. 19-40 years) are included in teenage years because Erikson's theory associates the final teen year as part of young adulthood. This is Erikson's stage of intimacy vs. isolation. Once adolescents have defined their personal identities, they progress forming intimate, loving relationships with other young adults. *Relationships* are the focus of this stage. Successful individuals develop *strong relationships*; those failing develop *isolation and loneliness.*

Albert Bandura's contributions to education

Albert Bandura's social learning theory emphasized the importance of social interaction in learning. Bandura accepted principles of behaviorist learning theories like antecedent stimuli, behaviors, and consequent stimuli that punished or rewarded (reinforced) behaviors. However, internal cognitive processes, and social contexts of learning, became more central in Bandura's theory. Also, he believes learning does not necessarily change behavior. Bandura discovered children learned indirectly by watching others—i.e., vicarious or observational learning: seeing others receiving rewards for certain behaviors, they imitated those actions to obtain similar rewards. This discovery contradicted the empiricist claim that learning requires direct experience. Bandura also discovered children witnessing violent actions by living persons (cf. his Bobo doll experiments) or by people they saw in video recordings would then display more aggressive behaviors imitating what they observed. This influenced education and parenting: adults, realizing children's behavior was influenced not just directly by experiencing violence, but also indirectly by observing it, became more concerned about controlling what children observed. Bandura identified attention, retention, reproduction, and motivation as conditions necessary to modeling and observational learning. Bandura's concept of reciprocal determinism states individuals and environments mutually influence each other. His concept of self-efficacy identifies belief in one's individual competence to perform specific tasks and skills.

Jerome Bruner's contributions to education

Bruner, like Piaget and many others, embraces constructivist philosopher, i.e., by interacting with their environments, children actively construct their learning, knowledge, and realities. His emphasis on discovery learning is based on constructivism. He defined learning as not only remembering existing, culturally imparted or acquired ideas and actions, but moreover inventing or creating these on one's own. Bruner feels "culturally invented technologies" amplify human abilities, rather than providing all knowledge. He influenced education by advising that its goal should be producing autonomous learners. Bruner posited three modes of representation in child cognitive development. 1) Enactive representation: action-based information based on motor responses, retained in muscle memory, emerging in infancy. 2) Iconic representation: visual image-based information, emerging around 1-6 years of age. 3) Symbolic representation: coded or symbolic storage of information, emerging c. 7 years and older. For example, the category "dogs" symbolically represents all dog breeds, types, and individuals. We remember information symbolically in words, numbers, etc. Bruner's concept of the spiral curriculum enabled teaching complex ideas to all ages by initially structuring them simply and increasing difficulty gradually. Bruner (with Wood and Ross) originated the concept *scaffolding*—temporary, gradually withdrawn support matching student needs.

John Dewey's contributions to education

Psychologist, philosopher, educator, and social activist John Dewey was a prominent member of the Progressive social reform movement, a president of the American Psychological Association, a functional psychology pioneer, a Pragmatist and Instrumentalist philosopher, and the foremost theorist in modern American education. Like Rousseau and Froebel, he believed in experiential "learning by doing." He shifted schools from authoritarian and teacher-centered, rote-learning methods to democratic classrooms, relevant curricula, and participatory activities. He emphasized the social, interactive nature of the learning and educational processes. Dewey believed education not only conferred knowledge, but moreover taught children how to live. His humanist psychology and instrumental philosophy informed his opinions that education should enable children to realize their full potential, and to apply those abilities toward the greater good. He also viewed education as an important force for social reform and change. He believed education should not concentrate exclusively on being either child-centered or curriculum content-centered, but balance the two. Like Bruner, he believed education should prepare autonomous learners—who were also ethical and reflective. He also professionalized the role of teachers as social service providers producing higher character and community intelligence standards, not merely vocational trainers preparing students for work with limited job skills and information.

Jean Piaget's theory of cognitive development

Piaget, like Bruner and others, believed in constructivism, i.e., children were not passive learners but actively constructed their own learning, knowledge, and worlds through interacting with their environments. He observed children as being "little scientists" from birth who experimented with and acted upon the environment to learn about it. Piaget formulated four stages of cognitive development. 1) Sensorimotor: infants respond to sensory input with motor responses. 2) Preoperational: wherein young children are *egocentric*, unable to see others' physical or mental perspectives. They think *intuitively*, not logically, unable to focus on more than one physical attribute of an object at a time (*centration*), categorize and classify, or follow structures and sequences of reasoning. They see things *animistically*, by attributing human qualities and behaviors to inanimate objects; and *magically*, by attributing events and others' actions to their own thoughts or words. 3) Concrete operations: school-age children can classify, perform other logical mental operations, and reverse them as long as they have concrete objects or events for reference. 4) Formal operations: preadolescents and adolescents develop the ability to perform abstract mental operations without concrete support, understanding and manipulating abstract concepts in math, philosophy, law, politics, etc. Piaget's theory influenced education, guiding educators not to present content to children who are not cognitively ready or able to understand; and introducing concepts and material appropriately to cognitive levels.

Lev Vygotsky's contributions on teaching practices today

Like theorists after him, e.g., Erikson, Bruner, Bandura, and others, Vygotsky, who lived during the Russian Revolution, stressed the importance of social interaction to learning. He differed from his contemporary Piaget's belief in invariant stages of cognitive development, believing instead that it varied among societies because culture heavily influenced it. Two of the most influential concepts in Vygotsky's theories were the more knowledgeable other (MKO), i.e., a person (or a computer, software program, etc. can be included) with a higher level of skill or understanding—whether peer, older child, or adult—than a given student; and the zone of proximal development (ZPD), which interact with one another. The ZPD is the distance between two levels of cognitive development: (1) the level of actual development, where a student can accomplish something independently; and (2) the level of potential development, where a student can accomplish something with guidance or assistance from an MKO. Vygotsky emphasized ability and potential above knowledge: what one could learn was more important than what one already knew. He also was first to prove that self-talk or inner speech (whose existence others agreed to, but not its cognitive value) was important to activity self-regulation, social competence, and learning.

Lawrence Kohlberg's theory of moral development

Kohlberg based his theory on Piaget's two stages of moral development, heteronomous (other-directed) morality and autonomous (self-directed) morality; but Kohlberg extended these to three distinct levels and six stages, with each level encompassing two stages. Similarly to Erikson's belief regarding psychosocial development, Kohlberg believed moral development continued throughout life. Kohlberg's level one is preconventional morality. In stage one, obedience and punishment, young children (and some adults) view rules as absolute and fixed; obedience averts punishment. In stage two, individualism and exchange, children judge actions by whether they meet one's own interests or needs. They can understand and appreciate *reciprocity,* but only if it also is in one's best interests. At level two, conventional morality, stage three involves interpersonal relationships, nicknamed *"good boy-good girl."* Conforming to meet social roles and expectations, concern for how choices affect relationships, and being "nice" predominate. Stage four, maintaining social order, focuses on respecting authority, doing one's duty, following rules, maintaining law and order, and considering overall society. Level three is postconventional morality. In stage five, social contract and individual rights, people still find laws and rules important, but only with individual members' agreement. By stage six, universal ethical principles, individuals apply internalized justice principles, regardless whether they conflict with rules and laws.

- 48 -

Bloom's taxonomy

Bloom organized learning into a hierarchy of six cognitive levels, from simplest to most challenging. Remembering involves retaining, recalling, retrieving, recognizing, reproducing, or repeating names, facts, lists, and other pieces of information. Understanding requires also being able to find, identify, select, describe, explain, discuss, review, restate, and/or translate information, rather than only remembering it. Applying requires learners to interpret information they understand; to use it appropriately, e.g., for solving problems; to illustrate, demonstrate, or dramatize it; write about it, etc. Analyzing means that learners must be able not only to remember, understand, and apply information, but moreover to break it down into component parts; assign information to different categories; make comparisons and contrasts between and among pieces or sets of information; use information to make calculations; differentiate and discriminate among different information; examine information; question its truth, accuracy, or credibility; experiment with it; test its veracity; and criticize information. Evaluating demands the learner assess and appraise information, make estimates and/or predictions based on it, rate it, judge it, and defend it. Creating, the highest level, involves proposing, developing, planning, designing, formulating, preparing, collecting, composing, organizing, and managing information, including both original ideas and/or original uses of existing information.

Physical and cognitive characteristics of typically developing children

Early Childhood

Physically, children gain c. 2.5 inches and 5-7 pounds, decreasing yearly. Preschoolers become taller and slimmer, losing baby fat. Preschooler heads are less oversized for bodies than top-heavier toddlers', but still somewhat large. *Cognitively*, continuing brain maturation plus wider life experiences enable significant progress in attention, planning, and language. Reasoning develops from 4-7 years, but is not logical. By 5 years, gross motor skills gain automaticity, and fine motor skills improve significantly.

Middle and late childhood

Physically, growth is slow and consistent—2-3 inches and 5-7 pounds annually. Heads and waists become smaller proportionately to height. Bones and muscle tissue strengthen. Motor skills gain coordination and smoothness. By 10-12 years, fine motor coordination and manipulative skills approximate adults'. *Cognitively*, brain circuitry continues developing, especially in the prefrontal cortex, improving cognitive control, attention, and reasoning. In Piaget's concrete operations stage, children can reason logically and reverse mental operations, but need physical objects, events, or examples for reference.

Adolescence

Physically, uberty combines physical and sexual maturation with hormonal changes. *Cognitively*, structural changes improve information-processing, reasoning, decision-making, and self-control. However, though the emotion-related amygdala matures earlier, the prefrontal cortex controlling emotions only matures by 18-25 years. Adolescents reach Piaget's formal operations, understanding abstract concepts and performing and manipulating entirely mental operations.

Linguistic, affective, and moral characteristics of children with typical development

<u>Early Childhood</u>

linguistic : greater sensitivity to spoken phonological features; linguistic rule systems understanding; learning and applying syntactic rules to speech; dramatic vocabulary development; changing speech "registers" and styles based on situation, improving conversational skills.

Affective: by 4-5 years, self-awareness; self-conscious emotions like guilt and pride; understanding of and ability to discuss both personal and others' emotions, causes and results, increase.

Moral: most are at Kohlberg's level one of preconventional reasoning with external punishments and rewards until c. 9 years.

<u>Middle and late Childhood</u>

Linguistic: understanding the alphabetic principle; categorizing; whereas younger children respond sentence-sequentially, e.g., prompted "dog" and saying "barks"; or "eat" and "lunch"; older children respond with like parts of speech, saying "cat" or "horse" to "dog," and "drink" to "eat." From age 6-11, vocabulary grows from c. 14,000-40,000 words. Complex grammar comprehension develops, and metalinguistic awareness, knowing, and thinking about language.

Affective: more varied coping strategies. Self-regulation and self-efficacy influence achievement.

Moral: many are at Kohlberg's level two conventional reasoning, stage 3, "good boy-good girl", adopting parental morality.

<u>Adolescence</u>

Linguistic: skills advance, including complex spoken and written sentences; writing stories following story grammar rules; consistently accurate inferences from text; understanding figurative language, idioms, and metaphors.

Moral: Kohlberg's postconventional reasoning is possible—recognizing alternatives, social contracts, and developing universal moral standards transcending laws.

Considerations for judging typical vs. atypical child development

Although the majority of children develop skills in each domain at similar ages and in similar patterns, individual differences dictate normal variance in each. Each child's personal history, characteristics, family history, and environment influence the rates and patterns of their development. This is why experts commonly indicate not exact ages, but ranges for normal developmental signs. Also, slowly emerging skills more often indicate delays; skills differing in form, function, and quality more often indicate disorders. While most children with typical motor development sit up unassisted at around 6 months, some take longer; if a child cannot maintain a sitting position by 10 months, this could indicate a movement or motor delay disorder. An infant whose legs stiffen whenever s/he attempts to roll over could also have a motor disorder. Older children who cannot dress or undress, eat with utensils, draw with crayons, or cut with scissors may have atypical motor development. Two-year-olds having vocabularies of below 50 words and using no or few two- or three-word combinations are considered "late talkers," who may have speech or language delays. Also, some children excel in receptive understanding of spoken language, yet have expressive verbal difficulties.

<u>Detecting atypical and typical cognitive, social, emotional, and moral development in children</u>

With intellectual development, the common standard for suspecting atypical or delayed development is an IQ score two standard deviations or more below the average for a standardized test. With adaptive development, age range-appropriate criteria are used; for example, a normal 3-year-old is expected to toilet independently, but not to tie shoes until about 5-6 years. Parents do not expect 6-year-olds to cook or sew. Typical adaptive development is often gauged through comparison to age peers. However, not all children lagging behind peers have developmental disorders or delays: considerable individual variance is normal. Parents can assess children's social skills development by downloading informal checklists, many available online, indicating social skills according to age levels. Innate temperament is one factor in emotional development: some children jump fearfully at unexpected noises, others laugh; some get angry, others cry at the same stimulus. Cognitive and emotional development interact, as evidenced in toddlers: most 3-year-olds begin developing self-control of their emotions via growing cognitive development. This progresses from initially separate cognitive and emotional processes—e.g., a child is immersed in stacking blocks until another child takes a block; emotion overwhelms the first child. Eventually, toddlers learn and remember other ways to respond than screaming or hitting.

Developmental milestones in physical, cognitive, and linguistic domains

2- to 6-month-olds

Physically, 2-month-olds can hold up their heads, start pushing up from stomach-lying, and their limb movements become smoother. Cognitively, they track moving objects visually, recognize people from distances, attend to faces, and fuss or cry showing boredom when activities do not change. Linguistically, they coo, gurgle, and turn heads toward sounds. Four-month-olds can hold heads steadily unsupported; may roll over stomach-to-back; bring hands to mouths; swing at hanging toys, or hold and shake toys; push down with legs when feet touch hard surfaces; and push up from stomach on elbows. They express happiness and sadness, respond to affection, reach for things they see, reach one-handed, track moving objects laterally, recognize familiar people and objects from distances, and closely observe faces. They start babbling, with expression; imitate heard sounds; and differentiate crying to express hunger, fatigue, or pain. Six-month-olds roll over front-to-back and back-to-front, begin sitting unsupported, support standing weight on legs, bounce, rock, and crawl backward and forward. They look at nearby objects, bring objects to mouth, display curiosity and try to obtain out-of-reach objects, and start passing objects hand-to-hand. They respond to sounds with vocalization, enjoy taking turns with parents making sounds, babble vowel strings, start including consonants, respond to their names, and vocalize pleasure and displeasure.

3-, 4-, and 5-year-olds

Socially and affectively, 3-year-olds typically show affection for others spontaneously; imitate adults and peers; show concern for crying friends; take turns during games and activities; display wide ranges of emotions; and understand the meanings of *mine, yours, his*, and *hers*. They easily separate from parents, can dress and undress themselves, and may become upset over major changes in daily routines. Four-year-olds pretend-play at being parents, become progressively more creative when playing make-believe, like new activities, prefer playing with other children to playing alone, cooperate with peers, frequently cannot distinguish between fantasy and reality, and enjoy talking about their preferences and interests. Five-year-olds are more likely to follow rules than younger children. They want to be like their friends and want to please them. They typically enjoy acting, singing, and dancing. They demonstrate sympathy and concern for other people. They have developed awareness of gender. Unlike 4-year-olds, 5-year-olds typically can tell the difference between fantasy and reality. They demonstrate more independence, e.g., going on their

- 51 -

own to visit a neighbor, though adults still need to supervise them. They are likely to alternate between being very cooperative and being very demanding.

Developmental milestones for adolescents

Physically, most adolescents will have completed puberty by the time they are around 15-17 years old. While girls are more likely to be mature physically by these ages, boys may still be in the process of physical maturation: girls are typically about two years ahead of boys in physical growth spurts and sexual maturity. It is common for adolescents to be concerned about their bodies, e.g., their weight, size, or shape. Adults need to be vigilant for eating disorders during later adolescence, particularly in girls. Cognitively, older teenagers may begin to learn more clearly defined work habits, especially if they begin to work after or before school, on weekends, and/or during the summers. They typically become more concerned about their future plans for attending post-secondary school, getting jobs, and what kinds of work they will want to do. They develop the ability to provide reasons for the choices they make more competently, including being able to explain their moral decisions regarding what is right and wrong. Adults should encourage adolescents' adequate sleep, exercising, and nutritious diets; and be available to provide support and advice while creating opportunities for and encouraging teens to use their judgment, problem-solving, and conflict resolution skills.

Emotionally and socially, teenagers around 15-17 experience decreased conflict with parents, and display more independence from them. Socially, they spend more time with friends, less with parents. They demonstrate more interest in dating and relationships, developing emotional capacities for sharing and caring more deeply and more intimacy. While it should not be ignored, it is also typical for teenagers to feel considerable depression or sadness. These emotions can contribute to reduced school performance, unprotected sex, and substance use or abuse. Morally, older teens can think abstractly according to Piaget and hence are capable of the highest moral development levels according to Kohlberg, understanding the concept of the social contract and even developing universal moral principles of human rights beyond legalities. Adults can show affection; spend time in mutually enjoyed activities with teenagers; encourage teen volunteerism and extracurricular interests and pursuits; ask about their feelings, including suicidal ideations; observe any behavior changes; respect teen opinions; show interest in teen activities; compliment and celebrate efforts and achievements; encourage responsible decisions, including regarding Internet and social media use; help teens plan ahead for difficult situations, e.g., involving peer pressure and/or others' risk behaviors; discuss responsibilities, expectations, and respectful behavior in workplaces and public; and respect teen privacy needs.

Ways in which different types of student development can respectively interact

When a student's cognitive development is ahead of his/her physical development, the child is likely to become frustrated when s/he can conceive of many things mentally, but cannot execute them physically. This is especially of younger children still having more physical development to achieve. Conversely, when a student's physical development is ahead of his/her cognitive development, young children are apt inadvertently to damage property and/or harm peers, younger children, or pets. Linguistic development affects social development in that more advanced language levels often facilitate social communication—but not always: some children show advanced language skills development, yet lack commensurate social skills. In another way, some less linguistically advanced students are skilled at using nonverbal communication skills to support social interactions. Some young students also have superior emotional intelligence (EQ) without necessarily having equally high academic or linguistic skills. More advanced affective development in elementary-age children can influence their moral development: the more children are able to

- 52 -

share, take others' perspectives, empathize, and engage in prosocial behaviors, the more able they are to understand and internalize less rigid, more mutual, and socially-oriented morality.

Linguistic development interacts with cognitive development: psychologists find very high positive correlations between vocabulary and intelligence test scores. Teachers can enhance adolescent linguistic mediation skills with exercises regarding literal vs. metaphorical word meanings, and enhance pragmatics (using language to meet needs) through question-asking skills instruction. Teens whose cognitive development precedes their physical development excel academically but not athletically may be stereotyped by peers as "nerds," and those with superior physical skills but lacking equal academic success as "jocks." Teens whose physical development far precedes their cognitive development may inadvertently harm others, particularly when rapidly gaining adult strength. Similarly, adolescent affective development influences cognitive development because the amygdala matures sooner, generating intense teen emotions; yet the prefrontal cortex, which will eventually control those emotions, does not mature until young adulthood. Affective maturity influences moral levels in that the more emotionally mature the student, the more able s/he is to relate to others' needs, use prosocial behaviors, and understand universal human rights. Teen social interactions are increasingly influenced by emotional intelligence (EQ) development. Both affective and social developments interact with moral development when teens must make difficult ethical decisions involving others in social contexts.

Supporting cognitive development during early childhood

Adults help children focus attention by preventing interruptions and distractions. Show interest in children's activities and offer observations and reflections about what they believe children are trying to achieve. Presenting learning materials in new ways piques curiosity: spread green "grass" cloth over blocks, making a hill; arrange toy farm animals on it; arrange dolls "reading" books in classroom reading or library corners. Observe nearby objects and events, inviting children to go see what they are. Support mastery motivation with materials sufficiently challenging for interest without being impossible, express interest, encourage children, and share their joy when they show what they accomplished. Offering multisensory exploration modes, e.g., scent bottles, water, sand, cornstarch, etc., supports sensorimotor learning. Encourage object permanence by playing peek-a-boo, reading stories with flaps hiding pictures, and about people leaving and returning. Toys reacting differentially to actions, e.g., push lights, busy boxes, balls, etc., teach cause-and-effect. Stacking rings or cups, tunnels, toy houses, etc. promote spatial understanding. Play tools, phones, keys, paint, water, markers, etc. promote tool use comprehension. Scaffold play to the next level; supply materials, ideas, and language slightly increasing complexity and elaborating play. Discuss time concepts like now and later, before and after, today, yesterday, tomorrow, etc. Use language and toys introducing shape awareness, one-on-one correspondence, amounts, size comparisons, and numbers.

Teacher considerations for students in early and later adolescence

Middle school teachers who find some 6th-graders acting out in class or not completing work may attribute these instances to behavior problems, but experienced teachers with developmental perspectives point out that they may actually be adjustment problems: transitions between schools can be difficult for students; teachers may not realize the extent of variation among schools. Distinguishing adjustment or developmental difficulties from more severe problems is easier for teachers who have worked with students of every age. Whereas elementary-age students have concrete operations, including reversibility, adolescents have formal operations, including application of abstract concepts to specific phenomena. For example, an 8-year-old understood objects that looked smaller underwater did not shrink because, with reversibility, s/he could see

- 53 -

they were the same size when removed; but did not understand why they looked smaller underwater. By the student's teens, s/he understands water is denser than air, light waves travel at differing speeds through media of different density, and applies this to understand why objects look smaller underwater. Teachers can use deductive reasoning with teens that younger students could not follow. Hypothetico-deductive reasoning or "if-then" propositions enable adolescents to speculate about possibilities, e.g., going to college, moral dilemmas about justifying killing, etc.

Home and community cultural influences on elementary school student achievement

Some research into high-ability or gifted talent development in bilingual Hispanic elementary school students has concluded that influential home factors include family values like respect, education, career, and family; maternal roles; extended family role models; emotional support; Spanish-language maintenance; trips to parental native countries; and Hispanic legacies. School factors include safe school environments, flexible grouping, and English-language support (when necessary). Research also finds teachers of high-ability or gifted Hispanic students frequently know little or nothing about home language spoken. They tend to assume if a student is not in ESL classes or programs, s/he is not bilingual; but in fact, many are both bilingual and biliterate. Teachers also demonstrate limited understanding of multicultural meanings and practices. Educational investigators advise, standards for assessing Hispanic students should reflect their cultural and ethnic backgrounds to be accurate and relevant. They state the need for establishing direct communication between Hispanic parents and schools, including information about gifted program identification procedures and home methods parents can use to help their children educationally. Another need is professional development to help faculty and staff understand differences in student cultural, language, and learning styles. Also, access for classroom teachers to information about Hispanic students' linguistic histories and present Spanish usage is advised.

Impacts of community, racial, and cultural differences

With American demographics rapidly changing, schools reflect societal racism. Racial and cultural differences cannot be overlooked anymore. It is not only necessary, but moreover healthy for minorities to express their racial and cultural identities. Teachers, administrators, school staff, parents—all school community members—must be involved in designing learning experiences founded on understanding and respect for racial and cultural diversity. While educational experts believe this requires the whole society to unite for success, they concede that as this has not occurred, the educational system must still strive for resolution of racial and cultural conflicts through collective efforts. While schools are desegregated, surrounding cities and suburbs are not. Neighborhoods, the foundations of American society, are subject to racial and economic limitations. Because children learn from each other, their education is strongly affected by community factors of housing costs, incomes, lending policies, and racial and institutional discrimination. While some Latino parents believe bilingual education can overcome discrimination and black parents believe desegregation promotes equality, some Latino parents see desegregation as impeding their objectives by dissipating Latin influence and destroying bilingual programs. Experts call for compromise, noting that both must coexist by law.

Considerations related to children's school readiness and learning readiness

The majority of children may enter school ready to learn, but not optimally; and have a range of cultural, environmental, and educational background experiences. Readiness works two ways: preparing children for school and preparing schools for children. For educators to promote all children's learning, they must offer school environments recognizing background diversity, enabling comfortable transitions to successive learning levels, and supplying community supports

- 54 -

as needed. School readiness is divided into readiness for school and readiness to learn. The former involves specific motor, cognitive, linguistic, and social skills enabling children to absorb school curriculum; the latter involves the developmental level where children are capable of learning specific materials. Educators differentiate traditional ideas of readiness placing responsibility on children vs. giving schools the responsibility to provide necessary services in the least restrictive environment to enable children to reach their full potentials. Also, readiness assessment criteria can have inappropriate expectations, not recognizing normal variations in individual development and learning natures and rates. Experts find three factors critical: recognizing and supporting individual cultural, linguistic, and other differences; addressing early life experience inequities to ensure that all children have access to opportunities promoting school success; and appropriate and reasonable expectations of children entering school.

Stages in adolescent development from the perspective of developmental psychology

Despite age variances and overlaps, early adolescents develop new self-images based on physiological changes and apply emergent logical cognitive and rational judgment skills. Mid-adolescents endeavor to separate from parents; their cognitive and emotional abilities expand. They become adventurous, experimenting with various ideas while exploring their relationships to self, the opposite sex, and groups; and struggling to differentiate or reconcile their own values vs. those of parents and authority figures. They develop responsibility and self-reliance, assume greater control of educational and vocational opportunities and activities, and seek to establish their place in and contribute to society. Late adolescent identity and social role stabilizes; they gain integration and consistency in psychology and worldview. Balance among fantasy, reality, and aspirations; shifts from immature self-interest toward caring for and giving to others; and establishment and pursuit of realistic life goals are characteristics. Teachers must determine overall class functioning levels for planning lessons. For instance, lessons should help adolescents advance cognitively from Piaget's concrete operations to formal operations stage. To resolve Erikson's conflict of industry vs. inferiority, younger adolescents must experience school success; to resolve identity vs. role confusion, older adolescents must form satisfying future action plans. Hands-on activities like those Piaget offered can further these goals.

Activities teachers can give students in grades K-6 to help them develop

Grades K-2

Explain different examples of school success. Realize the relation between what you want to achieve and goal-setting. Describe a behavior you want to change. Give examples of academic and personal goals to set. Divide a goal into manageable steps.

Grades 1-3

Identify a situation you want to change. Explain how becoming what you want and school success are related. Identify progress you have made toward your goal. Explain how to improve your classroom behavior, e.g., paying attention, finishing assignments, raising your hand more, etc. Make a plan for improving your work in a certain school subject. Make a plan for a personal goal. Reward yourself for achievements using self-talk. Teachers can use puppet shows wherein puppets apply planning and goal-setting skills.

Grades 3-4

Explain how literary characters, people studied in social sciences, friends, and you have overcome goal obstacles. Identify people and conditions contributing to your goal achievement. Name steps for doing homework, studying for tests, organizing materials and spaces, etc. Name things

- 55 -

interfering with goal achievement you could not change. Evaluate what you could have done differently to achieve a goal better.

<u>Grades 4-6</u>

Develop friendship and academic goals with action steps and dates, monitor progress, analyze step delays or changes, and evaluate your goal achievement level.

Assignments for developing goal-setting, peer interaction, and decision-making skills

<u>Grades 6-8</u>

Identify resources (e.g., research sources) furthering goal progress. Analyze influences of supports and obstacles in completing goal action steps, and better ways of overcoming barriers and using supports. Differentiate long- and short-term goals. Apply goal-setting skills to academic success development. Set a positive social interaction goal. Teachers: use interest or incentive inventories, planning sheets, discuss goal-setting steps, and lead self-regulation and self-monitoring games.

<u>Grades 8-10</u>

Set a goal in a sport, hobby, musical instrument, or interest to accomplish in a month or two. Plan goal timeframes and action steps. Monitor progress and adjust plans as necessary. Evaluate goal achievement levels, and identify contributing or detracting factors. Analyze what you learned and would do differently.

<u>Grades 9-11</u>

Identify who helped you achieve a goal and how. Analyze why you could or could not overcome goal obstacles, an unexpected opportunity's goal achievement impact, why schedule conflicts could require changing goal timeframes, how substance use could impede and academic achievement contribute to long-term goal achievement.

<u>Grades 10-12</u>

Set long-term academic or career goals with action steps and completion dates. Anticipate obstacles and make contingency plans. Analyze how current health behavior decisions might affect long-term educational or career goals. Evaluate summer job goal feasibility based on your ability to execute action steps timely. Self-evaluate goal achievement. Create a behavioral contract to enhance a coping strategy and document progress in a journal.

Instructional methods that reflect individual student differences and developmental levels

Elementary grade students include wide ranges of individual differences. Teachers must pay attention to and address these differences to maximize the potential of each individual student. Many educational theorists and research studies show that when students receive instruction that responds to their developmental levels, as well as their learning profiles and personal interests, they find school more satisfying and achieve more success in said school. Teachers who differentiate instruction according to variable individual student learning needs are also recognized as more professional, competent, and creative educators. For example, elementary school teachers can vary instructional content by providing students with materials at different reading levels. They can record or procure some texts on tape for students with visual weaknesses and auditory strengths. They can make different vocabulary and/or spelling lists according to differing student readiness levels. They can present concepts in both visual and auditory modalities. They can assign reading buddies to students who are struggling readers—and/or to all students to enhance their reading skills. They can assign small groups for re-teaching skills or concepts to struggling learners, and for enriching the skills or thought processes of advanced students.

Early adolescent cognitive development

Individual differences in early adolescent cognitive development vary widely. Young teens develop metacognition, independent thought, high curiosity, and broad interests, though they typically do not maintain most. They prefer learning peer interactions, active experiences over passive ones, and learning about subjects useful and interesting to them. These teens develop abstract thought, analyze and synthesize information, formulate and test hypotheses, think reflectively, tackle complex ideas, understand metaphorical nuances and traditional wisdom's meanings, consider ideological issues, argue positions, question authority, and appreciate sophisticated humor. As Piaget stated, they make sense of the world building on their background knowledge and individual experiences. Young adolescents are more interested in authentic and real-life learning than traditional academic content. They frequently observe adult behavior keenly and are inquisitive about adults. Their abilities to anticipate needs, develop personal goals, and consider the future improve. Teachers must offer widely varied educational materials and approaches, from structured to challenging for concrete to abstract learners; plan curriculum around real-life concepts; provide experimentation and other authentic activities; enable peer and adult discourse; hands-on experience and direct environmental interaction; acknowledge changing interests by ensuring exploration opportunities; supplying forums for exploring reasons for home, school, and societal rules; and teach by example as role models.

Adolescent moral development

The ability to make principled choices increases with moral development. Young adolescents, developing abstract thinking, typically become idealistic, highly valuing fairness in human interaction. They start reconciling their understanding of others caring about them with their own adolescent egocentrism as they advance into Kohlberg's moral development stage of interpersonal conformity. They graduate from self-centeredness to more consideration for others' feelings and rights. They ask impossible, sweeping questions, and do not tolerate trivial adult answers. They typically embrace parental values while developing personal values. They cease seeing complex ethical or moral issues in black-and-white, realizing shades of gray but unready to address these—putting them at risk for unsound ethical or moral decisions. Teachers must acknowledge and utilize the connection between teen cognitive and moral development by planning lessons cultivating critical thought, higher-order thinking skills, and higher moral reasoning levels. For example, writing assignments articulating their feelings and thoughts; opportunities for examining behavior options and consequences; experiences requiring contemplating ethical or moral dilemmas and potential responses—helping students solve problems, develop values, and set their own behavioral standards. Teachers can provide scenarios whereby students explore concepts of justice, equity, and fairness. Schools should also offer curricula and programs addressing racism, sexism, discrimination, and similar social issues.

Adolescent emotional and psychological development

Seeking unique personal identities and independence characterize adolescent emotional and psychological development. While searching for adult identities, teens try to balance peer approval with adult acceptance, experiencing conflict from competing family and peer allegiances. Self-discovery and identity quests can increase vulnerable feelings as sensitivity to self-other differences grows. Young adolescence is typified by unpredictability and intensity. Teens tend to display restless, moody, inconsistent, or erratic behavior, including alternating inferiority and superiority and swings between anxiety and bravado. Self-esteem is fragile or low at these ages. Teens are notoriously self-conscious, and hypersensitive to criticism of their exaggerated perceived flaws. Emotional situations can provoke childish behaviors, unilateral arguments, and naïve opinions. Emotional volatility places teens at risk for poor decisions. As David Elkind noted, adolescents think their experiences are unique in the "personal fable." Teachers and schools can support identity formation with curricular and instructional exploration opportunities, organizational structures, advisory programs, and educational practices supporting positive adult and peer relationships, group cohesion, and caring atmospheres. Other positive outcomes include building student self-esteem, explaining its importance to development; explaining friendship's importance and the normalcy of changing allegiances; avoiding sarcasm, humiliation, or harsh criticism; providing self-expression and self-assessment opportunities, including reading, role-play, and drama; and helping teens realize their problems are not unique.

Classroom instruction that teachers can differentiate among students

Based on each student's learning profile, interests, readiness, and learning levels, teachers can differentiate classroom instruction. Four elements for differentiating instruction are: (1) content to learn; (2) the process students use to master content; (3) products students will produce, requiring practice, application, and extension and elaboration of what they learn in a unit; and (4) learning environment, i.e., how the classroom functions and how students experience it. Some examples of differentiating processes include: (1) set up interest centers where students can explore subcategories of class subjects they find most interesting. (2) Assign tiered activities with different levels of complexity, challenge, or support for acquiring the same skills and understanding. (3) Provide hands-on supports, like manipulatives, for students needing these. (4) Combine work commonly assigned to the entire class with individualized work for specific students into lists of tasks, making personal agendas to complete during designated and/or spare time. (5) Differentiate durations students take to finish tasks, allowing advanced students to examine topics in-depth and enable added support for struggling students.

Elements of classroom instruction that teachers can differentiate among students

To address the needs of individual students in a class, teachers can differentiate things like (1) content; (2) processes and activities whereby students learn content; (3) products students create by applying and demonstrating what they learned; and (4) learning environment, i.e., how students perceive the classroom and how it functions. Some examples of differentiating products for elementary school students include: (1) design rubrics matching and extending various student skill levels. (2) Offer choices to students in how to demonstrate learning, like between writing a letter, creating a labeled art mural, or producing a puppet show. (3) Invite students to design their own product assignments, providing they include necessary components. (4) Give students options to work on projects in small groups or individually. Some examples of differentiating an elementary school learning environment include: (1) furnish materials reflecting diverse home and cultural backgrounds. (2) Establish clear guidelines matching individual student needs for independent work. (3) Ensure the classroom contains both areas for collaboration and areas for undistracted quiet work. (4) Help students realize some classmates need to sit quietly, while others must move about. (5) Develop routines enabling students to get help when teachers are temporarily busy with others.

Decision-making and goal-setting skills

Young people are able to develop some independence and recognize they have some control over their lives by learning to set goals. First, they must decide what they want to accomplish. This decision-making helps motivate children to achieve things, not for external rewards or to please other people, but for their own satisfaction. This helps them develop internal locus of control and intrinsic motivation. One step adults can help with is first defining what a goal is. They might use the analogy of a hockey or soccer goal. Explain that winning a goal is the end product of much hard work; setting a goal is describing what you want to get done or the place you want to get to, and that involves planning for something you want to understand or do better. Another step for adults to help children determine their priorities is by listening more than talking. Observing some strengths and needs is acceptable, but encourage children to talk about themselves. For example, observe a child has learned something, and ask what s/he next wants to do with this skill. Ask if a child is worried about anything in school that will be difficult.

Teach students how to talk about goals to understand and set them. For example, they must define what they want to accomplish, by when, and which related skills they already know. Children of any age may conceive unrealistic goals. For example, a child who has not learned how to ice skate may decide s/he wants to place ice hockey. Rather than squelching aspirations by telling the child this will be impossible or too difficult, help the child refine the goal into smaller associated goals as steps to the ultimate goal. For example, suggest setting the preliminary goal of learning ice skating. This generalizes to all goals: they are not accomplished all in one attempt, but rather involve series of many steps. Assist children with task analysis, breaking a goal down into its smaller component steps or skills. They can make each skill or step into a smaller or shorter-term goal toward the main goal. Help students make visual reminders, e.g., a worksheet with a drawing of a ladder, to list steps toward a goal on the rungs; a goal board with a drawing of a soccer goal, etc. Also help students track and mark their progress, and celebrate success.

Impacts of student substance use and abuse on development and learning

Not only are the physical and neurological development of younger children incomplete, even adolescents have yet to undergo full brain development. Therefore, using alcohol and other drugs can cause damage to their central nervous systems and other body systems and organs. Damage can be temporary or permanent, reversible or irreversible. In addition to interfering with attention in school, substance use can interfere with myelination, whereby brain and nerve cells develop coating sheaths, both protecting them and facilitating impulse and signal transmission. This process continues into young adulthood. The heart, lungs, liver, kidneys, other organs and systems are still developing and can be damaged, sometimes irreparably, at early ages. Substance use also undermines motivation to learn and achieve. Under the influence, students attend to the effects they experience, not acquiring new information or getting anything done. When use becomes abuse, addiction causes focus only on getting more of the needed substance to relieve withdrawal symptoms and reproduce the original high—which latter is impossible and leads to ingesting increasing amounts. Students neglect hygiene and schoolwork, attendance and grades fall, and dropouts become more common. Substance use and abuse triggers or exacerbates anxiety, depression, paranoia, schizophrenia, bipolar disorder, and other mental disorders.

Conditions leading to gang involvement

The organizational structures and activities of gangs are extremely complex social phenomena. In low socioeconomic urban neighborhoods, gangs often develop in part to protect members against violence from adult criminals and other gangs. This positive motivation and protective benefit are still accompanied by undesirable effects. Gang involvement is more likely during adolescence, when students search to form personal identities. Many economically disadvantaged urban youth lack adult supervision, mentoring, and role models. Gang membership fills needs for group affiliation, belonging, identity, rules, and behavioral direction (even if behaviors are undesirable). Youth struggling to reconcile newly discovered abstractions and complexities find security in adversarial relationships among gangs, defining "us vs. them" mentalities that are less equivocal or contradictory. These enmities also provide concrete foes for youth feeling helpless to control or combat larger, seemingly unassailable foes of social ills like poverty, illiteracy, crime, discrimination, lack of opportunity, etc. Even in affluent communities, gangs may form to fulfill the same needs for social acceptance, allegiance, group identity, rules, etc.—sometimes particularly with inadequate parental or adult involvement, communication, and role modeling. Youth with unformed or unstable identities, vulnerable to peer pressure, are at higher risk for committing criminal acts as gang members. This can curtail their education, work, freedom, and life.

Peer-related issues

Before adolescence, very young children first developing autonomy find it very important to become their own persons and do things independently. These early assertions of self are reflected in the very individual, sometimes bizarre way young children may dress or eat when allowed to select their own clothing, unusual dietary choices, etc. However, social acceptance and peer pressure are extremely powerful forces. By the time they are in school, children begin showing concern for belonging to groups and fitting into social contexts. Student responses to social pressures reach greatest prominence during adolescence. Although adolescent quests for personal identities and defining social roles seem to recapitulate early childhood's assertion of autonomy in some respects, teenagers are additionally both hypersensitive to peers' perceptions and opinions and highly concerned with social acceptance. Teens struggling with identity issues can also feel threatened about defining their individuality, which informs their impending adult identities—which signal accompanying adult responsibilities. Conforming to group norms assuages adolescent self-consciousness and hypersensitivity to criticism by preventing teens from standing out; and reassures them that, as group members, they are not facing adulthood and its responsibilities alone.

Middle and high school teachers find many students very concerned with wearing certain clothes, eating and drinking certain foods or drinks, listening to certain music, and doing many things simply because "everybody" is doing them. "Everybody" can be everyone in a class, a school, a certain grade or age group, a circle of friends, etc. Adolescents develop exaggerated self-consciousness and hypersensitivity, leading to preoccupation with others' opinions and fear of standing out, seeming different, and not fitting into a group. As teens are also working to define their individual identities, teachers can appeal to adolescent investment in this process by reinforcing their independent choices, individual decisions, and affirming their uniqueness as persons. They can support teens in resisting peer pressure, whereby adolescents take advantage of others' social vulnerability by attempting to control them to conform by asking them what is right for them, not others; and expressing and demonstrating their approval and pride in students' asserting and being themselves. Teachers can also exploit peer-related issues by assigning cooperative learning projects; encouraging and rewarding academic club participation; and emphasizing other learning experiences involving positive social interactions, whereby group identification and interdependence promote collective and individual learning.

Types of play identified by Mildred Parten

(1) Unoccupied: not truly playing, simply observing anything of interest; a child may travel, stay still, move randomly, follow others, etc. (2) Solitary or independent play: playing alone, unaware or uninterested in others' activities. Two- and 3-year-olds do this more often than older children. (3) Onlooker behavior: observing others playing without participating, also more frequent among younger children. The child may talk about or otherwise interact socially, but not join the activity. (4) Parallel play (also called social coaction or adjacent play): playing near other children, but

- 60 -

separately. The child might imitate other children's behaviors. This type is considered transitional from solitary and onlooker play to associative and cooperative play. (5) Associative play: showing interest in and interaction with others playing, but activities are not coordinated or organized. (6) Cooperative play: interested in both play activity and participants. Activities are organized; participants assume or assign roles. Group identification or identity may develop. Requiring greater organizational skills and social maturity, this is more common with children older than preschoolers and kindergarteners. Parten found these play types progressively more socially mature, as child communication skills and interaction opportunities increased. Others generally agree regarding types, but consider them not necessarily sequential and/or influenced by other factors, e.g., how well children know each other, etc.

Importance of play to early childhood development and learning

The UN High Commission for Human Rights declares play every child's right. Pediatric research finds playing essential for healthy brain development. Playing develops physical strength, dexterity, cognitive and emotional strength, imagination, and early engagement and interaction with the environment. While exposure to letters and numbers promotes literacy, children learn about what people do, how they behave, and what they are thinking from playing, not from letters or numbers. By playing, children create and explore worlds they can master, enabling their overcoming fears and practicing adult roles. This helps them develop new skills, increasing their self-confidence and developing resiliency, which they will need for future challenges. Children learn sharing, group cooperation, conflict resolution, negotiation, self-advocacy, and leadership skills through unstructured play. Through child-driven play, they progress at their own paces, practice decision-making skills, and discover and pursue their own interests. Playing involves more healthful physical activity than passively watching TV, playing video games, etc. When young children's physical development precedes verbal development, they can express frustrations, experiences, and viewpoints through play better than language. Emotional-social development should be integrated with cognitive and academic learning. Research finds play enhances learning readiness, learning behaviors, problem-solving skills, and school adjustment.

Contemporary model of the whole child approach

The Association for Supervision and Curriculum Development (ASCD) and US Centers for Disease Control and Prevention (CDC) have collaborated to produce the Whole School, Whole Community, Whole Child (WSCC) model to coordinate public health, school health, and educational processes, policies, and practices to improve health and learning, which are interrelated. They say a whole child approach to learning, teaching, and community involvement means each child deserves to be safe, healthy, supported, engaged, and challenged. Related to this model, ASCD's Whole Child Initiative aims to help educators, policymakers, families, and community members realize a vision of educating the whole child through collaborative, sustainable action. ASCD's School Improvement Tool is a totally online needs assessment that educators in schools and districts worldwide can use to determine what practices to implement or improve to realize the whole-child education vision. The tool enables educators to survey, numerically score, and color-code schools regarding key criteria, e.g., all students enter school healthy, and learn about and practice healthy lifestyles; learn in physically and emotionally safe environments; are actively engaged in learning, connected to school and community, and supported by caring, qualified adults; have access to personalized learning; are challenged academically, prepared for college or employment success; and school whole-child approaches are sustainable.

- 61 -

Models of developmentally appropriate instruction related to literacy development

Direct or explicit instruction

Whole-class, small-group, and one-on-one learning. A teacher shows a class of 4-year-olds how to hold a book; points to the cover picture, inviting brainstorming about the book's subject; points to and reads aloud each title word; then reads them the book.

Centers

Individually-themed classroom areas for student selection, including computers, arts and crafts, gross and fine motor skills, etc. to enable meaningful, self-initiated, self-directed activity at students' own paces, stimulating language development and social interaction. Free play: students explore the physical environment, pretend, converse; pursue curiosity; and practice gross and fine motor skills and oral language skills. Students might construct buildings, make cookies, walk balance beams, paint, dress in costumes, etc. Letting students choose play areas facilitates self-exploration and using real-life manipulatives, informing all literacy instruction areas. Students develop learning styles and sense of the world.

Small-group instruction

Teacher modeling print reading; discussion of story events per page; problem-solving or predicting story endings and reasons; open-ended learning opportunities, meaningful to each group, focusing on each student's needs.

Guided reading

Teacher and students read text fluently in unison with expression and connotation; then discuss the story, including teacher observations, reteaching; enrichment; self-monitoring; enabling analytical and critical reading patterns, enhancing phonemic awareness, phonics, comprehension, fluency, and reading confidence.

Typical challenges encountered by middle and high school students

Students entering puberty are experiencing rapid physiological and psychological changes. For some, the magnitude and speed of these changes present major adjustment challenges. For example, a formerly small boy suddenly grows a foot within one school year. Understanding limb pain and becoming winded easily are normal with growth spurts will help; he may also need help adjusting to his change in appearance. Though increased height and muscle mass are gratifying and get girls' attention, he must modify his self-image accordingly. A girl practicing gymnastics since childhood, formerly compliant with coaches' rigorous demands, begins rebelling at these now while developing her individual young adult identity. She resents pressures for weight control because she cannot stop her body from growing larger and developing new curves. Educators can help her decide if she wants to continue, possibly with different coaches, in less competitive capacities or reduced hours. Another girl practicing ballet since childhood, responding to external and internal pressures, over-exercises, severely restricts her diet, and purges for weight control, developing anorexia and bulimia. In addition to referral to counseling, educators can encourage her to talk, give her permission not to be perfect, avoid pressure, offer choices, and provide things and activities she can control other than her body.

Helping students address educational and career issues

Most adolescents are aware of which things they find interesting, but may need some assistance in relating these interests to higher education and career paths. For example, several students share a love of animals. However, one of them excels in and enjoys all math subjects, biology, and chemistry. Another absolutely hates math and science, but loves bathing, drying, combing, brushing pets and making them look beautiful, and has a talent for handling animals gently. A third student is extremely nurturing, always rescuing lost and hurt animals and nursing them back to health. A fourth student loves animals but admires wildlife more than pets; is concerned about endangered species and extinction, already volunteering for conservation efforts; and wants to improve habitats for captive animals. The first student may consider a career as a veterinarian, the second as a professional pet groomer, the third as a veterinary technician or in an animal rescue organization, and the fourth as a wildlife biologist and/or zoo curator. Some students need higher education to qualify for careers they want, others to explore further or discover career preferences, and others for additional life experience and social maturity.

Instructional Delivery

Questioning students

Questions cognitively lower on Bloom's taxonomy—for knowledge and comprehension—are better when imparting or retaining factual knowledge. Open-ended, higher-cognitive questions—for application, analysis, evaluation, and synthesis—should be more than half of those used in higher grades, but elementary-grade students need smaller proportions of these too. Research finds combining higher and lower questions more effective than using either one exclusively. Studies show older students' on-task behavior, response length, number of relevant contributions and questions, peer interactions, complete sentences, and speculative thinking correlate positively with using greater than or equal to 50 percent higher-level questions. Teachers may still need to include explicit instruction, not just many more questions, for complex concepts. Pre-reading questions are effective with older, higher-ability, and interested students, but not with poor readers and younger students, who focus only on material for answering them. Slightly increasing wait-time promotes achievement. Studies find teachers paradoxically allow less wait time for students perceived as poor or slow learners than those perceived more capable. Teachers encourage participation by inviting student responses non-critically, addressing incorrect answers with redirection, and partial answers with probing—both explicit to student answers. Vague feedback, e.g., "Wrong, try again" is ineffective for achievement. Active listening restates student responses, helping clarify student understanding and meaning and encouraging participation.

Teachers ask students questions for varied purposes, e.g., actively involving students in lessons, regardless of questions' cognitive levels. "When did this author live?" "In what period is this work set?" Even low-level knowledge questions involve students as they consider and/or respond. "Why do you think the author did...?" require cognitively higher responses. Teachers might ask "Have you ever...?" or "Do you know anybody who...?" This relates textual events and experiences to students' own lives. Connecting new material to prior knowledge increases motivation and interest. Questions can evaluate preparation and check on assignment completion: in classes with many students not typically hesitant to speak, if nobody answers basic questions about assigned reading, they likely did not do it. Students completing math assignments successfully can likely answer specific questions about the operations they used or solutions they got, while those not doing or understanding it cannot. Questions develop critical thinking skills when requiring students to apply concepts and analyze them, separate inference from fact, evaluate or judge ideas and products, and synthesize components to construct new meaning. Questions help teachers review prior lessons to assess, increase, or refresh student comprehension and retention. They cultivate insights by making students think about topics, assess goal achievement, and stimulate independent learning.

Managerial questions facilitate classroom operations. Rhetorical questions reinforce or emphasize statements and ideas. Closed questions check retention and focus thinking. Open questions promote student discussion and interaction. Probing questions, based on student responses, require students to go beyond first answers. Clarifying: "What do you mean? Can you elaborate?" Increasing critical awareness: "What are you assuming? What are your reasons? What would an opponent say?" Refocusing: "Then what are the implications for...? Can you relate that to...? Let's analyze your answer." Prompting: "What's the square root of 94?" (Student: "I don't know.") "What's the square root of 100?" (Student: "10.") "Of 81?" (Student: "Nine.") "Then what do we know about the square root of 94?" (Student: "It's between nine and 10.") Redirecting to another student: "Do you agree? Can you elaborate on his/her answer?" Factual questions elicit simple information, e.g., "Who wrote this? Who is the main character?" Or they elicit event sequences: "What are the steps for a bill to become law?" "How is hydrochloric acid produced?" "How did

Robinson Crusoe react to discovering footprints?" <u>Divergent</u> questions have no right or wrong answer, eliciting exploration of possibilities and both concrete and abstract thinking. For example: "If the Spanish Armada had defeated England in 1588, how would it have changed history?"

Rather than remembering answers, students must figure out answers by higher-order questions, which require generalizing in meaningful patterns relative to facts. <u>Evaluation</u>: requires valuation, judgment, or choice via comparing things and ideas with established standards. Assuming equal resources, would you rate General Ulysses S. Grant or Robert E. Lee more skillful? Why? Which of these two books do you think contributed more to understanding this era? Why? <u>Inference</u>: requires deductive or inductive reasoning. Deductive: if gas temperature remains constant but altitude is increased 4000 feet, what happens to gas pressure? Why? Inductive: considering these world leaders' shared qualities, what can we conclude about required leadership qualities? Why? <u>Comparison</u>: requires discerning similarities, differences, contradictions, and non-relations – How are Social Darwinism and late-19th-century Supreme Court rulings related? How are Pericles' Funeral Oration and Lincoln's Gettysburg Address similar or different? Are clams and mussels the same? <u>Application</u>: requires transferring concepts and principles to different contexts – How did Germany's Weimar Republic demonstrate Gresham's Law? <u>Problem-solving</u>: requires using acquired knowledge, seeing relationships, relating parts to whole – Imagine you grew up thinking dogs were bad, but none bit you; how would you react now? Would the dog's characteristics matter? Explain the idea of prejudice using this example.

Supporting students in articulating ideas

One strategy teachers use to support clear student expression is prompting. Verbal prompting: when a student does not know the answer to the teacher's initial question, the teacher asks additional questions to which the student does know the answers, leading the student to discover more about the answer to the original question. For example, a teacher asks a student a square root s/he does not know; the teacher asks the student two more square roots, one higher and the other lower; the student realizes the unknown answer is between the other two. Nonverbal prompting: nodding or making affirmative sounds and gestures indicating agreement to encourage continuing, pointing at objects or information to give hints, hand-over-hand guidance with manipulatives, etc. Restatement: repeating a student's message in the teacher's own words, either affirming the message or allowing the student to deny or correct the restatement or clarify the message. Student: "This assignment took me all night!" Teacher: "It was too hard?" Reflective listening statements mirror student messages, not just restating them but moreover interpreting implicit meanings. Student: "I will never get this right!" Teacher: "You feel frustrated?" Wait-time enables student processing: understanding questions, recalling information, formulating responses. Research finds three minutes optimal for factual or low-cognitive, and longer for high-cognitive questions.

Methods that promote higher thinking levels

(1) After assigned reading or video viewing, ask students what they would have done in a fictional character or nonfictional individual's situation. After students complete projects or assignments, have them write (a.) what they could have done differently, (b.) how, (c.) what they will do differently or additionally next time, and (d.) what they learned during the process of the project or assignment. These both require students to reflect on their experiences and articulate insights and thoughts. (2) In class discussion, have students identify a book or movie's main assumption(s). Ask how they know these are true. Have them research for proof or disproof, teaching the habit of questioning and investigating rather than simply accepting others' assumptions. (3) Have students compare similarities and contrast differences between or among books, movies, experiments, natural phenomena, etc., guiding them to find relationships. Have them make cause-and-effect

graphics identifying relationships among events or actions in history, fiction, or drama. Ask how fictional characters and historical or current figures influence(d) one another; how chemicals interact, causing reactions; why, etc. (4) Ask students to explain how information relates to current study topics. For examining validity, see (2) above; also have students test claims directly when feasible. (5) Review information identified in lessons and classwork, ask what students conclude based on it, and have them explain the logic leading to conclusions. (6) Assign applying newly-learned skills in other classes, field trips, homes, communities, and workplaces.

Setting the stage for effective classroom discussions

For teachers to get all students engaged in discussing a topic, they need to make it appealing. One way is connecting topics to existing student experience and knowledge, making them more personally relevant. Ask if they have encountered similar situations or felt similarly in other situations: find some commonality between the topic and every student's life experience. Teachers also need to show respect for all student opinions. Experts note teachers' natural inclinations to evaluate, approve or disapprove, and judge student contributions, increasing student fears against expressing thoughts. To create climates welcoming participation, teachers must suspend judgment; instead of responding with "Right," "Wrong," or "That wasn't what I was thinking about," etc., they can respond, "Tell me more about that," "Thank you for sharing your ideas with us," etc. Asking students to elaborate without judging makes them feel safe to progress in their thinking and share it. This teacher acceptance establishing safety also supports student risk-taking. In safe, non-threatening, non-judgmental atmospheres, teacher acceptance encourages students to express potentially controversial or minority views. Making all students feel safe and invited to participate facilitates collaboration: teachers model respecting others' ideas; students with non-judgmental teachers are less likely to fear classmates' judgment.

Critical thinking and creative thinking

Critical thinking includes the abilities to question, evaluate, and judge information or material. For example, students should learn to distinguish opinions from facts in what they read and hear; look for evidence supporting author or speaker arguments, or lack thereof; evaluate supporting evidence, e.g., consider whether its source is reputable, proven, accepted by experts in its field, etc.; judge the quality of information or material through comparison, experience, and intuition. Creative thinking includes generating original ideas, coming up with problem-solving alternatives that differ from usual solutions, applying knowledge in novel ways and contexts, and divergent thinking. Traditional academics tend to emphasize and require convergent thinking, wherein multiple concepts, ideas, facts, and information come together or converge to yield the same answer or conclusion. Divergent thinking, by contrast, involves generating concepts, ideas, facts, and information that differ or diverge to yield varying answers or conclusions. For example, some informal assessments of divergent thinking include thinking of as many *different* categories of use for paper clips, or bricks, etc. (Bricks as projectiles represent *one* category, despite different targets and/or projection methods; bricks as building materials, also *one* category despite construction types or methods; using paper clips as fasteners is *one* category regardless of things fastened.)

Questioning, inductive and deductive reasoning, and problem-solving

Questioning promotes inquiry learning; gives students purposes for reading; focuses attention on learning targets; fosters active thinking, metacognition, and self-monitoring; augments comprehension; and helps students review new material and connect it to their previous knowledge. Student question generation can help them identify important ideas in learning materials and synthesize information. Teacher and student questions help students clarify meaning, find new information; analyze information by wondering about author intentions, meanings, and choices of content, genres, and formats; and pursue personally interesting topics related to learning material. Inductive reasoning is a bottom-up, specific-to-general process, beginning from accumulating specific observations or information; identifying regularities or patterns; and ultimately drawing general conclusions or principles. Conversely, deductive reasoning is a top-down, general-to-specific process; beginning from a general theory, principle, or field of information; narrowing this down to more specific hypotheses; testing these by collecting observations, information, and data to confirm or refute the theory; and draw a specific conclusion. Problem-solving involves identifying a problem, generating alternative solutions, testing these through implementation, and evaluating their effectiveness. This requires focus for problem identification, divergent thinking to generate alternatives, and critical thinking to evaluate results.

Planning, memory, and recall

Planning is an essential cognitive process which many students fail to do before plunging into activities. It requires abstract thinking and imagination to envision the processes of a task before actually performing them. While many higher-order cognitive abilities seem located in the frontal lobe of the cerebral cortex, planning appears to be in the prefrontal lobe. It is high among the higher-order thinking skills. By planning before writing, for example, students are able to organize their compositions in advance, preventing many major problems, failures, and starting over from scratch. Students must plan projects before beginning them to give them organized structures, devote equal or appropriately weighted durations to different parts, stay on schedule, complete them within prescribed timeframes, etc. Moreover, planning academic tasks provides essential practice for planning in everyday life, which facilitates many activities in similar ways on a larger, even more practical scale. Students use working memory to rehearse information in short-term memory and move it into long-term memory for retention. They retrieve information from long-term memory by recalling it directly or recognizing it among provided alternatives. Without memory retention and retrieval, students could not demonstrate, apply, or build upon what they learn.

Direct instruction vs. indirect instruction

Teacher-centered, direct instruction is the oldest, most widely used teaching model. Teachers give explicit, structured instruction using uniform lesson plans. Exploration, discussions, etc. are excluded. Most contemporary K-12 schools use updated versions. Examples include DISTAR, Hooked on Phonics, etc. Some longitudinal research shows Montessori, Waldorf, and other more flexible methods more effective. However, direct instruction is among the few scientifically confirmed ways of improving curriculum. Siegfried Engelmann originated a more specific direct instruction (DI), comparing it with 21 other methods during the federally funded Project Follow Through (1968-1995), meant to extend preschooler education following Head Start programs. Although funding was discontinued when data showed little or no benefit for this purpose, empirical evidence proved DI most effective of 22 methods for teaching reading, language, spelling, arithmetic, and positive self-image—the only one producing positive results consistently. Indirect instruction is student-centered and interactive; teachers facilitate small-group and cooperative learning. Students construct or transform material into new or different, meaningful responses. Encompassing all Bloom's taxonomy levels, it includes reading for meaning, cloze, concept mapping, case studies, inductive and deductive reasoning, content organization, examples and non-examples, questions, student experiences, self-evaluation, and discussion. DI aids learning facts, rules, and sequences; breaking down textbook or workbook material; lower Bloom's taxonomy levels; piquing student interest. Indirect instruction aids learning abstractions, concepts, patterns, inquiry, problem-solving, and discovery learning.

Independent study

Independent study is not a single instructional method per se, but rather a type of instructional strategy that encompasses a range of different instructional methods. Teachers intentionally provide independent study types of methods for the purposes of developing initiative, self-determination, self-reliance, self-direction, and self-improvement in individual students. In addition to individual students working alone, the definition of independent study can also include paired, partnered, or small-group learning. In each case, the teacher functions as a facilitator and guide rather than directing or controlling the entire activity. Some advantages of independent study include giving students more choices of learning materials, topics, approaches, practices, and more autonomy in completing assignments. These increase student motivation. Another advantage is flexibility: teachers can use it with one, two, or several students and another strategy with the rest of the class; combine it with other strategies; or make it the main whole-class instructional strategy. An additional advantage is freeing teacher time. However, teachers must ensure students have developed skills required for it. Some examples of independent study activities and methods include doing homework, writing reports or essays, learning contracts, correspondence courses and lessons, computer-assisted instruction, research projects, learning activity packages, assigned questions, and learning centers.

Experiential learning

Experiential learning is a student-centered, activity-oriented instructional strategy whereby students use inductive reasoning to discover information and insights. Process takes precedence over product. Activities involve "hands-on" learning. Rather than passively listening to teachers, only reading text, or viewing video or other visuals, students actively participate in direct experiences. This participation increases student motivation, as does communicating their activities to classmates so that, in effect, they teach one another. Critical components of effective experiential learning include formulating plans to apply learning to other contexts, and reflecting personally about learning experiences. Studies find student comprehension and retention are much higher through experiential learning activities than passive or receptive activities. Examples include administering surveys, building models, taking field trips, making field observations, conducting simulations, playing games, role-playing, synectics, focused imaging, and conducting experiments. Experimental learning involves the scientific method: asking research questions; formulating hypotheses regarding answers; testing hypotheses by experimenting, e.g., qualitative research like surveys and observations, or quantitative like randomly selecting participants, not treating a control group and manipulating independent variables with a treatment group to see if dependent variables are affected or unaffected to support or refute the hypothesis; reporting results; drawing conclusions and communicating these.

Interactive instruction

Interactive instruction is a teaching strategy that enables a range of different interactive methods and ways of grouping students. It is interactive because it places a major emphasis on having students share and exchange ideas, questions, activities, and tasks, and engage in discussions of their work and learning with classmates. Students in pairs, threes, small groups, or whole classes may participate in interactive discussions, projects, or assignments. Some examples of activities involving interactive instruction include holding debates; participating in student panels; engaging in role-playing exercises, which are also used in experiential learning; discussion, which is also a feature of indirect instruction; group brainstorming to generate ideas; practicing academic skills and tasks with peers; cooperative learning groups, which are always interactive and sometimes also involve independent study; laboratory groups, which can also involve experimental and

- 68 -

experiential learning; problem-solving activities; circle of knowledge group activity sessions; tutorial groups, including peer tutoring; and conducting interviews with peers and/or others.

Organizing and implementing effective instruction

First review national and state standards, their course textbooks, supplementary materials, and any test preparation materials required, to ascertain which concepts they must teach. Create a plan of study based on this information. To visualize and organize instruction, make a personal lesson plan calendar. Using the plan of study and calendar, plan instructional units and timelines. Next, write detailed lesson plans for each unit. Effective lesson plans should include learning objectives; student activities; estimates of time needed; materials required; alternative plans for any students absent during lesson activities; and assessment methods, including tests, homework, and classwork. Transfer the general unit plan to a planning book, assembling all unit plans to get an overall picture of the school year, supporting organization, focus, and implementation. Write daily lesson outlines and agendas. Some teachers write detailed information and notes, while others make simple outlines including times. Being organized and making smooth transitions are important to maintain student attention. Collect or create required materials, e.g., lecture notes, overheads, handouts, manipulatives, any planned daily warmups, etc. Request media in advance. Create emergency lesson plans for substitutes and mini-lessons to fill extra or leftover time to plan for the unexpected.

Continuous monitoring and charting of student performance

Continuous monitoring and charting (1) gives teachers information on student progress with short-term, discrete objectives. They can respond flexibly to student understanding, engagement, lacks thereof, and feedback, adjusting instruction by re-teaching or reviewing skills and concepts immediately instead of only finding students did not learn certain things after having covered several topics; and (2) gives students visual depictions of their learning. Having students chart and graph their own performance can enhance their engagement in learning. Continuous monitoring functions as ongoing evaluation, visual representation, immediate feedback; a diagnostic tool; instructional planning guide; communication mechanism with students, parents, other teachers, and administrators; and an evaluation practice that can motivate and engage students. However, it is not an independent student practice activity. Critical elements are frequently assessing student understanding and performance of discrete skills and concepts; ability to replicate assessment procedures over several days; tally, graph, or chart student responses; and involve students in tracking that progress and setting goals. To implement, select a specific instructional objective; design an assessment sheet students can complete in a few minutes with items reflecting the target skill, and where indicated, concrete, representational, or abstract understanding level; administer and score; have students plot correct or incorrect responses on graphs; discuss; draw goal lines on graphs; repeat.

Scaffolding

Scaffolding, in a metaphorical iteration of literal building construction scaffolding, is temporary support enabling students to complete tasks they cannot accomplish on their own at the time. As students master these tasks, the scaffolding can be gradually withdrawn until students perform the tasks independently without support. During this process, the role of the teacher is shifted from being the dominant expert on academic content to becoming more of a facilitator of learning and a mentor. As students learn how to perform tasks with support and gain increasing proficiency and independence, the responsibility for learning shifts from the teacher to the student. Scaffolded instruction establishes a supportive learning environment wherein students are able to give

- 69 -

feedback, ask questions, and support one another in learning new material. Using scaffolding in teaching gives students motivation for adopting more active roles in their learning. Because teachers provide scaffolds for tasks students cannot initially achieve independently, scaffolding requires students to advance past their current knowledge and skill levels, sharing responsibility and taking ownership for teaching and learning.

Scaffolding can be implemented with individual students, small groups, or whole classes. It is useful whenever students cannot understand a certain concept or are not progressing in some aspects of tasks. Step 1: the teacher models how to perform a difficult or unfamiliar task, for example, how to use a graphic organizer when students have never done so. The teacher might prepare an incomplete graphic organizer with some parts completed for handouts and a projection. The teacher describes how the graphic organizer illustrates relationships, asking students to "think aloud" about this. Step 2: teacher and students work together on completing the graphic organizer. Students might suggest information to add. The teacher writes student suggestions on the board or overhead; students complete their copies of the organizer. Step 3: students work in pairs or small groups to complete a blank or partially filled graphic organizer. Teachers may need to provide multiple scaffolds at various times to help students master more complex content. Step 4: students practice independently, demonstrating mastery and gaining speed and automaticity. In each step, teacher and students have different roles and responsibilities.

Instructional approaches that emphasize student responsibility for learning

In the inquiry-guided instructional method, students investigate to answer questions, attaining understanding of concepts independently. This not only promotes the development of lifelong research skills, but also places the responsibility for learning with the student. In the learner-centered teaching method, teachers are responsible for facilitating learning, while students take responsibility for learning. This shifts classroom power from teacher to student. In the instructional method of establishing learning communities, every member participates, taking responsibility for accomplishing learning goals. With shared learning, responsibility is collective, not individual. Participants include students, teachers, other educators, staff, administrators, parents, community members, and other stakeholders. Service learning is an instructional approach combining academic content with community service projects. Teachers are responsible for structuring and supervising learning, enabling student reflection. Students learn to take civic responsibility. In team-based learning (TBL), unlike other group activities, students participate as members of permanent teams; group meetings occupy most of class. Students are more responsible for and reliant on each other (interdependent) for learning, and more responsible for arriving to class prepared. Research finds TBL increases both student engagement and responsibility.

Developing higher-order thinking skills

Align learning goals, objectives, ideas, skills, content, tasks, materials, aids, and assessments. Create organized routines and activities: explain established routines, e.g., starting on time and following planned activity sequences; follow them. Conduct task analysis of a thinking skill to learn: identify the specific skill, prerequisite knowledge and skills, related sub-skills sequence, and student readiness with prerequisites. Prepare examples, sample problems and explanations. Prepare questions transcending simple factual information recall, addressing advanced understanding, e.g., how? How well? Why? Plan strategies for diagnosis, guidance, practice, and remediation. Establish a comfortable, non-threatening atmosphere. Communicate clear expectations, genuine topic interest, enthusiasm, and a businesslike approach combined with warmth. Prepare and organize thoroughly to minimize between-activity transition times. Clearly explain tasks: set goals at beginnings of assignments, and furnish finished product examples. Introduce tasks with clear, simple organizing frameworks like single-paragraph overviews, previews, charts, or diagrams. Introduce key terms and concepts before proceeding. Focus attention on important information using questions. Use written signals, repetition, nonverbal behaviors, and verbal statements for emphasis. Use demonstrations, models, pictures, diagrams, examples, etc. to make ideas vivid. Signal transitions between ideas. Give frequent feedback, including clarifying or correcting incorrect responses.

Student development of higher-order thinking skills

Cognitive and learning strategies include organization, elaboration, rehearsal; and metacognition for self-evaluating and self-regulating one's thinking, entailing mnemonics, visualization, diagramming, highlighting; or more complex strategies, e.g., the Multipass reading comprehension procedure. To help students develop critical and creative thinking and learning skills, intentionally design lessons expressly for teaching specific thinking and learning strategies. Teach self-reflection and self-evaluation: give students inexplicable dilemmas, paradoxes, etc., challenging pre-existing beliefs. Guide systematic student inquiry. Encourage reflection and making sense of new information by having students write or discuss in their own words how to integrate it with their existing ideas, approaches, and opinions. Encourage and guide students in forming hypotheses, brainstorming, guessing, speculating about consequences, and discussing how their thought processes have changed their ideas. Monitor inefficient strategies and correct them. Encourage continuous student reflection of beliefs about thinking, thought processes, and evaluating effectiveness. Use advance organizers and cognitive maps to show main parts or steps when approaching various thinking and learning tasks. Teach PQ4R (*preview, question, read, reflect, recite, and review*) with written materials. Instruction in abstraction, analysis, outlining, summarization, and generalization enhances both reading and reasoning skills. Stress broad algorithms, heuristics, and problem-solving strategies; give enough practice to overlearn for effortless, consistent use. Teach specific strategies using modeling, think-alouds, discussion, and practice. Students develop self-confidence from teachers modeling self-confidence in thinking and reasoning processes.

Name and define each cognitive skill for students; ask them for examples and synonyms. Model steps for applying each skill. Explain appropriate and inappropriate skill application contexts. Assign cooperative learning groups to practice skills. To improve comprehension, problem-solving, decision-making; and concept, principle, and procedure application: ask probing questions to diagnose existing student conceptions and misconceptions. Furnish hands-on experiences enabling students to explore generating new explanations or interpreting raw data. Give question stems or examples requiring higher-order thinking; have students answer in groups, pairs, or independently. Give practice in brainstorming, decision-making, experimenting, identifying and solving problems in art, music, and writing as well as math and science. Incorporate individualized options in lesson plans, e.g., assignment choices, modalities for multiple intelligences, varying instruction and application sequences, open-ended participation tasks with multiple alternatives, multi-ability tasks and varied activities accommodating differences in abstraction, language proficiency, and emotional influences. Give opportunities to discover procedural knowledge; explain procedure goals, applicable situations or problems, and corresponding strategies and rationales; demonstrate stepwise procedure application; give students practice selecting and implementing procedures; give performance feedback. Promote internal locus of control by helping students perceive themselves as effective learners.

Integrating technology into instruction

Instructional technology integration is effective when it supports curriculum goals. Technology must support four essential learning elements: active student engagement, group participation, frequent interaction and feedback, and connections with real-life experts. In the 1960s, MIT

- 71 -

professor Seymour Papert collaborated with cognitive-developmental psychologist Jean Piaget, and then developed Logo, a programming language for children to use without advanced mathematical knowledge. Students using Logo could write and debug programs to control robot movements with minimal instruction. They learned more in-depth geometry concept understanding and programming skills—and were more engaged in learning than in traditional classroom exercises. Papert pointed out the ample overlap of education and fun with computers for promoting all students' internal motivation. Today technology learning tools abound; almost every US public school has Internet connection. When technology is used for more ambitious learning goals than basic skills, studies find it helps students develop creativity, research skills, and higher-order thinking.

Technology can further learning through building local and global communities including students, teachers, administrators, parents, scientists, and others; giving students and teachers more opportunities for reflection, feedback, and revision; offering learning tools and scaffolds, e.g., visualization tools and modeling programs; giving classrooms exciting, real-world problem-based curricula; and expanding teacher learning opportunities. Social media support collaboration, reinforcing learning's social nature. Technology enables learning communities and improves learning cultures. Students learn concepts in ways impossible or impracticable with other instructional methods through social networking, simulations, and digital gaming. Educational technology complements what exemplary teachers naturally do. Experts note that digital games, instead of separating instruction from assessment, constantly assess student problem-solving progress, giving students feedback and further practice. Letting students teach them how they engage with digital media both informs teachers about technology and develops student metacognition. Integration means using technology to learn content and demonstrate content understanding, not simply digital expertise. Students need guided practice and exploration to achieve this.

Computer mediation

Communicating using computers gives students opportunities to access remote data sources, collaborate with students in other places on group projects, and share their work with other students to obtain their responses or evaluations. Research finds that computer-based instruction (CBI) and computer-assisted instruction (CAI) combined with regular classroom instruction enhances student motivation, academic achievement, and attitudes. Moreover, the increasing prevalence, even requirement, of computers in workplaces demands student preparation; and federal and state standards increasingly require integrating technology into instruction and student computer literacy. Studies have shown that the following computer-mediated communication applications are effective for enhancing student learning of prerequisite skills and higher-order cognitive skills: building skills in logical reasoning, inductive reasoning, deductive reasoning, and making verbal analogies; practicing and drilling procedures that incorporate tests or probes; and practicing problem-solving strategies and skills in making inferences. In addition, interactive learning software programs give students more autonomy in learning, allow them to learn at individual paces, engage student interest, and often make learning more entertaining. Moreover, students need immediate, specific, corrective feedback on their learning progress, which interactive software programs can give more consistently than single teachers with large classes.

Active teaching and learning strategies

Active teaching and learning strategies make students active participants in learning. Rather than passively listening to teachers discuss, read about, or observe others perform skills, students practice skills to gain proficiency. Many students learn best by doing. Hands-on activities take students out of books and sometimes their seats, classrooms, schools, or even familiar thinking habits. In addition to engaging student interest and giving actual practice, they have the benefit of integrating subject-area content with all four language and literacy domains—listening, speaking, reading, and writing. Though research consistently shows students learn better through active content engagement, some teachers avoid active learning. Objections and dilemmas include: concerns they will never cover required content; losing class control by not lecturing; having trouble getting students to work in teams—some doing all the work, others none; students' not knowing how to answer higher-order questions; student resistance to active learning or a preference for habituated listening and note-taking; what to do with ELL or special education students during active learning and group activities. Guidelines include: vary partners and small-group teams via randomization, specific rotation schedules, or other systematic schemes. Vary required team tasks and techniques. Clearly identify team member roles, task purpose, outcome, and time allotted. Prepare all needed materials. Determine how to grade tasks. Start small or brief activities early. Establish a signal for students to stop discussion.

Giving students choices among assignments enables them to decide how to demonstrate their learning. For example, some might choose to write compositions, some to make spoken presentations, some to draw illustrations, and some to construct models to demonstrate the same knowledge. A language strategy is A-Z Taxonomy: small student groups write the alphabet vertically on paper and think of vocabulary terms in the content they are studying that start with each letter. This technique is effective as both pre- and post-instruction. Pairing students to debate some controversial issue related to learning content, having pairs explain pro and con positions to each other and agree to an overall recommendation gives students practice in negotiating and compromising skills, plus listening and speaking opportunities. Brainstorming evokes creativity, originality, and quantity: ask open-ended questions; never criticize ideas. Providing a suitable target number of ideas sometimes helps. Some linguistically diverse students may feel more comfortable responding as members of a small student team or group.

In a "carousel questions" strategy, the teacher writes several questions about a content topic being learned on large posters or paper stations posted around the classroom. Small student groups, each with a different color marker, rotate every few minutes among question sets. At every station, teams add ideas, responses, or answers not already included. Then the class shares all student responses, gaining multiple and varied answers to the questions. In case studies, students are given real-world stories about things that happened to an individual, family, school, or community; students apply their content knowledge and skills to authentic situations. In critical explanation, teachers ask students to consider reasons or factors that might explain some content-related issues or problems. Use "might" and "could," not "why" to avoid implying right, wrong, or only one correct answer. In discussion webs, students consider a content-related issue or problem in small groups, then regroup and share their work and information with classmates from other groups. In field studies, students have opportunities to learn about and study issues in their community related to the content they are learning. Health classes might study community nutrition, disease, safety, environmental issues, consumer health, or healthcare services; earth science classes might collect rock samples, identify them, and determine local distribution patterns; social studies classes might study local landmarks and associated history, etc.

Long-term goals, short-term objectives, instructional objectives, and lesson plan objectives

Long-term goals typically are mastered over a school year and are stated in very broad, general terms. Goal areas typically correspond to content areas like reading, writing, math, and other subjects. Teachers derive short-term objectives from long-term goals. Short-term objectives can be completed in shorter time periods, ranging from two weeks to three months. Teachers then derive instructional objectives from short-term objectives. Students can generally master instructional objectives within one lesson. From smaller numbers of long-term goals, teachers should be able to generate a larger number of short-term objectives and even larger numbers of instructional objectives from short-term objectives. As an example, if a long-term goal is for students to read at grade level, then related short-term objectives could include recognizing vocabulary sight words; using phonics, context clues, and structural analysis to identify unfamiliar words; and demonstrating text comprehension on literal, inferential, and critical levels. From these, a teacher could break down phonics into rules for short and long vowels, digraphs, initial and final single consonants, and consonant blends to write individual instructional objectives.

Correctly written objectives include: student orientation, behavioral terminology, a criterion, and a condition statement. "Review long and short vowels in one-syllable words" or "teach fire safety" are teacher-oriented. To clarify their significance and use for students, they should be student-oriented: "correctly read aloud words containing long or short vowels"; "identify fire safety rules." Behavioral terminology is observable and measurable. This is why Bloom's taxonomy supplies action verbs for each complexity level in the hierarchy and each domain. Experts remark that while knowledge-level objectives, e.g., to read sight words aloud or recite multiplication tables, are prerequisites for more advanced learning, teachers should still not dwell primarily on these as most easily observable or identifiable, but ensure they give equal time in their lessons to higher-level cognitive skills. Experts also remind teachers not to confine objectives to Bloom's cognitive domain, but include the psychomotor and affective domains as well. Objectives can include all three. For example, an instructional objective for a student to answer comprehension questions orally with 90 percent accuracy after silently reading a passage from a grade-level basal text can include requesting assistance by raising one's hand, using a person's name to get his or her attention, asking a question, and saying "please" or other social amenity.

SWOT

SWOT analysis stands for *strengths*, *weaknesses*, *opportunities*, and *threats*. While frequently used by anyone analyzing market trends, identifying target markets, and/or developing marketing plans (which includes not only salespeople, but also therapists and other practitioners who must promote their services), it is also useful to apply to education. For example, teachers can use it with high school students in career counseling to identify the job-relevant skills they possess (strengths) and those they lack (weaknesses); jobs open, job growth probabilities, and chances for advancement in a student's preferred career field (opportunities); and competition for jobs, dead-end positions, and downsizing probabilities (threats). Accompanying the SWOT analysis, a gap analysis tool identifies employer needs and job requirements; student and candidate knowledge and skills; differences between these, which represent gaps; an action plan to fill gaps; a timeframe to complete the plan; and people who can help. For example, an employer might require knowledge of Excel or other spreadsheet software; the student might only know Word or other word-processing software. The action plan is to learn Excel or other spreadsheet programs through a short community college course, school enrichment program, library-offered class, interactive computer tutorial, etc. Teachers can also use these tools to identify and address other, non-career-related academic gaps.

Hypothetical situation wherein a teacher identifies and analyzes student knowledge gaps

Suppose a teacher has designed a unit on a content subject and has taught the class a number of individual one-day lessons within this unit. The teacher's regular practice is to conduct formative assessments, e.g., pop quizzes, oral Q&A sessions, whips (going around the room quickly, having every student answer an open-ended content question), etc. near the end of each day's lesson. So

- 74 -

far, each formative assessment has shown 80-100 percent of students grasped main lesson concepts, facts, and points. But on this day, the teacher finds 90 percent of the students fail to demonstrate knowledge or understanding of lesson content. It is highly unlikely 90 percent of students did not pay attention or lacked cognitive ability to comprehend the lesson, and highly likely the lesson was ineffective. Also, the 10 percent displaying knowledge and understanding may have been the most conscientious students and/or had the highest cognitive ability levels; and/or some, most, or all of the 10 percent may already have had existing knowledge of the lesson topic. Therefore the teacher re-teaches this lesson, using different instructional strategies than the first time. This time the formative assessment shows 95 percent of the class knowing and understanding key concepts and information.

Teacher assessment literacy, practices, and needs

Various research finds teachers viewing learning as memorization assesses student information recall; teachers viewing learning as constructing knowledge and understanding use formative assessment to create continuous information flow about student understanding and adapt instruction to be more effective. Studies also show assessment-literate teachers do not limit assessment to multiple-choice or true-false questions but apply many, varied strategies, selecting those strongest and most relevant for specific learning goals. Pre-service teachers are found having inadequate repertoires of assessment strategies. One study showed the teacher asking the most conceptual questions and having the biggest variety of ways to adapt instruction according to assessment results had the highest student performance level. Also, some researchers (Gottheiner and Seigel, 2012) conclude others frequently overlook how teachers interpret formative assessment data in their studies, and more resources for doing so are needed. Teachers in their study reported that, although student group discussions of questions could contribute to new misconceptions, they also triggered discourse—building on classmate ideas and enabling concept discovery and construction before even learning corresponding terminology.

Addressing student conceptions, misconceptions, and preconceptions

Multiple teachers agree to the value of having students discuss scientific concepts and struggle to define these on their own before teachers supply them with the scientific terminology. They find this process enables students to construct and own their knowledge. Teachers also observe students from diverse cultural backgrounds may have different ways of making sense of problems, making it important to provide real-life contexts giving them personal relevance to students and accessing prior student knowledge for understanding them. Teachers emphasize structured activities, which afford students chances to develop their thoughts before sharing them; and allowing each student time to share ideas increases participation. Starting with small groups and progressing to whole-class discussion allows teachers to circulate, monitoring or assessing many more student responses; allows students to exchange and develop ideas in smaller, non-threatening groups; and improves subsequent whole-class discussion levels. Teachers emphasize needing to address previous student knowledge. They realize misconceptions can be based on cultural beliefs and personal experiences, making them resistant to change. Researchers report that, although teachers can often predict common student misconceptions, students frequently give wider response ranges than teachers can predict; and that many teachers propose re-teaching for preconceptions, but more experienced teachers try different instructional strategies.

Differentiated instruction practices effective for enhancing student literacy

Teaching experts advise using common instructional texts for read-alouds to facilitate differentiation. Teachers can use teaching text read-alouds to build background knowledge, demonstrate strategy application to students, introduce issues and invite student journal responses, and assure every student access to the information and skills they need to improve their reading. Researchers find that using multiple texts at varied reading levels—not just one—to teach units enables all students to obtain information from materials they can read best. Rather than teaching "the textbook," teachers need to organize every individual instructional unit around a topic, issue, or genre. This applies whether teachers assign students to small-group work, or use whole-class differentiated instruction approaches. By organizing for instruction this way, teachers can meet all student reading levels. Because students can only become better readers if they understand how to construct meaning while they read, teachers must show them this process by modeling the ways in which they think about texts during read-alouds; work with small reading groups; and one-on-one instructional conferences with individual students. This gives students multiple opportunities to learn how to construct meaning from text.

Expert teachers find discussion particularly important when differentiating reading instruction. Student discussion effectively builds on every individual student's factual knowledge and understanding, and gives students opportunities to build comprehension and clarify meaning. Students deepen recall and understanding when teachers ask them to progress past fact memorization to discussion applying those facts to problems and issues. In-depth small-group or whole-class topic discussions demonstrate how classmates think and reason, build background knowledge, and can make information relevant to students' personal lives. Teachers must never assume every student absorbs the same information from a lesson or demonstration; also, students not having absorbed lesson content can write little or nothing about it because they can only write what they know and understand. Writing strengthens comprehension and enables thinking, exploration, and learning. Teachers can glean insights from reading student journals about student text analysis and inferential thinking skills, supporting intervention planning. Ongoing assessments enable teachers to reveal individual student need areas and successes and target instruction accordingly to support every student. Experts also advise teachers to think through every unit to determine what they want students to learn about genres, issues, and reading strategies; carefully plan units accordingly; and assemble appropriate read-aloud texts, plus reading materials to meet every student's needs.

Culturally responsive teaching

Culturally responsive teaching utilizes diverse students' cultural background knowledge, previous experiences, and performance styles, increasing the effectiveness and appropriateness of learning for them by teaching through and to their strengths. Culturally responsive instruction recognizes various ethnic groups' cultural heritages as legitimate—both as legacies influencing student attitudes, approaches, and dispositions to learning; and as content worth including in formal curricula. Culturally responsive approaches establish meaningful connections—both between students' school and home experiences, and between abstract academic concepts and the sociocultural realities that they live. It employs a broad range of instructional strategies addressing different student learning styles. It teaches students not only knowledge about their own and others' cultural traditions and heritages, but moreover to praise one another's cultural legacies and practices. Instructional practices that are culturally responsive incorporate multicultural information, materials, and resources in all skills and subjects schools routinely teach. Classroom environment considerations include using literature reflecting various literary genres and ethnic perspectives; incorporating everyday living concepts like jobs, economics, and consumer behaviors of different ethnic groups into math instruction; and activities that reflect a range of visual, auditory, tactile, and other sensory experiences to accommodate different student learning styles.

Culturally responsive teachers maintain cultural identity and heritage as well as academic performance. They teach the whole student, using cultural references to develop cognitive, affective, social, and political learning. Students develop interpersonal relationships, acting as extended family members supporting, encouraging, and helping one another. Group accountability makes individual success everybody's responsibility in academic communities. Teachers satisfy student needs regarding human dignity, sense of belonging, and individual self-concepts. Multidisciplinary teacher teams may collaborate, teaching single cultural concepts; students can actively participate in their own evaluations. Classroom climate, learning context, student-teacher relationships, curriculum content, instructional techniques, and assessments are included in culturally responsive teaching, which is multidimensional. It empowers students as learners and people by sharing teacher and student authority; relating personal growth to public life; developing critical curiosity and inquiry habits as well as strong knowledge and skills; and treating individual development as a social, cooperative, active process wherein students explore society, power, inequality, and change. It uses varied cultural experiences, not traditional practices, as teaching and learning resources. Students learn reflection, decision-making, and effective action—personally, socially, economically, and politically; more humane, caring interpersonal understandings and skills; more insightful, clearer thinking; and continual knowledge criticism, revision, renewal, and sharing.

Cooperative learning

Cooperative learning requires positive interdependence (students sink-or-swim together): assign assembly line-style and synergistic task completion. Establish collective goals, resources, and rewards; assign group roles; arrange group furniture and environment; have groups compete against each other. Face-to-face interaction entails seating groups in circles or pairs facing each other. Promote individual accountability through checking with random group members, assigning individual tasks, bonus group credit or rewards if all members perform well individually, and having students bring individual work to their groups. Social skills including decision-making, communication, trust-building, leadership, and conflict management must not be assumed but taught. Teachers should record their observations of students on observation forms to provide feedback. Social skills include categories of group formation and assembly, group functioning, and the formulation and fermentation of ideas and knowledge. Group processing can be accomplished orally and/or in writing by small group reflection; teacher provision of feedback to small groups or whole classes; teacher and small group observations; and goal-setting, by students with teacher guidance as needed, for students' next work sessions, e.g., regarding further social skills development.

Promoting student use and refinement of higher-order thinking skills

To get students to explore ideas from diverse perspectives, plan and ask questions prompting them to use their imaginations. For example, during a lesson on agriculture, ask students what they would think and feel about certain policies and practices if they were, respectively, legislators, corporate executives, factory farmers, small farmers, migrant farm workers, consumers paying for groceries, families eating groceries, etc. In a history lesson, ask students to take the perspectives of Native American tribes and of European settlers; or consider both the viewpoints of American revolutionaries and British colonial governors, etc. To promote problem-solving, instead of telling students how to solve problems—mathematical, scientific, economic, logistical, creative, etc.—ask students how, also promoting inquiry; have them brainstorm to generate many ideas as a group; guide their consideration of alternatives and speculation about potential consequences; and let them practice implementing solutions, analyzing and discussing results. Rather than "yes" or "no" questions, asking open-ended questions allows for many varied responses. To develop research skills, have students form research questions, guiding revision of overly broad or narrow questions; guide them through steps of formulating hypotheses, conducting experiments testing hypotheses; collecting, analyzing, and interpreting data; reporting results; and drawing and communicating conclusions.

Areas of executive functioning that commonly pose challenges for students.

Parents frequently identify <u>time management</u>, <u>planning</u>, and <u>organization</u> as challenges for their children. These are three among many areas involving executive function. Executive function skills start developing during infancy, continuing development into adulthood. Considering this duration for full development, children need solid foundations. Executive functioning involves cognitive skills utilized for executing tasks. A single task requires several executive function skills. For example, to get dressed for school, a student must plan ahead for the weather, sustain attention long enough for task completion, manage emotions regarding wanting or not wanting to go to school, and start and finish the task in a timely fashion. Students use executive functioning skills to help them do homework and chores, keep track of belongings, follow rules, save money for things they want, and many other things. Some signs that a student may be experiencing difficulty developing and/or applying executive function skills include: the student has trouble estimating how long it will take to complete a school project, and/or planning the project; telling a story with the details sequenced correctly; or remembering information while performing an activity.

Helping students develop time management, planning, and organizational skills

<u>Time management</u>: have students color portions of a clock face using dry-erase markers to represent time segments, e.g., five minutes, 15 minutes, etc., helping them visualize elapsed and remaining time; and check in halfway through time allotted. Give students halfway-point questions, e.g., are they halfway finished? Are they still focused on the task's goal? Are any distractions robbing them of on-task time? Must they speed or slow their work pace? <u>Planning</u>: one application is helping students plan homework. Ask them what a given homework assignment would look like; have them sketch it on paper divided into two columns, e.g., with a vocabulary assignment, students write vocabulary words and definitions in the left column, and draw pictures illustrating each definition in the right column. This helps them identify where to start, what they need, and how completed homework will look, promoting more independent work. Post-it note calendars help students visualize longer-term assignment due dates, and divide assignments into more manageable chunks. <u>Organization</u>: workspaces with Post-it notes or baskets labeled "Prepare," "Do," and "Done" support both planning and organization. Dual-pocket folders, one pocket for homework or materials to take home and another for completed homework to turn in, facilitate organization.

Procedural steps for teaching that follow direct instruction principles

(1) <u>Introduction and review</u>: get student attention to introduce new information, or review or build on previously learned information. Identify the lesson's learning goal and relevance or significance. (2) <u>Development</u>: model the skill, knowledge, or behavior students will need to demonstrate. Clearly explain and give sufficient examples of material to be learned. Check for understanding by asking key questions or otherwise eliciting student questions. Use visual aids, multimedia presentations, or other prompts to facilitate successful student information processing. (3) <u>Guided practice</u>: once students respond positively to modeling, explanations, and examples, assign tasks for student practice and monitor them closely. Offer help and additional direct instruction (repeating the second step) to students not having mastered the material yet. (4) <u>Closure</u>: conclude the lesson, recapping what it covered; remind students of the learning goal; prepare them for the next step: (5)

- 78 -

Independent practice: assign tasks or activities to students who demonstrated proficiency and competency in step (3) to eliminate any teacher prompts and assess degrees of student mastery. This can include homework. (6) Evaluation: assess progress formatively through classroom assignments, worksheets, etc.; and/or summatively through projects, tests, etc. Determine if learning goals are met or need revisiting in future lessons through evaluation feedback.

Indirect instruction strategies

Indirect instruction is student-centered. Students actively discover or construct knowledge through inquiry, hands-on exploration, experimentation, and problem-solving activities. Teachers are facilitators assigning and guiding student activity selection, supervising and supporting work. In inquiry learning, students formulate, ask, and answer questions and solve problems rather than teachers' giving answers or solutions. Students apply content knowledge and skills analyzing and explaining teacher-supplied case studies—detailed, in-depth histories and observations of individual real-life persons, families, groups, schools, communities, etc. Concept mapping facilitates students' visualizing, organizing, and applying learned concepts. Teachers guide student project and assignment preparation, identifying focus, participants, schedules, etc.; idea generation and listing; idea sorting and rating for structure; developing maps using software for multidimensional scaling, cluster analysis, etc.; interpreting; and applying maps. Reading for meaning involves active reading, previewing and predicting before, seeking relevant information during, and reflecting after reading. Students identify explicit textual messages; make logical inferences; identify main themes and ideas; analyze development, connection, interaction of people and characters, events and plot, and ideas; evaluate purpose or viewpoint influences on text content and style; differentiate objective and subjective; integrate and evaluate visual and numerical as well as verbal content; comparatively analyze multiple text topics, themes, approaches, and information. Cloze procedures—requiring student meaning determination from context to supply missing words— teach sequencing awareness, linguistic relationships, searching, prediction, and reconstruction.

Independent instruction promotes individual student autonomy, initiative, self-determination, self-direction, self-reliance, self-improvement, self-confidence, self-efficacy, and self-esteem. Students can pursue individual interests using individual styles and paces. Its applications are highly flexible and adaptable. One caveat is that teachers must ensure students have acquired the skills necessary before beginning. In learning contracts, students agree to complete specified tasks within designated conditions and schedules and sign them, promoting accountability and responsibility. In research projects, students independently develop research questions; locate, access, and consult multiple information sources; use the information to answer research questions; and write reports or papers organizing and communicating results (with teacher guidance as needed). Learning centers are self-contained areas within classrooms containing easily accessible, varied learning materials where students independently engage in self-directed learning activities. They include skill development centers, exploratory and interest centers, and enrichment centers. In computer-mediated instruction, students interact with software programs rather than teachers or classmates, working more autonomously at their own paces. In distance learning, students access information remotely, eliminating restrictions from geographic locations.

Field trips, experiments, simulations, role-plays, games, and observations

Students generally love field trips for getting them out of classrooms and providing real-world adventures, experiences, and materials. However, they also benefit from applying knowledge and skills acquired in classrooms to real-life situations for authentic, hands-on learning experiences. For example, in a geology lab, rock samples are usually distributed equally; but on field trips, students discover some rock types (e.g., quartz) are far more plentiful; find samples with mixed types; and enjoy independence and excitement in seeking and procuring samples—while additionally interacting with nature. In experiments, instead of reading or hearing about scientific concepts and procedures, students practice these, encountering and solving involved problems and challenges first-hand. They experience direct ownership of their learning. Instead of abstractions, concepts become real to them. Simulations, while not real, are realistic, enabling students to engage in activities not experienced in real life, e.g., developing military strategies, planning battles, and fighting wars; working in various occupations; marrying, raising families; building and managing cities, farms, corporations, etc. Technology makes simulations increasingly accessible, interactive, and vivid. Role-plays enable students to envision different perspectives, developing understanding, empathy, and social interactions. Games apply skills and knowledge in entertaining contexts, structured by rules. Observations develop student perception, detail-orientation, and objectivity.

Interactive strategies

All interactive strategies promote interpersonal and social skills. Brainstorming eliminates or minimizes student inhibitions and promotes self-expression, originality, and creativity by asking students to generate and express as many different ideas as possible without teacher or classmate criticism, censure, or rejection. Quantity supersedes quality. Students acquire more ideas from classmates than they could produce alone. Cooperative learning groups promote both collective and individual accountability, responsibility, and teamwork. They access and utilize the cooperative, noncompetitive orientations of students from collectivist cultures; and enable ELL and LEP students to ask classmates questions their cultural backgrounds might inhibit their asking teachers. Interviews help students learn about one another, show them they can serve as helpful resources for one another, and develop student communication skills. Discussions let students exchange ideas, information, and opinions; ask and answer questions; consider problems, questions, or ideas classmates propose that did not occur to them; use evidence to support their arguments; learn to disagree civilly; and consider differing perspectives. Peer practice affords classmate support, interaction, and greater comfort levels and identification than individual or teacher-led practice. Debates teach students to apply logic, support arguments with evidence, attend and respond to opponent arguments, take turns, follow rules, and interact formally.

Helping students develop complex thinking processes

When students learn concepts, they are not merely memorizing facts, the lowest level of Bloom's taxonomy. They also understand ideas, which is the next level. Problem-solving involves multiple steps: first, students must identify the specific problem, requiring observational and analytical skills. Then they generate multiple possible alternative solutions, requiring understanding relationships between needs and actions, plus independent and divergent thinking. Third, they anticipate various potential consequences of different alternatives, requiring abstraction, imagination, relating hypothetical situations to their own background experiences, and speculation. The next step, implementing solutions, requires active, hands-on, experiential learning. Then students evaluate solution results, requiring analytical thinking, cost-benefit analysis, judging effectiveness, value, etc. Analysis is Bloom's fourth level, evaluation Bloom's fifth. Metacognition involves thinking about one's own thought processes, requiring objectivity, analytical skills, reflection, and application—using metacognitive insights to inform, self-improve, and refine one's own learning strategies and processes for greater effectiveness. Critical thinking requires intellectual standards; discipline; open-mindedness; fairness; empathy, humility, and integrity; distinguishing objective from subjective information; evaluating and judging information and sources for validity and quality; applying logic and reasoning to unfamiliar or new ideas; informing thought with evidence; accuracy, clarity, precision, relevance, consistency, depth, and breadth.

- 80 -

Transferring knowledge and skills requires application—Bloom's third level—to different contexts and situations.

The directed reading and thinking activity (DR-TA; Stauffer, 1969) helps students analyze text, determine purpose, question, clarify, and predict in all content subjects. Students examine the title to predict text subject matter. Following reading, open-ended questions elicit student predictions, opinions, and opinion-text connections. Comparison-contrast: make students develop questions about similarities and differences, writing them in graphic organizers, e.g., students might ask, "If circles were squares, what would happen?" "How are dogs and cats different and similar?" "How are gloves like hands? How are they not like hands?" Inferring: provide political cartoons or comic strips, and ask students to infer meaning. Student pairs or small groups identify inferences and connections they must make to interpret the cartoonist's point. Categorizing: with younger students, play 20 Questions or "animal, vegetable, mineral"-type games; provide manipulatives, having them sort objects into three different category containers. Give older students a controversial question or statement; have small groups research the topic; sort information into columns headed "Pro," "Con," and "Interesting Facts"; form opinions, and discuss. Summarizing: model first; have student partners or small groups read, stopping regularly to paraphrase; have them summarize key ideas in three or fewer textbook sections in no more than 20 words. Synthesizing: have students contribute to an idea web mural, adding and connecting ideas and comments about a central topic or question.

Modeling, developing self-regulation skills, scaffolding, guided practice, and coaching

Modeling: many students learn better from witnessing demonstration than only hearing or reading verbal description, particularly when learning procedures they must execute physically. Modeling also allows teachers to demonstrate correct techniques and sequences. Additionally, modeling helps students develop self-regulation skills including managing emotions, overcoming discomfort, taking turns, listening, demonstrating, and communicating. Teachers modeling appropriate behaviors show students how to perform tasks, and use self-regulation to complete them. They also teach self-regulation through hints, cues, and scaffolding: temporary support students need to complete tasks that are gradually removed as students gain skills. Differentiating instruction: teachers recognize diverse student experience and expertise levels in content knowledge, thinking, problem-solving, listening, speaking, reading, and writing; through ongoing assessments, develop differentiated lessons to meet each student's needs. Having students learn in pairs or small groups promotes meaningful discussion, observation, and learning from each other. Differentiation focuses on concepts and issues, not chapters or books, encouraging students to expand concept understanding and explore so-called "big ideas." Choices of experiences and tasks or projects motivate students. Guided practice: after modeling, explaining, and examples, assign tasks or activities, monitoring closely; offer assistance as needed. Coaching: helps students understand impacts of time management, organization, and disorganization on studies; examine and strengthen study skills, problem-solving, strategic thinking, and effective interaction and collaboration.

Phases of self-regulated learning

One popular model of self-regulated learning defines three phases. (1) Forethought and planning: students analyze learning tasks, setting specific goals for completion. Students learning new or unfamiliar material may not recognize appropriate goals, best task approaches; teachers instruct them about these. (2) Performance monitoring: students apply strategies for task progress, monitoring strategy effectiveness and their motivation to continue. Students may react to discomfort with new strategies by falling back on more familiar, less effective strategies. Teachers help students overcome frustration and gain fluency with new strategies through close monitoring and specific feedback. They also support self-monitoring by having students keep records of how many times they worked on specific tasks, amounts of time working, and strategies they used, enabling students to visualize progress and make needed changes. (3) Reflections on performance: students evaluate strategy effectiveness, their task performance, and manage emotions regarding outcomes. Self-reflections influence subsequent planning and goals. Encouraging setting short-term goals helps students track progress. Goal-setting and planning are complementary: planning includes and supports establishing goals. Teaching students to approach tasks with plans promotes self-regulation and learning. Self-monitoring involves goal-setting and planning. Instructional strategies promoting self-regulation include direct instruction, guided and independent practice, reflective practice, social support, and feedback.

Instructional grouping configurations

The whole-class group configuration is the traditional, most widely used model. Teachers deliver lectures or lessons, assign classwork to, ask questions of, and lead discussions with the entire class at once. Small-group instruction, a more recent development, divides classes into groups, usually three to six students each. Each group collaborates, researching and discussing topics. Group members may be assigned different group roles, e.g., leader, facilitator, recorder, summarizer, timekeeper, presenter, errand monitor, etc. Teachers may assign individual tasks to each group member or have everyone contribute to a larger task. Students benefit from sharing, discussing, developing, and preparing their ideas in less threatening smaller groups before doing so in the whole class; and learning and practicing social interaction skills with fewer classmates under more controlled conditions. Small groups can benefit ELL/LEP students culturally intimidated about questioning teachers by enabling questions of classmates, and students with autism spectrum disorders (ASDs) overwhelmed by larger group interactions. Independent learning allows proceeding at students' own paces, using their own learning styles and strategies. One-on-one instruction benefits students needing intensive, direct instruction, remedial intervention, and/or personal student-teacher interactions and relationships. Think-pair-share structures student discussion, limiting off-task thinking and behavior, and builds in accountability through reporting to partners and the class.

Cooperative learning groups are very structured, typically containing three or four students working several days or weeks. Teachers clearly define assignments, goals, and plan of operation, and spend time teaching member roles, e.g., questioner, reporter, recorder, etc. Within designated roles, team members share leadership. All must contribute for team progress: group interdependence dictates groups win or lose together. End products represent whole teams. Cooperation, goal achievement, task completion, and group process awareness are equally important. Highly individualistic or creative students may chafe at restrictions and students preferring whole-class anonymity feel pressured, but learn cooperative teamwork skills. Collaborative groups feature three to six students working days, weeks, or months on open-ended problems or tasks which can cover much content. Flexible student roles can change throughout assignments and projects. Students help others, observing, evaluating, critiquing, explaining, and suggesting improvements. Team goals, product, and collaborative communication process awareness is constant; meeting goals justifies changing direction. Students honestly discuss ideas, information, resources, procedures, results, their own and/or others' work; multiple approaches and open communication are important. Students needing structure may prefer cooperative teams, but collaborative groups learn flexibility and communication. Homogeneous groups may feel more comfort and commonality than heterogeneous, gender-inclusive and multi-age groups, but lack their exposure to diverse perspectives expanding experience. Multi-age grouping can facilitate helping and mentoring relationships.

Short-term, working, and long-term memory

When we temporarily retain information for about three to 20 seconds, this involves short-term memory—a receptacle for visual and auditory information we rehearse, consider, analyze, interpret, or otherwise manipulate using working memory. For example, repeating a phone number to oneself silently or under one's breath until dialing or telling it to someone is in short-term memory. When we encode or consolidate and transfer information from short-term memory to long-term memory, that information is stored for an indefinite time period. Depending on individual cognitive characteristics, relative importance and meaningfulness of information, its affective impacts and associations, whether and how often one accesses the information, etc., long-term memories can last a lifetime, years, or less. Via top-down processing, prior knowledge in long-term memory strongly influences sensory perceptions; expectations about sensory experiences influence their interpretation, contributing to bias. Instructional design implications include making information sufficiently meaningful and relevant for transfer to long-term memory; and dividing information into chunks to facilitate transfer. Chunking enables the brain to automatically group some items for better retention and learning. Long-term memory, organized into interrelated schema networks, enables recalling relevant knowledge and relating new information to existing knowledge, which teachers activate using curiosity-piquing questions, graphic organizers, video, etc.

Teachable moment

Teachable moments, unlike instruction teachers plan in advance, are unplanned situations arising in classrooms, offering teachers ideal opportunities to impart some understanding or insight to students regarding some concept or topic. Teachers cannot design or plan for teachable moments. They occur momentarily; therefore, teachers must be observant, notice them, and seize the opportunity to take advantage of them. Because they are unexpected, making use of teachable moments can insert temporary detours into a teacher's original lesson plan in order to explain some idea which has aroused collective student curiosity and/or captured their interest. As an example, a teacher describes a morning class meeting wherein one student asked why the previous day had been a school holiday to observe Veterans Day. The teacher took advantage of this question as a teachable moment to discuss military service personnel's historical and current sacrifices on behalf of our country. Students were so fascinated with this topic, they discussed neighbors, relatives, and friends serving and the meaning of the military to the country's future for 20 minutes. The benefit of following such tangents is their maximal impact on students through their natural timing. Teachable moments can ultimately develop into complete lesson plans or instructional units.

Useful feedback

Useful feedback must be consistent, formative, timely, and ongoing to enable student performance adjustments. It must be user-friendly: students must understand feedback to apply it, so it must be age-appropriate or developmentally appropriate, not containing excessive or overly technical information for students to handle. Expert educators communicate observation of one important behavior, which changing can produce noticeable improvement immediately, not offering advice until ensuring students understand the significance of observations. Effective feedback is actionable: grades, "wrong," and "good job" are not feedback. Inferences from data without presenting data are not descriptive enough. For example, "Many students were bored in your class" is judgment, not observation. "Twelve of 25 students texted or passed notes during your lecture; only one did during the small-group activity" is less arguable, more neutral and useful. Feedback must include explicit goals and tangible, goal-related results. Students can be too occupied with performing to attend to results: video recordings help. Most school district "formative" test grades refer to recently taught objectives, not final performance standards. Evaluating fall and winter performance against spring standards, measuring progress using more pre- and post-assessments, and using item analysis to identify individual student performance improvement needs are more effective.

Diverse student backgrounds and needs

Today's classroom diversity includes students with different native languages, cultural backgrounds, previous educational and personal experiences, and knowledge. Disabilities are also a possibility. Regardless of background, gender, or other characteristics, all students need teachers to behave and communicate in considerate ways. Teachers who consider how peers and faculty may misjudge some students and how this affects them, and are aware of stereotypes and their consequences, can develop true awareness of others' perspectives. Using language, examples, and behaviors to treat students with interest and consideration and encourage others to follow suit facilitates establishing welcoming environments where students feel comfortable participating, enabling their success. Even though teachers may have student records, they need to inform themselves of individual students' background knowledge. They can begin school years surveying student knowledge prerequisite to their subject or class; give students lists of basic content-area vocabulary they expect students to understand, asking them to identify unfamiliar or problematic words; consult Individualized Education Program (IEP) information, special educators, and parents about how student disabilities can affect attendance and participation; and ask students, parents, school social workers, and/or others about student religion, family obligations, and other unique factors to consider.

Motivation theory

Self-determination: student propensity for initiating activities independently, as opposed to only doing what teachers tell them to do. Achievement motivation research finds student motivation to learn and perform is stronger based on internalized motives, e.g., interest in subject matter, self-efficacy, desire to know things, desire to succeed, career ambitions, etc. By comparison, externalized motives, e.g., to gain rewards from teachers, schools, or parents; to avoid punishment; to impress teachers, classmates, friends, parents, etc. are not as effective. Attribution: how and where we assign cause. Students with more internal locus of control attribute their success or failure to personal abilities and actions; students with more external locus of control attribute successes or failures to people, actions, events, or situations outside themselves. Cognitive dissonance: discomfort with contradictory information; we adjust our schemas (mental representations) to reflect new information, form new schemas, or reject the information to restore congruence and resolve the discomfort. Classical conditioning: associating an unrelated stimulus with one that elicits a certain reflexive reaction can condition it to evoke the same reaction. Pavlov repeatedly paired bell-ringing with meat powder to make a dog salivate; eventually bell-ringing alone evoked salivation. Operant conditioning: manipulating antecedents and consequences shapes behavior; positive reinforcement strengthens probability of repeating behavior; punishment weakens it. Negative reinforcement removes a reinforcer or reward, decreasing behavior repetition.

Promoting student motivation

Teachers delivering instruction with enthusiasm and energy are role models: demonstrating their motivation and passion motivates students. Teachers showing why they are interested in subject content personalize it for students. Getting to know students, belief in student ability, strong

- 84 -

interest in their learning, and personal interest in student backgrounds and concerns inspire personal student loyalty. Many students want to know the application, utility, or real-life relevance of content before further engagement. To do this, use many examples and explain how it prepares them for future opportunities. Design activities directly engaging students in material, offering mastery opportunities: discovery learning requiring reasoning through problems to discover underlying principles independently satisfies students. Positive social pressure makes cooperative learning activities effective. Design assignments with challenges appropriate to student abilities and experiences. Set realistic performance goals; help students set and achieve reasonable goals. Tests and grades should show mastery, not shortcomings. Allow all students opportunities to achieve the highest grades and standards; avoid grading on curves. Make criticism constructive, feedback nonjudgmental. Criticize specific performances, not performers. Seek means of stimulating advancement; emphasize improvement opportunities. Avoid classifying students as leaders or followers. Give students as much choice and control over their learning, assessment, and performance as possible.

Intrinsic motivation

Students intrinsically motivated to learn are attracted to and fascinated by subjects, recognize their relevance to real life, feel a sense of accomplishment from mastering them, and feel called to them. Their reasons for learning are typically because the content interests them, they find it improves their thinking skills, and/or they find school success rewarding. Advantages include that intrinsic motivation sustains itself and has more longevity than external rewards; teacher efforts to build internal motivation typically involve efforts to further student learning as well, typically focusing not on rewards or punishments but on subject matter. Disadvantages include more specialized preparation, taking longer to produce behavior change, and requiring teachers utilize a variety of approaches in different students. Getting to know individual students and what interests them, connecting student interests to subject content, and strong teacher interest in subject content (and demonstration thereof) support developing intrinsic motivation in students.

According to one model, students offered opportunities to engage in learning activities first decide whether an activity is interesting to them or not. They engage in activities that interest them. If not immediately finding interest in an activity, they then evaluate it according to two criteria: whether or to what extent it is stimulating, i.e., it attracts their curiosity, affords a challenge, and/or appeals to their sense of fantasy; and whether or to what degree it affords them personal control—i.e., it is not too difficult for them to accomplish, and allows them some measure of free choice in the specific topics, learning styles, methods, procedures, materials, and forms of assessment they can use to acquire knowledge and demonstrate understanding. If students perceive an activity as both stimulating and controllable, they consider it potentially interesting or valuable and engage in it. If either or both conditions become inadequate, students disengage unless influenced by some extrinsic motivation. Students are more likely to repeat engagement in activities they find repeatedly stimulating and controllable, and discard those repeatedly not satisfying these criteria. Research finds the more constructive teacher criticism is and the more freely and often teachers praise student efforts, the more encouraged and self-motivated students become.

Including students in instructional decisions

All human beings want some control over their circumstances and activities. This is especially important to K-12 students: as minors, they have less legal and practical power and control over their lives than adults. Students perceiving teachers as having all the control over their instruction are more likely to respond only to external rewards and punishments and less likely to develop internal motivation to learn and achieve academically. When teachers include students in

- 85 -

instructional decisions, students feel ownership of the content and their learning. For example, teachers can ask students which aspects and topics within curriculum subjects interest them and let students choose topics they are interested in for papers and projects. They can give students choices among working independently, in pairs, or in small groups for some learning activities. Teachers can offer students options for how to weigh different assignments and assessments to determine their grades. Including papers, projects, tests, presentations, and other varied ways of assessing students allows them more control over how they demonstrate their learning. Participation and control in their instruction increases student motivation for acquiring and demonstrating knowledge.

Internal vs. external motivation

External motivations include teacher and parent expectations of students; rewards students can earn by demonstrating learning; and grades, which determine passing, promotion, retention, graduation, future opportunities, college admissions, scholarships, etc. Applying external motivators typically requires little preparation or effort, frequently does not require much teacher knowledge about individual students and their interests, and produces more immediate behavior changes. However, designating appropriate rewards and punishments becomes challenging when students become habituated, requiring escalation over time. External rewards frequently distract students from learning subject matter. They are not durable: students lose motivation once rewards and punishments are discontinued. Additionally, multiple experiments (e.g., Lepper, Deci) show external rewards can decrease internal motivation: students of all ages continued to engage in activities without rewards as they found them inherently interesting, whereas those given rewards for engaging in them discontinued engagement when rewards ceased; extrinsic rewards apparently reduced intrinsic interest. Internal motivations, including student interest in subject matter and learning and desire for knowledge and success, require more teacher time and effort and take longer to change behavior, but are durable, not dependent on rewards or punishments. Additional factors affecting student motivation include how stimulating activities are and how much control students have over them.

Contrasting with internal motives that students have for learning and succeeding academically, grades are external motivators. While they provide an index of how a student performed in classroom activities and assessments—which can vary in accuracy—grades by themselves do not give students intrinsic reasons to learn or achieve. Students displaying extrinsic motivation might say they need certain letter or number grades to pass courses and accomplish graduation from high school, to the next grade, receive rewards promised by teachers or parents, or avoid punishment. This differs from students saying that certain grades prove they know, understand, or have mastered subjects. Though some view formative assessment grades as feedback, these often do not inform adjusting performance. In an expert's (Wiggins, 2012) analogy, suppose a student's goal in PE is to run a five-minute mile, already having achieved 5:09. Suppose at the end of the first lap of a mile race, her coach yelled, "B-plus on that lap!" This does not support progress toward the goal. But the coach's yelling individual lap times, feedback, and advice: "You're on pace for 5:15," "You're not swinging your arms," "You need two seconds off the next lap to finish under 5:10—pick it up," provides specific information and advice for progress toward the goal.

Showing students the appeal of instructional content

Teachers can encourage student interest in subject content by showing its appeal. To show novelty, comment how you have not seen anything quite like a certain topic or activity. To show utility, describe a topic as including valuable ideas you will use later in the course and being a topic they will use over and over in both school and life. To show applicability, point out how relevant certain

- 86 -

subject matter is to the course and everyday life. To show anticipation, prompt students to ask themselves while reading what next logical step the text foreshadows. To show surprise, remark that the class has used some subject matter in many different ways, and then whet their interest, saying, "If you think you've seen them all, just wait until our next activity." To show challenge, suggest students will find the upcoming material very interesting and invite them to rise to a challenge. To show feedback, predict that when students try an assigned activity, they will discover whether they really understood the previous lesson or not. To show closure, announce that many students have asked about a topic or phenomenon, telling them they will now finally find out more and why.

Problem-solving learning tasks and learning project activities

Technology is an enormous asset to both teachers and students. For example, word processing programs, e.g., Microsoft Word, streamline teachers' work creating instructional documents like learning units, lesson plans, student handouts, worksheets, rubrics, checklists, progress reports, written parent communications, etc. Students can write essays, research reports, papers, short stories, plays, poetry, books, etc. They can type and save preliminary notes and outlines, then easily copy and paste portions into compositions. Students benefit from being able to delete and restore text paragraphs and sections instantly, and easily move paragraphs and sections to other locations as they learn how to organize their writing. Spell-checkers and grammar-checkers, while not substitutes for student knowledge, alert students to typing and mechanical errors for correction. Microsoft Excel and similar spreadsheet programs facilitate organizing numerical data and verbal information. Students can type in figures or lists with little or no editing and Excel displays and prints them in spreadsheet format. Databases give teachers and students large amounts of easily accessible information about specified topics, enabling them to search and sort it. Graphic tools enable students and teachers lacking artistic ability to create colorful, effective, professional-looking visual images to illustrate, organize, and understand information and concepts. Students and teachers can establish, use, and contribute to online communities to communicate and share information remotely, often instantaneously.

Communicating and publishing information with various technology tools

Teachers and students alike can use available technology productivity tools to organize, share, and present information in different formats. For example, in preparing a lesson plan, a teacher might create a PowerPoint slide presentation to project while delivering a lesson. By entering summary statements of main ideas, important concepts, major facts, etc. on each slide, teachers call student attention to the most significant aspects of the lesson, reinforcing these even as they provide additional information and details through lectures, discussions, textbooks, etc. Not only are slide presentations good for identifying main points, they also reinforce information presented in other ways (speech, textbooks, handouts), providing the redundancy students need to learn and retain it. In addition to PowerPoints, slide shows are good ways to illustrate lectures, lessons, and student presentations with visual imagery that engages viewers. Teachers can make videos of class for objective feedback and analysis; students can produce videos for class projects. Teachers can create multimedia presentations to access different student learning styles, helping all students benefit from instruction. Teachers can write parent newsletters, and students can create and publish classroom or school newsletters. Students, parents, and school personnel can view documents via websites and programs on monitor screens and/or print copies.

Assessing learning that students demonstrate through technological activities and projects

Teachers newly integrating technology into student work often wonder how to grade it. Evaluating student processes and actions is the same as with traditional written work, though it differs with the divergent potentials and unique features of each medium. For example, a notebook contains handwritten notes and drawings; a blog can contain hypertext, interactive imagery, embedded video, etc. Teachers must distinguish a technology tool's capabilities from the performance of the student using it. For example, iMovie has built-in, user-friendly professional effects enabling anybody to produce visually impressive video presentations. Hence teachers cannot grade the end product but the process, i.e., the student's research, writing, image selection, and other activities. In this sense, assessment must be more formative than summative to avoid focusing only on flashy end products and observe learning activities throughout the project. Teachers can create assessment rubrics using online generators like Rubistar, Digital Media Scoring Guides, Matrix Rubric with Points, PBL Checklists, Scholastic Rubric Maker, and Common Core Rubric Creator; or use available rubrics designed for general assessment; student blogs, wikis, websites, digital portfolios, social media, effective technology use, videos, digital storytelling, podcasts, graphic organizers, programming, coding, and gaming.

Providing unique growth opportunity for modern students

Many technologies (e.g., calculators and iPads) are student-centered. They were developed to provide a one-on-one interactive experience with some form of learning. Research has shown that learning technologies act as cognitive amplifiers. Students can learn more efficiently and effectively with technology. Technology, however, is not a silver bullet. Simple access to technology will not empower students to learn better. Teachers will require training to learn how to properly implement classroom technology (in coordination with pedagogy) and students will have to learn to appropriately and responsibly use technology. In coordination with technology and new pedagogical innovations (e.g., flipped classrooms, collaborative problem solving, or inquiry-based learning), teachers are able to provide their students with engagement opportunities previously unavailable. Students who have access to technology are able to directly engage with concepts and contexts any time of day or night. No longer are teachers the sole facilitators of quality learning. With traditional pedagogies (e.g., lecture), technology may be more distracting and less helpful. Technology is not best utilized as a replacement for old modes of knowledge transfer (e.g., note-taking or board presentation). A professional educator can adapt to both the new devices and new modes of thinking that empower student learning at trajectories not previously attainable.

Incorporating social media in the classroom

Social media is virtually ubiquitous in 21st century America. Our students are immersed in a society dominated by social media and this offers teachers an opportunity to model asynchronous (i.e., outside the time and vicinity constraints of standard class periods) learning processes that help students become lifelong learners. Examples of positive classroom social media outlets include *YouTube* where students can view or develop podcasts directly applicable to classroom topics. Teachers can use *Twitter* to post updates about assignments or deadlines. Teachers and students can blog about classroom experiences and practice academic writing skills. Students can receive more immediate feedback on academic pursuits with *Facebook*. Through all of these social media interactions, teachers can monitor students and model appropriate etiquette for online interactions as they help students become responsible and respectful citizens in a digital world.

Although there are a number of great benefits of social media in the classroom learning environment, these benefits do not come without the possibility of distractions. Students may try to tweet or snapchat with friends during class time. Teachers can always use less common social media tools to provide an opportunity for technologically empowered student engagement without the distraction associated with the most popular social networking platforms. For example, *Edmodo* enables educators to communicate with students, share materials, and distribute assessments in an efficient and non-distracting manner. Teachers and students can share work and gain efficient feedback through shared *Google Docs* that allow limitations on who contributes to social interactions. *Edublogs* allow teachers to share materials, encourage student contributions, incorporate videos, and facilitate online discussions.

Acceptable use policies

Like many businesses, most schools have acceptable use policies (AUPs) in place to stipulate the practices and constraints that users must agree to when accessing the Internet or local network. Many schools require students and staff to sign their AUP document before providing them with a network ID to gain access. AUPs are also required by Internet service providers (ISPs) of users when they sign up for the company's Internet access services. Users who sign AUPs agree to comply with such rules as not using the service to contribute to violating any law, not trying to violate any user's or network's security, not posting commercial messages to Usenet groups (sets of collected messages or notes on various topics submitted by users and posted to servers on a global network) unless they have obtained permission in advance, not trying to send spam or junk emails to anybody not wanting to receive it, and not trying to "mail-bomb" websites by flooding their servers with mass numbers of emails.

Electronic information

To locate information on digital networks, many search engines exist, e.g., Google, Bing, Yahoo, Lycos, Excite, AltaVista, McAfee Secure Search (from the anti-virus program publisher), Trovi, and DuckDuckGo (a "trackless" search engine keeping search history and information private); and search engines offered by websites known as online marketplaces, social media, or information sources like eBay, Amazon, Twitter, Wikipedia, etc. These user-friendly sites create huge databases indexing millions of websites, locating sites relevant to the search terms (words or phrases) that users enter. Software applications enable accessing and manipulating information from remote devices. Similarly to how technical support agents access user devices remotely to resolve technical issues, users with applicable permissions and software can access information remotely. Both software programs and websites commonly include help features: the user clicks a *help* button loading a window, webpage, or website with information like step-by-step instructions, FAQs, and answers; indexes to look up specific Help topics; interactive tools; and chat windows. To evaluate e-information, first appraise author credentials, publication date, revision and edition, publisher, and journal title. Then critically analyze content, including intended audience, objective reasoning, coverage, writing style, and consult evaluative reviews.

Evaluating electronic information critically

Initial appraisal: what are the author's education, degree(s), experience, publications, and institutional affiliation? Is the institution reputable? Is the source about a topic in the author's expertise area? Look in the source's biographical information and/or *Who's Who* publications. Is the author cited frequently in multiple bibliographies or other sources? What is the publication date? Is the information current? Is the publication a first edition or a revision? Are revision dates given? Who is the publisher? University presses are typically scholarly and reputable. Is a journal scholarly or popular? These differ in complexity levels. Content analysis: read the preface, foreword, or abstract to discern author intent. For a broad overview of covered material, scan tables of contents, indexes, and bibliographies. Read chapters specifically addressing your topic. Is the intended audience general or specialized? Is the source too advanced, technical, or elementary? Or is it suitable for your needs? Is the information fact, opinion, or propaganda? Good writers can convince readers their interpretations are facts. Is information valid and well-researched, or questionable and unsupported? Are assumptions reasonable? Are ideas or arguments fairly consistent with other works on the topic? Is author viewpoint impartial, objective, and unbiased? Does it substantiate, update, or supplement other sources? Are sources primary or secondary? Is the style logical, organized, clear, and readable? Read critical reviews of the publication in online reviewing sources.

Equity issues arising from differences in technology access and use

Although most schools have Internet access and some policies targeting minority, low-income and rural schools have succeeded, recent research still observes "digital divides" between poor and rich countries; differences in access among ethnic groups; unequal distribution of technology across regions and schools by socioeconomic status, minority enrollments, rural and urban vs. suburban schools; more access to computers in schools and homes for boys than girls; and slower Internet connections and unreliable, outdated hardware in poorer schools. Schools often poorly integrate and underuse available technology in classrooms. Even though technology can help students with disabilities access educational content, girls, disabled, rural, urban, poor, and minority students do not receive educational technology's full potential. Most homes have computers, but they are middle-class; in other families, lack of home access exacerbates gaps in school access when students with home access have more technology experience and confidence, dominate school technology, and reap more educational achievement and advancement. Parental support, modeling, and influence are also affected by socioeconomic status, lack of home access, and lack of parental digital knowledge. Girls use Internet and computer technology more confidently and often at home than in school. Even with apparently equal access, boys dominate home equipment, free access, and school computer clubs.

Ways in which individual student differences influence classroom communication

Younger students need concrete terms, examples, and materials; older students can handle increasing abstraction. Teachers should give students of all ages concepts and vocabulary slightly above their current levels for challenge and growth. Both student and teacher communication can be influenced by gender, e.g., volunteering, calling out, or waiting to be called on regardless of knowledge and preparation. Teachers may perceive or treat identical student responses differently according to student gender and/or race, e.g., as assertive vs. aggressive or enthusiastic vs. disruptive. ELL and LEP students may know content, but lack English to express it, or feel uncomfortable with their ELP levels. Numerous studies show when teachers communicate high learning expectations for all students, including ELLs and students with disabilities, they perform better. Emotionally engaging anecdotes, examples, and connecting topics to student prior knowledge, experience, interests, value, and utility stimulate student curiosity and interest. To clarify class goals and purposes, focus on major points, letting students find additional information in other activities. Repeat key concepts and ideas, compare and contrast, summarize, use analogies and metaphors to aid student comprehension and emphasize importance. Structure classes logically: present problems, then develop solutions; frame topics as stories; chronologically recount processes and events; show interconnected ideas' relationship to overarching themes; share outlines; explicitly transition between topics using mini-summaries, connections, or verbal signals.

Ensuring engagement and understanding of all students

Verbally, vary vocal speeds and tones to keep speech interesting to students. Vocal projection facilitates student hearing and also demonstrates teachers' confidence in what they say. Pausing strategically gets student attention, emphasizes transitions in topics, and gives students time to process information. Give ELLs and students with hearing, cognitive, learning, and other disabilities more wait time to allow for translating and processing teacher questions and formulating and translating their answers. Nonverbally, stand up straight and maintain eye contact to project confidence. Smiling communicates valuing what you say. While avoiding distracting apparel and excessive gestures, use movement to express enthusiasm, excitement, and energy. To help explain, illustrate, or clarify complex ideas, use media—not to distract from but to enhance instructional communication. Use chalkboards, dry-erase boards and overheads to demonstrate reasoning behind derivations, illustrate processes, and teach dynamically. Use slide presentations to organize varied visual, audio, and animated content, summarize ideas, and emphasize key points. Animations and videos offer sense of scale and illustrate dynamic processes. Audio can illustrate sounds associated with physical processes and introduce new, historical, or remote voices into classrooms. Artifacts can incorporate real-life elements, and print or electronic handouts give students detailed images and information. Redundant and multimodal presentations benefit ELL, exceptional, and all students.

Classroom question types to access different levels of Bloom's taxonomy

Levels, question types: knowledge and comprehension: what are the main points? What happened when...? Why did...? Application: can you think of other words meaning the same thing? Can you use this word in a different context? Can you think of another example of this? Does the same idea apply to...? Analysis: what effect does this achieve? Why do you think the author chose to do this? Does this fit into a pattern? What is suggested by...? How...? Why do you agree or disagree with this? Evaluation: which of these are most effective? What do you think of this? Do you think this works well? What are the strongest and weakest aspects of this? Synthesis: can you create your own version of this? How can you change the audience, features, etc. of this text? Where else can you see examples of this? Student activities, levels: analysis: debate a topic. Create text-based questions. Draw concept maps exploring connections. Mind-map aspects of a topic or text. Synthesis: study pastiche and parody. Analyze authors and writing styles closely; adopt styles. Experiment with genres, audiences, and text type features. Evaluation: devise reader expectation criteria for various text types. Apply assessment criteria to own and others' work.

Active listening strategies

Effective, active listening strategies accomplish multiple goals: teachers show students they care about them, demonstrate attention to their concerns, make them feel understood, establish and develop student-teacher relationships, give students emotional connections with school, model effective listening strategies for students to learn and use, and motivate student learning. Research shows student learning motivation requires feeling connected. In active listening, the listener uses verbal and nonverbal signals, asks questions to clarify, and restates main points for the speaker to confirm or correct. Restating in one's own words can also involve interpreting the speaker's message. For example, a student says, "I don't like this school as much as my other school. People aren't nice." The teacher responds, "You're unhappy here?" The student answers, "Yes. I haven't made any friends. Nobody includes me in anything." The teacher responds, "You feel left out here?" The student confirms, "Yes, I wish I knew more people." Questions, restating, and interpreting clarify factual and emotional message content. When speakers refine listener interpretations, they feel heard, gain insights into their own feelings, and may experience catharsis. Listeners enhance their skills in focusing on speakers and considering implied meanings.

Nonverbal communication

Open postures communicate receptivity; crossed arms and legs or similar averted body positions communicate the opposite. Ways of walking, sitting, standing, holding one's head, and subtle movements all convey attitudes and feelings. Gestures supplement speech, often unconsciously. Because different cultures assign different meanings to the same gestures, awareness is important to prevent misunderstanding or misinterpretation. Vocal tones and inflections express confidence, affection, anger, and sarcasm; and can even indicate understanding, agreement, and many more. Listeners also attend to speaker loudness, speed, and timing. Eye contact demonstrates interest in our culture; in some other cultures, it is perceived as confrontational and avoiding it shows respect. We communicate affection, attraction, or hostility as well as interest through eye contact; gauge others' responses; and maintain conversational flow. Facial expressions universally show happiness, sadness, anger, fear, surprise, disgust, and other emotions. Personal and social physical space or distance vary by individual, relationship, situation, and culture and can communicate intimacy, dominance, or aggression. Nonverbal communication informs verbal communication by repeating verbal messages; contradicting them; substituting for them; complementing or adding to them, e.g., patting on the back while verbally praising; accenting them; or emphasizing them, e.g., pounding the table, desk, lectern, dais, or pulpit with spoken points.

Professional organizations

In addition to research, mentors, supervisors, and colleagues, professional development resources for educators include professional organizations. Discipline-specific and other organizations enhance educator knowledge, expertise, and skills through conventions, conferences, workshops, trainings, publications, online courses, networking, local chapters, etc. Organizations include: the American Association of School Administrators, National Association of Elementary School Principals, National Art Education Association, American Counseling Association, American School Counselors Association, National Association for the Education of Young Children, American Library Association, International Reading Association, National Council of Teachers of English, American Council on the Teaching of Foreign Languages, Teachers of English to Speakers of Other Languages, Council for Exceptional Education, National Association for Gifted Children, National Council of Teachers of Mathematics, American Association of Physics Teachers, National Association of Biology Teachers, National Science Teachers Association, National Council for the Social Studies, Council for Exceptional Education, National Association for Sport and Physical Education, American Educational Research Association, Association for Educational Communication and Technology, American Federation of Teachers (AFL-CIO union), National Education Association (union), Association for Childhood Education International, Association for Supervision and Curriculum Development, National Middle School Association, National PTA, National School Boards Association, and National Staff Development Council.

Determining professional development goals

US states typically certify or license college graduates to teach in public schools for two years or similar periods with the expectation they will attain master's degrees or some other additional certification during that time. Teachers meeting state-established goals earn more advanced licensure. Even teachers with advanced graduate degrees must continue throughout their careers to set and achieve goals. Mentor teachers help new teachers set personal goals, develop personal development plans (PDPs), and document ongoing professional activities. Goals can include reading professional literature, attending educational conferences and seminars, etc., as well as taking college and graduate courses, accruing continuing education units (CEUs), etc. School district professional development committees (PDCs) work with new teachers and mentors to assure goals meet established district guidelines, sometimes paying workshop tuition. Teacher PDP approval by PDCs gives state licensure boards documentation of new teacher efforts to meet state requirements. PDCs and district administrators collaboratively set district-wide professional teacher goals, both subject-specific and interdisciplinary—e.g., aligning curricula with state standards and raising standardized test scores. PDCs offer all teachers training that targets district goals. Teacher, mentor, and PDC goal-setting must meet state education department standards. Goals should also be SMART—*specific, measurable, attainable, relevant/result-oriented*, and *time-limited*.

Professional development resources

Educational research studies often evaluate the effectiveness of various instructional practices. Educators benefit from many available literature reviews, meta-analyses, compilations, or other syntheses identifying consensus on effective practices to implement. Federal and state education departments, boards, and local school districts frequently adopt research-based instructional practices for individual teachers to follow. Professional organizations also disseminate research findings and provide courses, workshops, and conferences where members can learn additional information, insights, skills, and techniques to improve their teaching and student learning. A common route for teachers to improve knowledge and practical expertise is through graduate courses. Some teachers begin with bachelor's degrees, then complete master's degrees while working, obtaining more advanced knowledge of pedagogy and specific subject-area content, higher-level teaching certification, and salaries. Some certified in general education subsequently complete graduate courses in educational specialties. Some get degrees or certificates in additional subjects and specialties, e.g., math plus science, multiple languages, English plus ESL, special education plus early childhood education, etc. Mentors personally and individually advance PD, helping educators with PD plans; observing and providing feedback; sharing their knowledge, experience, and expertise; and providing reassurance, encouragement, and support. Pre-service internships provide closely supervised on-the-job practice and experience. Study groups and learning communities enable information sharing; learning communities also allow workshop and presentation collaborations, etc.

Helping educators utilize and integrate technology into instructional design and delivery

Contemporary technology not only greatly facilitates and enhances instruction, learning, and education overall, but integrating technology into instruction has become a necessity now that society depends on and requires its use so heavily. Among many available resources, one is the International Society for Technology in Education (ISTE), offering consulting services and helping educators develop customized PD learning programs. Workshops include one providing in-depth examination of worldwide educational initiatives using technology. Another, for teachers and educational leaders with advanced technology skills, teaches ISTE Standards and how to teach others these in schools or through peer coaching. A virtual workshop gives lead teachers hands-on experiences in designing learning activities embedding ISTE Standards, measuring activity effectiveness, and working district-wide with faculty teams to integrate these standards across the curriculum. A three-day onsite leadership academy provides in-depth PD knowledge and understanding of ISTE Standards; and instruction from experts in these standards regarding the conditions essential to implementing them at district, school, and classroom levels. ISTE mobile learning support services help educators and stakeholders apply prevalent (and popular with students) mobile technology for learning. ISTE's classroom observation tool measures effective classroom technology integration. ISTE offers school administrators and principals digital citizenship, technology leadership institutes, a standards readiness workshop, and essential conditions readiness Survey.

Reflection

Reflection enables teachers to gain some distance and objectivity to analyze their instructional practices and interactions with students, which in turn enables them to identify, plan, and implement measures to improve these for improved student learning. To track their effectiveness in the classroom, teachers should establish baselines early in the school year. They can keep journals, writing their reflections about classroom interactions as often as possible. Selecting one high-achieving and one low-achieving student in a class and charting how the teacher's professional relationship with each student develops can often accurately reflect learning opportunities the teacher provides for all students. Writing honestly and rereading previous entries regularly help teachers change their behaviors to improve student-teacher relationships, hence learning. Many pre-designed self-assessment checklists, questionnaires, and tools help teachers evaluate their practices systematically and use their responses to reinforce or expand teaching strengths and address weaknesses. Through peer assessment, teachers have colleagues observe and provide feedback on their instruction: others often see behaviors and omissions we cannot, and/or provide alternate perspectives. The "critical friend" method is similar. Systematic incident analysis enables teacher insights into student behaviors and teacher-student interactions and how changing teacher behaviors can change student behaviors. Portfolios enable teachers to review work development and changes longitudinally.

Reflection questions that a teacher might ask him or herself after a classroom activity

1. What were the learning objectives for this experience? Did I expect too much or too little of the students?
2. Did this experience work well? Did the students react positively or negatively? What data do I have that this experience was (un)successful?
3. What can I change about this lesson? Is it possible to better prepare my students for this lesson next year?
4. What questions should I have asked before the experience? Which questions should I have asked after the experience?
5. What student behavior was most notable? Did any circumstances from outside the classroom affect this behavior?
6. How do my students learn? Would my students learn better in some different way?
7. Were all my students actively participating in this experience? How can I adapt my lesson to make it more student-centered?
8. What data do I need to make an informed decision about this activity's effectiveness? What plans should I make to get this data in the future?
9. What do my data tell me? How can I adjust my expectations and my activity based upon the data I got?
10. Can my students meet the objectives in a more efficient manner? Does this activity need less time or more time? How can I adjust for next year?

Practices that apply research data finding them effective for instructing students

Cognitive research studies have established that comparing, contrasting, and classifying help students understand complex concepts. Teaching students to identify idea similarities and differences applies these findings. Research shows students' higher-order cognitive skills for analysis and synthesis, in-depth analysis, and reading comprehension improve through effectively summarizing information and note-taking. Teaching students how and assigning them to summarize and take notes efficiently applies research to improve instruction and achievement. Educational achievement motivation research demonstrates the impact of recognition for reinforcing and monitoring student effort, e.g., symbolic or abstract recognition is more effective than concrete rewards; rewards contingent on meeting some performance standard are most effective; 8-year-olds' learning strategies differ radically from 12-year-olds' and adults' strategies; and 8-year-olds learn mainly from positive feedback, not negative. Teachers raise student achievement by recognizing, rewarding, and praising specific goal achievements. Studies show learning occurs linguistically and non-linguistically; visual or other non-linguistic representations help students understand, retain, retrieve, connect, and apply knowledge; and the more students combine linguistic and non-linguistic systems, the better they learn and think. Teachers apply these findings using multimodal instruction. Additional research-based effective teaching practices include practice, homework, objectives, feedback, generating hypotheses, testing hypotheses, advance organizers, questions, cues, cooperative learning, and teaching and assigning nonfictional writing.

Feedback

Teachers receive feedback from a number of sources (e.g., students, parents, colleagues, department leaders, and school administrators). Some (but not all) of the feedback will be useful. Feedback like "I don't like your class" does not give a teacher the opportunity to improve his or her classroom practice. Other feedback like, "Try to allow more wait time between asking a question and calling upon a student to answer" is more specific and teachers can act on this. Helpful feedback and less helpful feedback both provide a teacher with the opportunity to initiate a conversation on his or her pedagogy. In response to non-anonymous feedback, a teacher can ask follow-up questions to clear up any vagueness. Feedback can be something to talk over with a mentor, an invitation to initiate a discussion within a professional learning community, or even a starting point at which to begin a process of action research in the classroom. Unfortunately the feedback a teacher receives (particularly from students) is not always helpful and in some cases can be hurtful. A beginning teacher must remember not to take feedback personally. A professional teacher is only expected to do the best that he or she can to improve based upon the appropriate feedback he or she receives.

Characteristics associated with helpful feedback (TOTAL)

1. **Targeted**: Feedback should be targeted towards a goal and allow the subject of the feedback to adjust his or her actions in an effort to improve. Vague or imprecise feedback is not only unhelpful but can also be misleading.
2. **Ongoing**: For feedback to be useful, individuals must have the ongoing opportunity to improve.
3. **Timely**: Feedback must be timely. Late arriving feedback deprives an individual of the opportunity to improve recent behavior or efficiently affect better results.
4. **Actionable**: "Great Work" or "This is not right" are not examples of good feedback. Both lack the specificity necessary to be useful. Good feedback can be acted upon. Adjustments can be made in response to specific and useful suggestions on how to improve.
5. **Level-Headed**: Feedback must be genuine, trustworthy, and not overly ambitious. Improvement in any endeavor is an incremental process that is best accomplished slowly, in short increments over long intervals of time. A feedback recipient must be able to trust that a critique is both sensible and prudent.

Resources available to help professional development and enhance effectiveness

Every educator in the world (at universities, colleges, and schools of every type) is a part of a professional learning community, in the broadest sense of that phrase. The growth of the internet and data resources have made teacher professional development more available than it has ever been before. Websites like *Edutopia* can help a teacher stay current with the latest technology or innovative pedagogy. National organizations (e.g., NCTE, NCTM, NCSS, and NSTA) offer memberships for teachers in every field and each offers publications and web based resources. National and state-based organizations organize conferences at which educators come together to share and collaborate. Numerous research journals are published regularly and are searchable via indexing services (e.g., ERIC and JSTOR). Journals regularly publish peer-reviewed articles featuring the best new ideas in teaching and learning in their fields. A virtually innumerable amount of resources is available for every teacher who wishes to stay current. A modern professional teacher is one that is open to new ideas and is willing to put forth the effort to learn about new pedagogical methods. A modern professional teacher is willing to try to implement new classroom methods based upon new learning about the best practices.

Implicit teacher bias

Implicit teacher biases are stereotypes or attitudes that are manifested unconsciously in the classroom. In some cases these biases may adversely affect student learning. One pervasive stereotype is that girls are not able to do mathematics as well as boys. A math teacher may subconsciously call on boys more often or praise girls less often. Boys may do better in this math class because they are given more opportunities or praise, which may not be available to girls because of a stereotype. As a teacher, awareness of potential biases is the first step in overcoming them. Teachers should reflect on their teaching practice and collect/analyze classroom evidence (data) to determine if biases are present. In order for each student to have a fair chance to succeed, teachers must recognize each as an individual, rather than a member of some stereotypical group (e.g., athletic team, ethnic group, gender, or those with past behavioral issues).

Mentors as a resource for strengthening teacher knowledge, skills, and effectiveness

Collegial collaboration is the basis of quality educational practice. No individual can reach every student or solve every problem. In recent years, a number of school systems have begun formal programs to help train veteran teachers to serve as mentors for younger teachers. A mentor is a veteran teacher who is accepting of a new teacher, is effective in a variety of different interpersonal contexts, and adept at providing instructional support. A mentor is empathetic, optimistic, and open to development in new aspects of the teaching profession. A mentor is a resource who can provide insight into the culture of a school, share tips and tricks that he or she has picked up over the years, and talk about how to resolve challenging circumstances. A mentor is a colleague who can put issues into their proper perspective and reassure a new teacher who may feel isolated or overwhelmed.

Professional learning community (PLC)

Although the phrase "professional learning community" can have multiple meanings, PLCs are most often small groups of educators who meet on a regular basis to discuss and collaborate to improve teaching skills and student academic performance. Professional learning communities might discuss the creation or editing of class materials, completed student work as exemplars of student learning, data from student assessments, or professional literature pertinent to classroom experience. The focus of professional learning communities is learning: student learning and teacher learning about student learning. Professional learning communities can offer an opportunity for teachers to engage in reflection on teaching practice and cycles of action research or other evidence-based adaptations of classroom activities/assessments towards better student performance.

Professional versatility

Education has never been and will never be a one-size-fits-all endeavor. No two learners are exactly the same and no two classes are exactly the same. What works for one student or class may not work for another. Given the diversity of students in the classroom, open-mindedness and a willingness to adapt are arguably the most important characteristics of successful teachers. Both as an individual in the classroom and as a part of a professional learning community outside of the classroom, an openness to the possibility of a new approach allows a teacher to persevere through the most challenging of circumstances. Challenges encountered might arise due to: behavioral problems, learning differences, student exceptionalities, technology, and any of a number of possible distractions originating inside or outside the classroom. A versatile teacher open to collaboration with colleagues, creative problem solving, and trying new methods can overcome almost any challenge.

Action research

Action research is a process of reflective classroom inquiry performed by the teacher. Action research is a technique through which a teacher might refine his or her teaching practice by using available data to inform new methods or mechanisms of student learning. The four generic stages for action research are: Plan, Act, Observe, and Reflect. A teacher plans a learning experience for his or her students and then puts that plan into action. The teacher observes his or her students' reactions during the experience and the learning results (positive or negative) through either formative or summative assessment. After analyzing the available quantitative and/or qualitative data, the teacher formulates a new plan of action for future student learning experiences and the action research process begins again. Action-based research is the most natural mechanism of classroom study for the teacher. The teacher is using the evidence available in a scientific process to improve his or her educational practice. Action research is one example of the evidence-based educational practice advocated by the standards.

Investigating a problem using a mixed methods study

Quantitative methodologies are adept at answering "if" questions. Numerical-based methods can help answer questions regarding whether there is evidence that a particular pattern is occurring. For example, a study of test scores will tell you **if** your students understand a given concept. Qualitative (text-based) methods are adept at answering "how" or "why" questions. For example, qualitative (text-based) methods would be required to determine **why** students have not learned a given concept well. Mixed method inquiry (including both quantitative and qualitative aspects) can greatly benefit an educator seeking to grow as a professional by providing both direct verdicts and indirect contexts to questions of pedagogical effectiveness.

Quantitative and qualitative research methods

Quantitative methods are deductive in nature. Quantitative investigators will collect and analyze numerical data with mathematical and statistical tools. An example of a quantitative method would be to compare the results of a pre-test (before a lesson) and a post-test (after a lesson) to determine **if** a lesson was effective. Quantitative methods are commonly applied in scientific fields in which numerical data is available (e.g., biology and physics).

Qualitative methods are inductive in nature. Qualitative investigators will collect and analyze textual data collected from interviews, observations, or conversations. An example of a qualitative method would be to discuss a lesson (after the fact) and ask the students for their perceptions about the effectiveness of the lesson. Qualitative methods will help determine **why** students were or were not successful on a given assessment. Qualitative methods are commonly applied in fields studying human behavior (e.g., marketing and sociology).

Pros and cons of quantitative and qualitative research methods:

- Quantitative methods are number-based. Qualitative methods are text-based. Numerical methods can determine **if** students are learning about a particular concept. Qualitative methods would be required if a teacher wished to understand **why** students were not learning a given concept.
- Quantitative methods are more objective; numerical data is gathered using unbiased measurements. Qualitative methods are more subjective. Researchers must interpret the results of interviews or discussions and can be susceptible to implicit or explicit biases.
- Quantitative methods tend to require more planning time before implementation while qualitative measures require more time after the implementation. Numerical data are more straightforward to analyze but more difficult to collect. Textual data are more challenging to analyze but less cumbersome to collect.
- Quantitative methods are stricter in their design; collected responses must be numerical. Qualitative methods are more open-ended in their design; a greater variety of responses can be accepted and analyzed.
- Both quantitative and qualitative methods can be shown as valid and reliable.

Classroom Management and Organization

Relationship between academic instruction and classroom management

When educators teach and encourage students to take responsibility for their own behaviors rather than taking total responsibility for guiding student behaviors, teachers and students approach and understand content differently. Moreover, when instruction is more demanding (e.g., students address novel problems and/or create products), teachers must make more complex management decisions. This relationship between instructional activity levels and management complexity supports research evidence of the inseparable, complex interrelationship of instructional curriculum and classroom management. Teachers must help students learn to meet concurrent academic demands for comprehending and manipulating content, and social demands for interacting with others to demonstrate that content knowledge effectively. This broader view of classroom management has redirected research from controlling behavior to creating and sustaining learning environments—including furniture arrangements, classroom decorations, developing and communicating rules and routines, and interacting with students. Research shows teachers implementing systematic classroom management approaches when school years begin have students demonstrating higher task engagement and academic achievement. Researchers also identify strategies eliciting low misbehavior and high involvement as communicating awareness of student behavior, overlapping activities, smooth transitions, instructional momentum, and whole-class-focused attention alerting.

Understanding student group dynamics and managing their behavior

Be aware of individual students' group roles, e.g., leader, instigator, conscience, intimidator, enforcer, procurer, or negotiator; develop friendly relationships with the first three, and keep the first two on-task. Know group-required behaviors, conversation topics and interests, and what maintains a group's cooperation and unity. Place a daily "do-now" activity on the board or students' desks to start upon arrival before lessons, preparing students for lessons and continuing ongoing group or team tasks and activities. Greet and converse with students, always respectfully. Pleasantly remind and encourage desired behaviors before classes begin. Engage group leaders in task preparations (equipment setup, writing assignments on boards or overheads, reading assignment directions, handing out worksheets): others follow. Include cooperative learning groups, and allow collaborative team answers. Recognize and reward good behavior. Never embarrass students in front of classmates, which provokes individual and group rebellion. Determine behavior reasons and functions, e.g., boredom, overly easy or difficult assignments, confronting or embarrassing students, favoritism, group leader behavior contagion, pre-existing issues, distracters, etc. Prevent escalation using low-impact interventions: interest in student work, encouragement, good-natured humor, physical proximity, touch, interrupting oneself mid-sentence and using the "teacher glare," reminding classes and groups of times they did well, and changing lesson presentation to become more interesting than any distraction(s).

Productive classroom environments for students at different developmental levels

Teachers must take into account the developmental levels of their students to establish positive classroom environments for them. For example, teachers should not expect young children to begin preschool having already learned to share with other children. Teachers can model sharing and cooperation for them, and encourage and reward their imitating teacher examples as well as spontaneous prosocial behaviors, which researchers have observed in young children. Teachers can also observe whether young students engage in unoccupied behavior; independent or solitary play;

onlooker behavior; parallel, associative, or cooperative play; and influencing factors, e.g., how well children know each other, offer matching activities, and introduce experiences at the next higher level. Teachers can offer peer collaboration opportunities to older elementary and middle school students by assigning study buddies, partners for peer tutoring, working together, or think-pair-share and similar activities. Small groups can also be formed for planning, organizing, and implementing team or group learning projects, although teachers must remember that students have typically not developed social interaction skills to the extent of high school students, and so must guide them accordingly. In high school, teachers can extend productive learning environments beyond classrooms to surrounding communities, engaging students' abstract cognitive skills to promote respect, social conscience, and action through service projects.

Respecting diversity and promoting the active engagement of all students

Honor student experiences: create safe spaces, enrich curriculum using student experiences, and give students opportunities to learn from each other's perspectives and experiences. View different identity groups from asset-based orientations, let students define their own identities, and avoid or challenge stereotypes. Select texts reflecting demographics of and relevant to specific classes, and assign discussions or reflective writing about reading. Share personal anecdotes inviting student sharing. Student-centered classroom setups should include multicultural decorations or imagery reflecting our society's diversity and student backgrounds. Arrange furniture and materials to support comfort, ownership, dialogue, and collaboration. Structure classrooms for maximal student voice and participation. Involve students in setting norms and expectations, considering gender, language, and cultural and communication differences. Give students daily classroom jobs accommodating different learning styles, innovative student approaches, and real-life responsibility and work skills. Use gender-neutral categories and practices and let students choose group identifications. Build shared inquiry and dialogue through respect, trust, voice, humility, and active listening skills. Revisit participation norms: include and value small-group participation, written and artistic responses, and active listening as well as verbal communication. To create safe climates, actively teach emotional-social skills, work to create positive relationships, build community, prevent or intervene with bullying, focus explicitly on understanding and appreciating differences, practice and teach meaningful conflict resolution, and teach students to challenge exclusion and bias.

Instructional strategy for communicating high expectations

Experts (Marzano, 2010) advise: (1) as early as possible, identify students for whom you have lower expectations. Once formed, negative expectations are hard to admit and change. (2) Identify student similarities. Though teachers resist admitting they automatically form expectations based on student appearance, speech style, or ethnicity, research finds early expectations based on such characteristics. Expectation patterns do not indicate bigotry or racism when people actively work to keep biases from controlling their thoughts and behaviors. (3) Identify your differential behaviors toward low-expectancy students, which are far more important than your expectations. Students observe and make inferences based on teacher behaviors. Affectively, teachers make less eye and physical contact, smile less, and lightly or playfully converse less with low-expectancy students. Academically, they ask them less challenging questions, call on them less frequently, explore their answers in less depth, and reward less rigorous responses from them. (4) Consciously treat high-expectancy and low-expectancy students the same way. Affectively this is relatively easy, but academically more challenging: students habituated to low teacher expectations may experience discomfort when teachers challenge them more. However, ultimately this enables students to ask clarifying questions and risk communicating new ideas.

Responding to all student cultural, linguistic, and familial backgrounds and needs

Students learn more when challenged by high teacher expectations, including open-ended questions and assignments requiring critical thinking skills. Explicitly teaching skills for studying, working with teachers, and completing college applications to students whose parents never attended college fills "cultural capital" gaps, preparing underrepresented students for college. Give students adult responsibilities for collaboratively contributing to planning, coaching, financial activities, etc. Diversity becomes a resource; students learn varied skills. Teacher knowledge and caring about individual students promotes their participation. Understanding student home cultures aids educator understanding of student behavior inside and outside classrooms. Encouraging active parental participation greatly supports student academic success through mutually understanding parent, classroom, and school expectations of teachers and students; helping parents converse to prepare children for classroom communication; helping parents pursue GED or ESL programs; and referring parents to community resources for arts, sports, science programs, and homework help. Eliciting and validating student background experiences, e.g., using semantic webbing to inform lesson planning and increase student engagement. Selecting curriculum for cultural relevance—student ethnic groups' contributions to US history and culture—enhances student self-esteem, makes lesson topics meaningful, and enables authentic, interactive language, literacy, and thinking skills. Culturally compatible social learning organization and communication expectations and norms make teaching and learning more effective.

Developing student oral and written communication skills

Oral: the inside-outside circle – students, facing each other in two concentric circles, pair up; take turns speaking and listening; and rotate partners. Choral response – teacher asks a question, gives a signal, allows wait-time, says "Everyone..." and initiates signal, and the students respond in unison. Think-pair-share – students rehearse responses with partners, getting corrective feedback or elaboration help before whole-class sharing. Dialogic reading – teachers read books with individual students or small groups using "CROWD" prompts: sentence *completion*; asking questions requiring student text *recall*; *open-ended* questions about book pictures; *w-questions* (who, what, when, etc.) about pictures; and *distancing* book pictures and words to students' own life experiences. PEER prompts: *prompting* students to talk about text, *evaluating* responses, *expanding* responses, and *repeating* prompts at higher levels. Written: written responses, same answers – teachers ask questions; students write answers on whiteboards; teachers allow wait-time, say "Everyone..." and students hold up written responses. Written responses, varying answers – like same answers, but students check answers with partners, revise as needed; teachers call on individual students. Think-pair-share activities also enable students to get peer feedback about written responses before sharing them with the whole class.

Communicating expectations to students

By always behaving fairly and consistently in class, teachers model integrity for students, who understand better what is expected of them by witnessing the teacher meeting his/her own high expectations. Reinforce expectations daily, and repeat continually—sometimes through gentle reminders, other times interrupting instruction to discuss expectations as indicated—to change student attitudes. Support and inform student success through parent-teacher collaboration by communicating to parents your expectations of both students and parents. Prepare "achievement contracts" outlining mutual expectations students sign when the school year begins. Give students time to find answers themselves, only giving hints or ideas, not supplying correct answers immediately. Periodically, have students write about how they think they are doing and suggestions for improving the class. Always speak to students positively, emphasizing their ability to learn your instruction. Let students view you as a real person; get to know them. This attitude motivates some students to work harder to please teachers. However, avoid the trap of being students' friend; maintain authority as their teacher. Tell students exactly what you expect, making activity and assignment standards perfectly clear. Ensure every student knows s/he can earn high grades by working hard enough. Let students revise poorly-graded work, promoting mastery learning.

Good student-teacher interactions and relationships

Good student-teacher interactions and relationships enhance classroom atmosphere. Research has generated a significant body of literature showing that the quality of teacher-student relationships influences student academic achievement and behavior. Teachers showing students respect and guiding them to respect each other encourage active learners. Learning more about students, interacting and communicating with them, and providing appropriate feedback establish relationships promoting effective teaching and learning. When students have opportunities to communicate with one another, they share responsibility for learning, discuss diverse viewpoints, and shape class direction. Classes with predominant lecture formats are frequently well-organized; teachers typically know content well and clearly present material, but student-student interaction opportunities are lacking. More student-focused classes present small-group, paired, and whole-class discussion opportunities. Tasks having multiple potential solutions or answers can shift lesson direction, generate deeper thought processes, and enhance discussion quality. Small-group discussions particularly enable enough chances to listen, consider others' ideas, and all students to have a voice. Gallery walks, professional communication projects, classroom data explorations, structured academic controversy discussions, open-ended teacher questions, cooperative learning methods, structured jigsaw activities and other discussion exercises, conceptual multiple-choice questions about lesson themes combined with peer instruction, and in-class think-pair-share assignments are all ways to improve classroom interactions.

Teacher enthusiasm

Numerous studies identify teacher enthusiasm as a behavior which prominently affects student learning. Research also shows that a combination of teacher enthusiasm and constructive feedback enables students to learn more. Investigators find more enthusiastic teachers spend more time on presentation and positive performance feedback. Enthusiastic teacher behaviors include the following: variation in vocal tone, pitch, volume, and pace is important. Teachers with monotonous, droning voices inspire student boredom. Teachers reflect their excitement with teaching and learning through their eyes by making eye contact with students; using their eyes expressively, e.g., raising eyebrows, opening eyes wide, etc.; and using their eyes as well as their ears to listen to students. Judicious teacher use of body language, gestures, and other nonverbal communications also communicate enthusiasm. Effective teachers clap hands, give high-fives, make OK signs, thumbs-up, etc. Sweeping arm motions, energetic body swinging, hand gestures, and facial expressions showing pleasure or displeasure, amusement, disappointment, and approval express enthusiasm. Moving around the classroom not only enables teachers to monitor students, but also makes them less predictable and boring. Nonverbal behaviors also reinforce verbally encouraging students.

Instructional skills and practices that foster innovation

One expert (Hiam, 2011) identifies "five I's" as components of innovation curriculum: imagination, inquiry, invention, implementation, and initiative. Initiative is the foundation enabling the four others. Although daydreaming is discouraged in classrooms, teachers must learn creative expression skills to encourage student imagination. Master teacher collaboration with invention and creativity experts on curriculum design is one recommended solution. To fuel imagination, educators must connect seemingly unrelated topics, skill-sets, and ideas. Most inventions are innovative combinations of multiple domains. Writing across the curriculum, combining arts and sciences, etc., stimulates imagination. To encourage inquiry, students—not teachers—must ask most of the questions. Students must question, explore, and research curiously to innovate. Teachers can incorporate student question-asking exercises following activities into established curricula. Educators must challenge students to invent new and better ways to solve problems and apply learning to real life more often—weekly, not once or twice throughout school or only through science fairs. Implementation must also be increased: students get insufficient practice putting ideas into action, learning from mistakes, refining plans, and persevering. Initiative is more common in non-hierarchical and individualistic societies. Teachers need preparation for mentoring and coaching students in initiative-based learning; schools must support teachers' guiding students by supplying resources and valuing decentralized activities. Challenge, encouragement, and support develop self-efficacy and agency, promoting invention.

Aspects of how information and communication technology (ICT) supports student learning

Education is socially oriented and greater teacher-student personal contact is associated with quality education; ICT is compatible with and supportive of student-centered learning environments. ICT can have a transformational role in teaching and learning. Student-centered learning incorporates experiential and hands-on learning, self-directed student learning, and flexible learning activities. Students must not simply remember information to understand and apply it; they must question, grapple with ideas, discover things on their own, and construct knowledge, with teachers not being information presenters but facilitators—which also enhance their attention, interest, and motivation. Contrasting with teacher-directed learning, student-centered learning is more congruent with constructivist learning. Researchers conclude that to make complex information their own, students must individually discover and transform it. As facilitators, teachers provide opportunities for students to discover ideas, apply them, and consciously utilize their own learning strategies. Thus curriculum design is shifting from emphasizing informational content to competencies and how information will be used. Teachers use ICT in lesson planning and presentation; students use ICT for exploration, practice, and preparing assignments and presentations; administrators and teachers use ICT to complete administrative tasks more efficiently. Technology-facilitated, student-centered approaches facilitate multimedia presentation, enhancing learning; and encourage student responsibility for learning.

Assistive communication technology

Some students have speech and language disorders; some with autism spectrum disorders, cognitive, or other disorders may have limited communication skills or be completely nonverbal. Because academic success depends on communication, assistive communication technology can help students overcome learning obstacles. Visual representation systems are effective for students having difficulty with auditory receptive and verbal expressive, but greater visual processing abilities. augmentative and alternative communication (AAC) systems and devices are assistive technologies facilitating communication. They range from low-technology to high-technology. Low-tech systems and devices are typically easy to use and inexpensive, including dry-erase boards, albums, folders, binders, and other ways of storing and transmitting images. Mid-tech systems and devices include simple, battery-operated or electronic voice output communication aids (VOCAs); overhead projectors; and tape recorders. High-tech systems and devices are more complex and expensive, including computers; software programs, e.g., speech-to-text and text-to-speech software; adaptive keyboards and other hardware; and more complex VOCAs. Special education student Individualized Education Programs (IEPs) must include any kinds of assistive technology required for them to achieve learning objectives and succeed in school. AAC systems and devices enable interactive student-teacher communication, effectively giving voices to students appearing to lack them.

Inclusive classroom environments that promote equity and respect for students

When teachers initiate open dialogues, they engage students in a democratic process and provide opportunities for group decision-making requiring compromise, not competition. Teachers can rearrange classrooms to facilitate group decision-making and student interaction, e.g., sitting in circles, moving all desks to one side, reversing the room's front and back, and letting students learn from their decisions to democratize classroom spaces. They can assign group projects, which should be multidimensional, equally emphasizing textual, graphic, creative, presentation, and other components to address different skills and learning styles. Group projects also require member interdependency for successful completion, and vary in group composition. Rather than the typical forms of talking and writing for classroom sharing, wherein the loudest or fastest student gains the floor, teachers can vary protocols, e.g., visual art; paired and/or small-group sharing; allowing more time for reflecting, organizing their thoughts, and writing; and activities enabling thinkers, talkers, writers, and visual artists to share ideas. During class discussions, creating conflict regarding topics gives students more realistic experiences of complex issues. When students take various views of issues, not for competition or winning but for consensus, it affords experiences that demonstrate the complicated, messy nature of real-life democratic processes.

Organization of classroom desks

The classic rows and columns model of student desk placement facilitates a teacher-centered learning environment. All students are facing the teacher who, because of the orientation of student desks, is the fulcrum of every discussion. Eye-contact between dialoguing students in rows and columns of desks may be impractical or impossible. Students can be easily distracted and hard to monitor. Alternatively, teachers might choose to use a U-shaped configuration in which every student has a "front-row" seat. U-configurations are conducive to lively discussion; any student can maintain eye contact with any other student. However, U-configurations may not allow a teacher to reach every student's position. A third option might be pods of three or four. Although pods are not good for lectures and whole class discussions, they are particularly useful for student-centered pedagogy incorporating group projects or collaborative problem solving. Pods will most efficiently allow students to be in close proximity to their neighbors while also allowing a teacher more efficient access to every student and the opportunity to coach them through difficulties when they arise.

Flipped classrooms

A "flipped" classroom is a pedagogical model in which the traditional uses of time inside and outside of the classroom are reversed. Traditional time inside the classroom is devoted to teacher-centered (i.e., passive) activities like lecture. In a "flipped" classroom passive learning exercises are reserved for outside of the classroom. Either the teacher will record audio or video segments for students to consume at home or the teacher will make use of pre-existing content (e.g., Mometrix Academy or Khan Academy). Traditionally time outside of the classroom is devoted to more student-centered (i.e., active) experiences such as problem solving. Because traditional homework is generally individual, problems are often less challenging and less instructive. In a "flipped" classroom, problem solving and other traditional homework is done inside the classroom allowing students to collaborate on more challenging problems with additional assistance from the teacher.

- 104 -

In the student-centered "flipped" classroom model, student learning effectiveness is increased because both halves of the reversal facilitate deeper understanding. Students have more time to digest material at home and can pause or replay lectures as often as they like. In the classroom students can solve more challenging and instructive problems through the assistance of classmates and their instructor.

Cooperative games for preschoolers

Musical chairs, duck-duck-goose, and similar traditional games exclude children from the fun by emphasizing competition; cooperative games teach preschoolers to listen, follow directions, develop movement and problem-solving skills, and collaborate. "Help": balancing paper napkins on heads, children move about, freezing if napkins fall; touch to unfreeze classmates. "Robots": pairs take turns as robot and commander. Commanders direct robot movements to negotiate obstacles, reaching preset goals. "Balloon keep-up": outdoors or in gyms, children collaborate to keep balloons aloft. "Cooperative musical chairs," or "islands": when music stops, children share, not compete for, remaining chairs or islands. "Roll it": children sitting in a circle, feet touching, roll a ball to others, keeping it steadily moving; as children master rolling, add more balls. The goal is to keep control rolling as many balls as possible. "Cooperative duck-duck-goose": children walk in place in a circle; "it" chooses a goose, who walks, runs, or skips around the circle, chooses another goose, giving everybody a chance. "Cows and ducks" (also known as "frogs and dogs," "cats and snakes," or "chickens and goats"): whisper animal names in children's ears; each moos, quacks, etc., traveling; children making the same sounds group and move together like their animals. "Find it": call a color to moving children; first one finding something that color touches it; second holds the first's hand, etc., until all connect.

Kindergarten schedules balancing active vs. restful activities

Kindergarteners apparently have boundless energy, yet fatigue quickly; short attention spans demand change. Teachers therefore must alternate active movement with restful activities to prevent both exhaustion and boredom. Kindergarteners thrive through independently and cooperatively working with small peer groups, conversing, choosing activities, and practicing and applying skills they are learning. Organizing and managing learning environments via learning centers matches kindergartener identities and ways of learning, developing "learning to learn" skills of autonomy, initiative, persistence, creativity, resourcefulness, risk-taking, reasoning, and problem-solving. For example, children decide to create their own board game: they collect materials from learning centers; make a game board, markers, dice, rule book, timer, and (using a computer graphics program) design and print play money; use classroom word walls, charts, or ask the teacher and peers for help writing numbers and words; play their finished game repeatedly, and teach others how. This includes student choice; multiple learning domains; all curriculum areas; teacher guidance; and physical, cognitive, language, emotional, and social development. Skills play develops: literacy is learned through print concepts, reading, writing, linguistic communication, and purposeful writing; mathematics is learned through shapes, number concepts, language, predicting, measuring money, and time; science through exploring materials' physical properties and recycling materials; social studies through collaboratively developing, following rules, geographic thinking and mapping, and money use; arts through drawing and creating; and technology through basic computer use and software navigation.

Establishing and managing productive classroom learning environments

For students to take risks, engage effectively in challenging activities, and collaborate, teachers must make classrooms emotionally safe. Establish a rule for students and yourself, e.g., "We do not laugh at others, tell them to shut up, put them down, or insult them." For all students to participate, teachers must make classrooms intellectually safe. Habituate them to starting work whenever you say, "Please begin," starting with easier tasks, ensuring they know more challenging tasks will follow. Make tasks complex and rich, giving diverse students opportunities to excel and assist peers. Accomplished teachers establish active-learning environments—students thinking, speaking on-task, and working collaboratively near 100 percent of the time—and not only closely observe and measure the quantity (number or proportion of students, amount or proportion of time) of on-task behavior, but also the quality (strength, depth) of student attention and engagement. Newer teachers can start developing lessons and skills for creating ongoing active-learning environments by analyzing which activities really engage their students. Make participation inclusive every day by identifying some questions every student can answer simply; have them raise an index finger when ready; when all do, have them whisper answers or signal, e.g., thumbs-up, thumbs-down, or thumbs-sideways.

Facilitating student conflict resolution

Researchers (Crawford and Bodine, 2001) from the National Center for Conflict Resolution Education report most major conflicts escalating into violence begin as more minor incidents, e.g., unprovoked contact, using others' belongings without permission, etc. Few interactions are initially predatory, yet conflicts rapidly escalate. Most conflicts happen between or among acquaintances, either at school or in the home. Violent behaviors commonly share a retribution goal. Violent acts reflect not lack of values, but value systems accepting violence. Based on these findings, experts (Concordia Online Education, 2013) offer four instructional strategies for effective classroom conflict resolution. (1) Role-playing requires viewing behaviors from others' perspectives, teaches empathy, can add humor to resolving conflicts, and enable examining conflicts more objectively for insights about sources. (2) Have students track conflicts they partake in or witness over time, recording observations in journals (keeping identities anonymous), and discuss student reactions pros and cons. (3) Teach good listening behaviors: eye contact, not interrupting, asking questions, avoiding giving suggestions or advice, nodding and smiling as positive reinforcement, and restating messages in one's own words. (4) Have involved students write about conflicts, providing cooling-off or time-out periods and requiring reflection, including how they felt and retrospectively better alternatives. For example, listing three things they would do differently; model and teach using conflicts as learning opportunities.

Student behavior management approaches

To curtail misbehavior by exercising authority while eliciting minimal emotional distress, and additionally model reasonable, respectful use of authority, a "simple authority statement" promptly and authoritatively expresses disapproval as objectively as possible. If it is either unnecessary or unwise to confront students directly, teachers can redirect student energy to other behaviors, e.g., learning activities. This stops or interrupts misbehavior without provoking student hostility. For example, younger students or those with attention deficit hyperactivity disorder (ADHD) may not be intentionally misbehaving, but lack impulse control; redirection can restore on-task behavior without damaging a student's self-esteem or self-image. Reminding students calmly of assigned tasks enhances their understanding of target behaviors without communicating unpleasant emotions or judgments. Telling students what they should do "next time" gives students behavioral correction, but avoids discouraging them by focusing on the future instead of what they did wrong this time. Teachers can prevent responding inappropriately in haste by responding with silence to misbehaviors not significantly disrupting class. Silence also enables teachers to make mental notes and consider later which actions (if any) apply, and gives students opportunities for solving their own problems.

Helping students develop and exercise accountability, responsibility, and self-regulation

Any time students display careless or unacceptable behaviors, responding with a "check yourself" message advises students to check what they just did, implicitly communicating that by checking, they will realize what they must do to correct their behavior. This reminds students to practice responsible self-management. When students, especially younger ones assigned individual classwork, become restless and off-task, settle them down and increase their concentration powers through a "clock focus" strategy: on the teacher's prearranged cue, students stand and watch the clock's second hand complete full one-minute rotations, choose how many to watch, and then sit down and resume working once the last rotation is complete. This provides scaffolding for students to develop better behavioral self-awareness, self-management, and self-control. Clock-watching, standing, and teacher cues can be gradually eliminated toward independent on-task self-regulation. Placing a student near the teacher in a "visitor's chair," with returning to regular seating allowed whenever the student feels ready to self-manage responsibly, avoids expressing disapproval. When upsetting emotions arise, model honest communication and interpersonal skills without provoking guilt or defensiveness through "I" statements about personal feelings and needs; avoid "you" accusations or comments.

Classroom transitions between activities and lessons

During transitions, students frequently become distracted, restless, and misbehave because the lessons and activities before and after, and the transitions themselves, are not standardized. Hence teachers must build bridges for students for efficient transitions. Bridges must be totally consistent, using the exact same prompts, cues, and steps in exactly the same way every time, so students can rely on them. This makes activities and events both before and after transitions immaterial because students always know what teachers expect of them. Teachers can design a uniform transition by chaining several mini-routines, which they must model, teach, and practice. (1) Signal for class attention. (2) Once all students are attending and making eye contact, start directions with "In a moment... (e.g., we're going to start another lesson)" to maintain student attention. (3) Give precisely detailed directions, including prearranging cues, e.g., "When I say 'go,' you will put away your materials, clean off your desks, and quietly meet me in the learning center." (4) Ask if anybody does not know what to do. Once everybody understands, use the prearranged cue (e.g., "go") to impel students toward learning objectives. (5) Observe student activity and confirm they are following directions. Avoid interrupting transitional activity. To address noncompliance, have students repeat the sequence.

Classroom routines and procedures

Effective teachers devote school's first few weeks not to teaching content, but to establishing classroom routines and procedures: research finds lacking these causes most behavior problems. Routines and procedures decrease instruction interruptions, increasing smooth class flow. Experts advise handing out copies of routines and procedures to every student on the first day, retaining extra copies for new students arriving later. Do not expect compliance after merely handing out and going over them once. Teach key procedures once or twice daily over several days. Explain reasons for each routine and procedure, model each for students, give students non-examples of compliance, and have one or more students model each. Go over less important routines and procedures, monitor, and reinforce as needed. Consistency is critical: teaching, monitoring, and reinforcing routines and procedures, and firmly establishing these over the first three weeks of school offers enormous benefits; do not give up after a few days. Routines and procedures include entering and exiting; starting work; attendance; lunch counts; announcements; lateness; absence; makeup classwork and tests; out-of-seat; teacher attention signal; assignments; pencil-sharpening;

collecting supplies; carrying, handling, or using equipment; forming groups; group, learning center, and independent work; lining up; restrooms; water or snacks; other school locations; submitting homework and papers; exchanging papers; getting help; asking questions; finishing classwork early; classroom visitors; fire drills, codes, and alerts; sudden illness or injury; checking out materials; end-of-day cleanup; organizing materials; changing classes; homework; dismissal.

Theoretically based classroom behavior management and monitoring techniques

Based on behaviorism, functional behavior analysis identifies functions, reasons, and purposes of behaviors, enabling identifying and teaching preferable replacement behaviors meeting the same needs and functions. For example, pay attention to students who raise their hands, but not to students who call out answers. Behavior contracts specify precisely what students agree to do, and for what reward. For example, a first-grader becomes bored with teacher read-aloud story time after three minutes, wandering around the room. An initial two-week contract specifies s/he stay seated and attend for five minutes in return for quietly playing with a toy nearby for the remaining time. Future contracts gradually increase attending durations. Contracts teach students verbal obligation, responsibility, self-control, self-monitoring, negotiation, and compromise. Applying the behaviorist principle that positive reinforcement is more powerful than punishment, and the social learning theory principle of vicarious or observational learning, the "catch them being good" technique involves identifying disruptive and non-disruptive behavior instances. At class beginnings, use a randomized beeper or recording; ignoring disruptive student behaviors (whenever possible) and praising nearby students displaying appropriate behavior. (Use time-outs for severe disruptions.) Instead of a teacher singling out or scolding a student and thereby reinforcing disruptive behaviors, students imitate praised classmates for similar rewards. This teaches students they receive no attention of any kind for disruptive behavior, but favorable attention for appropriate behavior.

Establishing developmentally appropriate behavioral expectations of students

Teachers may observe some developmentally unrealistic parental expectations for their children, e.g., expecting them to "do as I say, not as I do" when their own behaviors are not positive models; expecting children to predict how present behaviors will influence future outcomes. While teachers should involve students in behavior changes, teachers cannot expect students to implement changes autonomously. Teachers should consider developmental, not chronological ages of students with cognitive delays or disabilities regarding appropriate expectations. School-aged children and adolescents generally share these cognitive characteristics: they are present-oriented, i.e., they focus on the here and now; usually cannot consider future consequences, which do not seem real to them; have difficulty anticipating consequences of their behaviors beforehand; can understand basic cause-and-effect relationships, provided these are sequenced closely together; have still-developing concepts of time, and difficulty with planning skills. Not standing out as different but fitting in—particularly for adolescents—is a major concern. Expect students to help track goals, not create and track them without reminders; and learn about and select among various choices, not independently make positive choices without concrete rewards and positive parental and adult models.

Promoting ethical academic work habits

Rather than threatening students with punishment for cheating, teachers can better promote ethical work habits by serving as positive role models; explaining and initiating class discussions about honesty and responsibility, how these are compromised by using others' work without giving credit, etc.; and praising and otherwise rewarding individual student work as examples of ethical

- 108 -

academic practices. Research finds that, just as with academic expectations, having behavioral expectations high enough to challenge students, but realistic enough that they can achieve them with effort, is more effective than lowering expectations—including for mainstreamed students with disabilities. Rather than doing all the work for students in monitoring their behavior, teachers can engage students in monitoring processes and procedures, gradually teaching them the skills and responsibilities needed to self-monitor and self-regulate their behaviors. Teaching monitoring skills also supports teaching students about conflict management and resolution skills. Teaching students active listening skills reduces miscommunications, misunderstandings, and thus conflicts. Having them role-play opposing positions teaches empathy, objectivity, and insight; and advances conflict resolution, as does having them reflect and write about actual conflicts and potential alternative responses.

Communicating with parents

Ask individual students' parents which communication methods work best for them; use multiple methods. Though traditional written notes and phone calls take more time, some parents prefer them. Many parents email; others want text messages; some can be reached on Twitter or Facebook; others want classroom blogs, websites, and/or videos. SnappSchool.com and similar online tools enable simultaneous multiple communication methods. Target goals—recruiting more parents to share workplace experiences with students, improving student attendance, etc.—when planning communications. Establishing and communicating high standards and expectations at the beginning of the year and regularly thereafter make parents allies to reinforce your expectations at home: studies find parental expectations among the strongest predictors of student achievement; later communications about problems receive more objective, supportive responses. Communicating about the class, not just their child, helps parents see your viewpoint if some decisions that are not ideal for one student are best for the class. Remember the school also communicates with parents, so avoid duplicating fundraising appeals. But inform and advise them of all school resources, including after-school and summer programs or other services supporting shared goals for students. Measure effectiveness by whether parents return permission slips and/or visit, students come to class prepared; note which methods elicit more responses for future reference.

Partnering with parents to increase student achievement

While preparing educators with information and training for involving parents, ED's model for parent involvement through parent-educator partnership to enhance student achievement prepares parents by communicating, in appropriate formats and languages, timely accountability data, core subject teacher qualifications, supplemental education services, home and school involvement opportunities, and parental rights and roles. ED also provides training and materials for helping children achieve academically; recruiting and training parent leaders in data interpretation, advocacy skills, and training other parents; involving parents in helping to monitor and evaluate the effectiveness of school policies for parental involvement; facilitating meaningful two-way engagement; and training parent leaders for participating on school advisory boards, school site-based parental advisory councils, and other groups that influence educational policymaking. Educators are informed of parent involvement policies and procedures, opportunities to involve parents, accountability data, and options among supplemental education services available to students. Educators and school staff receive training to prepare parents and other educators; assess needs; create family-friendly schools; identify, recruit, and train staff in parental involvement's value; monitor compliance with parental involvement requirements; evaluate parent involvement policy effectiveness including parent input; engage parents in

- 109 -

developing plans for increasing student achievement; and collaborate with parents on advisory boards and site councils.

Engaging families from diverse backgrounds

In recent decades, education research shows parental involvement and student achievement correlate directly. Multiple studies find that, regardless of background or income, students with involved parents more likely attend school regularly, adapt well, enroll in higher-level programs, achieve higher test scores and grades, display better behavior and social skills, graduate, and pursue post-secondary education. Research reveals three key practices of schools successfully engaging families from diverse backgrounds: recognizing, respecting, and addressing cultural and class differences and family needs; focusing on building trusting, collaborative relationships among families, community members, and teachers; and espousing partnership philosophies with shared power and responsibility. Every Student Succeeds Act's (ESSA) Title I lists parental involvement requirements for Title I schools, other schools, districts, and state education agencies. Immigrant parents may have cultural beliefs of not questioning teachers; low-income, homeless, multi-job, single, and/or LEP parents and those with past negative school experiences care about children's education, but may have difficulty expressing it. They may not know how to engage, feel incapable of making meaningful contributions, or do not feel welcome. The US Department of Education has therefore established a nationwide system of Parental Information and Resource Centers (PIRCs) under the Elementary and Secondary Education Act (ESEA) to provide parents, schools, and organizations with training, technical assistance, information, organizational partnerships, and support regarding child development and school success needs.

Helping parents understand school data about student progress

Under federal ED establishment of nationwide Parental Information and Resource Centers (PIRCs), state family centers have produced digital media explaining information related to the Every Student Succeeds Act (ESSA), including on school accountability, testing, school choice, and socioeconomic status. Trainers use these DVDs at PTA, school board, advisory board, school staff, and community organization meetings and site council trainings to reach wider audiences. Some have produced Spanish versions. DVDs are especially useful to inform non-reading parents, and can trigger questions and discussions which PIRC staff and volunteers can address or facilitate. Center staffs ask parent advisory councils and focus groups, including immigrants, to review materials and give feedback whether it is comprehensible and interesting. The American Development Institute's (ADI) PIRC offers workshops helping parents understand school (not student) report card data including demographics, academic performance, and Adequate Yearly Progress (AYP). ED guidelines for teachers to help parents access and understand education-related information include: rather than "reinvent the wheel," look for and distribute existing tools and publications. Design NCLB-related materials that are short, clear, and concise. Ask parent representatives to review drafts of new materials for reader-friendliness before production. Make informational DVDs for group meetings and non-reading parents. Initiate guidance sessions, websites, and workshops to communicate and help parents understand relevant educational issues.

Conducting conferences with parents

A parent-teacher conference is a two-way conversation focused on student learning. A teacher should use concrete examples and avoid abstract assessments of a student. A teacher should seek collaborative solutions to issues that have arisen and should seek to open the lines of communication for future dialogue on improving student learning. A teacher should remain positive and discuss a student's growth and progress. Though some negative aspects of a

- 110 -

conversation may be inevitable, a teacher can always pivot back to future positive opportunities and building on a student's previous successes. One of the core aspects of cultural responsive curricula is positive perspectives on students' families. A parent conference is an excellent opportunity to build rapport and establish a collaborative relationship that will positively affect student learning both in the classroom and in the home. A teacher should ask questions of parents and listen actively. A family will be able to provide input into a student's learning styles and background that are not otherwise easily accessible.

Include students in parent conferences when possible. Hearing teacher praise benefits them. For criticisms of performance, study habits, or behaviors, attending students are present to participate in correction plans. Come prepared with test results, work samples, anecdotal observation notes, etc., presenting concrete evidence to discuss with parents rather than vague references. Ask parents to inform you about their child's performance in previous school years. Approach problems positively, focusing on plans for correction with student and parent agreement. Propose any ideas you have for implementing assistance as specifically as possible, including what parents can expect of you in progress reporting and how to stay in communication in the immediate future and throughout the year. Take care not to overextend yourself with phone calls or written reports on just one of many students, which can also irritate busy parents. Impress upon parents that you are a team to recruit their participation, e.g., monitoring children's studying, checking homework, and/or signing your weekly or daily reports. Avoid defending your policies or yourself: reflect on the student and how s/he can best work with existing classroom procedures and rules. Give parents contact information. Regardless of effort required, begin and end conferences with something positive about the student.

Classroom Assessment

Statistical reliability and validity

Reliability: whether a test gets consistent results over repeated administrations. Test-retest reliability retests the same respondents with the same test, e.g., two weeks or a month later. Difficulties include having to write different questions on the same material, etc., to control for memory and practice effects. Internal consistency reliability compares two versions of a test concurrently, evaluating whether they correlate or measure the same construct. Validity: whether a test measures what it purports or intends to measure. Criterion validity: whether a test reflects certain abilities. One type is concurrent validity: whether a test correlates with benchmark or criterion tests. Another type is predictive validity: how well a test predicts abilities by testing respondents for a given construct, then comparing future results. Content validity: whether a test represents all of a given construct. Construct validity: whether a test measures its identified construct and not others—e.g., depression, not stress or anxiety. Convergent validity: whether constructs we believe are related are actually related. Divergent or discriminant validity: whether constructs we believe unrelated are unrelated. Bias: subjective slant toward expected results. Example: IQ test item "cup and (a.) saucer, (b.) fork, (c.) table," presumed student familiarity with cup-and-saucer sets; but low-income students chose "table," having experience only with cups on tables, not cups in saucers.

Formal and informal assessments

Standardized tests are a primary example of formal assessments. They have been used to test large numbers of students; data from results are mathematically calculated and summarized; standard scores, percentiles, or stanines are provided. Statistical analyses support conclusions based on test results, e.g., a certain score range is the average for representative samples of the student population in a given grade, hence other scores can be defined as above or below average and by how much. These are typically norm-referenced tests. Informal assessments are performance- and content-driven, not data-driven. For example, a running record of how well a student is reading a particular book is an informal assessment. Typical scores are most rubric scores; percentage of words read correctly; 15 correct answers out of 20 questions, etc. These are typically criterion-referenced or performance-based tests. To compare students to peers their own age, compare student strengths and weaknesses with those of peers, or assess overall achievement, formal assessments suit these purposes. To inform and improve ongoing instruction, as in formative assessment, informal assessments meet those purposes. Formal tests, statistically proven, are good for summative, not formative assessment and generalized data, not individualized data. Informal tests, more individualized, are good for ongoing assessment but less objective or statistically supported.

Formal assessments all include standardized methods for their administration, scoring, and interpretation of the scores. Some examples of formal assessments include all standardized achievement tests, which are often national or statewide; so-called high-stakes examinations; standardized intelligence or IQ tests; many standardized screening tests; and many standardized diagnostic measures. Standardized testing instruments have been statistically proven valid, i.e., they test what they are meant to test; and reliable, i.e., they yield consistent results across repeated administrations. Their manuals include statistical methods for scoring and interpreting the scores, and tables or charts showing the average scores of samples of students that represent the test-taking population, plus other scores and how many standard deviations these are from the average. Quizzes and exercises at the ends of educational textbook chapters, sections, and units are also examples of formal assessments. Informal assessments do not typically include standardized instruments, though some exist, e.g., standardized reading fluency measures. Teacher observations, class or student question-and-answer sessions, running reports, student projects, presentations, and experiments, student portfolios, and performance assessments are examples of informal assessment measures. Some find peer teaching and debates informal assessments as well.

Formal assessments provide quantitative data because they are standardized and report standard scores. Informal assessments provide qualitative data because they are not standardized, so the results reported by teachers using them are more subjective. Formal assessments enable comparison of individual students with peer groups, but typically not specific details about individual students. Informal assessments can give more detail about an individual student's strengths, needs, and performance; but less objective comparison of individual student performance with age, grade, or peer performance. Formal assessments are norm-referenced tests comparing student performance to norms for their developmental level, age, or grade. Informal assessments are typically criterion-referenced tests comparing student performance to pre-established criteria students are expected or intended to achieve and teachers are expected or intended to teach. Some students experience significant test anxiety when standardized formal tests are administered in whole-class or group settings. Some students also experience significant anxiety, even panic, when teachers single them out to answer questions in class as informal assessment. Hence it is important that teachers obtain sufficient results from both formal and informal assessment, and multiple forms of each, to develop more comprehensive pictures of student abilities and achievements.

Student scores from standardized intelligence scales and standardized scales of adaptive functioning are often used to inform student placements into specific schools, grades, and types of classes most compatible with their educational strengths and needs. While tracking is generally unpopular these days, educators seek to place students into groups where ability levels are similar and teachers can offer material (even if via differentiated instruction) that is sufficiently challenging, neither impossibly, inappropriately, or overwhelmingly difficult nor overly easy or boring. For students with certain disabilities, e.g., autism spectrum disorders (ASDs), many formal assessments exist to inform educators where a student is on the spectrum; intellectual and adaptive functioning levels; individual interests, difficulty areas, and specific behaviors, which can be both typical of the disorder and vary widely individually. Formal assessments are given at ends of school years to measure student achievement. These results are used for purposes of individual student grade promotions; to compare year-end student performance to baseline scores to assess student progress toward instructional objectives; and school accountability, to compare school effectiveness by comparing rates and percentages of student achievement to those of other schools, inform school improvement plans, and secure or continue government school funding.

One of the most valuable and prevalent uses of informal assessment findings is to inform ongoing instruction. While teachers plan instruction based on initial student assessments, during implementation they may find some students are not responding to their methods or having difficulty learning new material. With new students and large classes, teachers can discover new individual student characteristics throughout the school year. For example, by using informal measures regularly as formative assessments, teachers may find early on a student(s) not progressing at the rate(s) projected. They can then either (1) change the timeframe when the student is expected to achieve certain objectives; (2) change objectives to represent smaller increments, amounts, or lower levels to achieve within the timeframe; or (3) change the instructional approach, techniques, or strategies to be more compatible or effective with particular students. Conversely, when students progress much faster than anticipated, teachers can adjust instruction to provide higher difficulty, enriched content, etc. Formative assessments also monitor and document on-target student progress. In addition to formative assessment, informal measures afford alternative ways of evaluating student performance that formal standardized tests cannot measure, e.g., performances, portfolios, creative projects, etc. Some students cannot respond to objective examinations but demonstrate their competencies in different formats.

Essay questions vs. selected response questions and written tests vs. performance measures

Essay questions have one obvious advantage of testing composition and writing skills as well as subject content knowledge when testing subjects other than English composition. They also enable students to go into depth and detail about topics, showing the extent of their knowledge. Essays afford students choices of subtopics, points they make, examples they use, how much they emphasize certain subtopics and points, how they organize their essays; allow them to persuade or convince readers through argumentation; require recall, not recognition; and showcase student higher-order thinking skills. Disadvantages include being more time-consuming to administer and write; requiring writing skills, which if deficient can obscure a student's other subject knowledge; and requiring far more time and subjective judgment to grade. Selected-choice questions are much faster to administer; can cover larger numbers of smaller points; allow teachers and testers more control of subject matter; are easier for students, requiring recognition, not recall; have more clear-cut right and wrong answers; are graded more objectively, and far faster, even electronically or automatically. Disadvantages include less information about individual students' overall knowledge; lacking elaboration or depth; and enabling some correct answers from sheer guesswork through probability. Written tests can be more objective; performance measures enable students to show what they can actually do, an advantage for those who do not write well.

Portfolio assessments

Portfolio assessments involve reviewing a collection of student work products gathered cumulatively over a period of time, e.g., a semester or school year. One of their advantages is that they can provide clear evidence of student progress, growth, and other longitudinal changes that a written test or single term paper will not show as clearly. Another is that products may be artworks, models, and other concrete objects, not just test answers, written essays, or papers. These are more individualized, demonstrating more student skills than tests or papers, including nonverbal skills like artistic ability, creativity, divergent thinking, spatial awareness, mechanical ability, nonlinguistic organization, etc. Students with different learning styles, who may not use the linear thinking needed for objective tests and/or lack organizational, language processing, and/or verbal skills for writing, but excel in other areas, can produce evidence of those strengths in portfolios. Another advantage is avoiding test anxiety for many students. Students also have less time pressure and can devote more total time to creating things more gradually. Portfolios can be used for both formative and summative assessment. Some disadvantages include more subjective teacher grading, time required to accumulate portfolio products, teacher time and effort to match products with learning objectives, and lack of standardization.

Considerations for selecting assessment formats and instruments

When choosing assessment instruments, educators and testers should first always remember that any comprehensive assessment must include multiple and varied methods, instruments, tools, and (when feasible) formats. They should never rely on a single test. One test might be most indicated for assessing a very specific skill, but even for single domains, e.g., language or adaptive functioning, multiple tests are better, as responses and scores can differ and some reveal abilities others overlooked. Age-appropriateness is important. For example, to use Wechsler's IQ scales with a young child, one would administer the Wechsler Preschool and Primary Scales of Intelligence (WPPSI), not the Wechsler Intelligence Scales for Children (WISC) or Wechsler Adult Intelligence Scales (WAIS). (If a gifted child exceeded WPPSI's top levels, administering the WISC would be interesting, though other giftedness instruments would also be indicated.) Students who are nonverbal—e.g., some with autism spectrum disorder (ASD), cerebral palsy (CP), intellectual disability (ID), or other disorders—can be evaluated using the Leiter, Raven's Progressive Matrices, UNIT, etc. Young and/or disabled students with receptive language understanding but absent or limited expression can respond to the Peabody Picture Vocabulary and other receptive tests.

A student's age or grade level are not the only factors to consider for selecting assessments. The educational context is also a key to format and instrument choice. For example, while intelligence scales give an idea of a child's intellectual capacity for purposes of educational placement, curricular and instructional design, individualized or differentiated instructional planning, etc., intelligence testing is not necessarily relevant or even significant to define adaptive functioning levels. Some children, due to innate characteristics, life experience, and training, function significantly higher in daily living and social skills than intellectually. Other children function adaptively much lower than their intellectual capacities would suggest due to behavior disorders like attention deficit hyperactivity disorder (ADHD), autism spectrum disorders (ASDs), learning disabilities (LDs), major mental disorders, etc. To ascertain daily living activities a child can perform compared to age peers and inform instructional design for developing adaptive skills, tests like the Vineland Adaptive Behavior Scales are indicated. When developmental delay is suspected in young children, tests like the Bayley Scales of Infant and Toddler Development help evaluate developmental levels. Because many school districts model their goals on their state education department's standards, the best way to align assessment with campus and district goals is often to administer standardized tests provided by statewide assessment systems.

Aligning instructional design and goals with statewide assessments

Teachers need not view the process of aligning their instruction with assessment as "teaching to the test." Instead, they first need to read the standards on which the statewide assessments are based. As an example, many states are now basing their statewide assessments on the Common Core State Standards (CCSS). This means that what students in the state are expected to learn to know and do via the instruction they receive is encapsulated within the CCSS. A teacher whose students will be taking a test based on the CCSS would need to first review the standards and align their teaching to ensure that everything included in those standards is also included in their planned curriculum for the year. Because the state tests are written to align exactly with the standards on which they are based, teachers can be assured that students who are adequately instructed in the knowledge and skills outlined in the standards will be measured appropriately by the exam, without the need for focusing on the test itself.

Monitoring student understanding and guide instruction

Rather than teach an entire unit and administer an end-of-unit test, only to discover most or all students did not understand key or major points the teacher wanted to convey, it is more useful to monitor student understanding early and often. For example, at any grade level, after a teacher makes introductory statements in a lesson, s/he can stop and ask the class questions whose answers should reflect whether they heard and remember the few main points, whether they can repeat one or a few key definitions the teacher gave, whether they understood the concepts communicated, etc. Seeing few or no volunteers or many students looking perplexed indicates a need to reteach and/or explain or demonstrate concepts differently. Quizzes at ends of lessons within units also monitor student understanding of shorter segments. When teachers assign small-

- 115 -

group projects, they may have a member of each group orally report current group or project status and progress to the teacher or class periodically. Teachers can offer time-management strategies if they are falling behind schedule or advise reducing project scope, information amounts, etc. Teachers who find the majority of students not understanding or learning need to revisit and revise their instructional levels, approaches, methods, and/or techniques.

Formative and summative assessment

Formative assessments are conducted during instruction. Teachers use them to obtain feedback that they and their students can both utilize for improving the teaching and learning that will occur as it continues. For example, after giving a lecture, a teacher might ask middle or high school students to write down a sentence or two that identify the lecture's main point(s). Similarly, kindergarten and first-grade teachers can review an orally taught lesson by asking students to repeat one or two key vocabulary terms included, and/or one or two main points. When a teacher has told older students they will be assigned a paper as part of a unit, once the class has completed enough reading, teacher lessons, lectures, classwork, discussions, etc., the teacher can have students write and turn in outlines for the papers they will write. Summative assessments are conducted after instruction. They may evaluate learning from a unit, semester, or school year. Teachers use these to determine course grades, student grade promotion, and evaluate class, grade, and school achievement compared to those of other schools for accountability purposes. For example, grading final exams, critiquing senior music recitals or art projects, etc. help determine final course grades.

Research finds that formative assessment reduces learning gaps. It also helps teachers design instruction targeting specific learning goals; supporting student learning; monitoring student progress; identifying strengths, needs, learning gains; differentiating instruction; evaluating instructional effectiveness; informing and adjusting ongoing instruction; promoting effective teaching practices; enhancing learning for struggling students, ELLs, and students with disabilities; improving all student learning outcomes; augmenting coherence through alignment or connection with state comprehensive assessment systems; and reforming curricula. Hence federal legislation like the Every Student Succeeds Act (ESSA), replacements for the ESEA and NCLB Acts, the Individuals with Disabilities Education Act (IDEA), and state policies promote using formative assessment to narrow learning gaps. Researchers find: (1) to identify learning gaps, educators must understand differences between what students know and need to know to design instructional support enabling student progress toward learning goals. (2) Teachers must give clear, detailed feedback designed to close instructional gaps. Reciprocal teacher-student feedback informs student learning status and next instructional steps. (3) Active student involvement in learning and assessments, and student-teacher collaboration to develop shared knowledge regarding current learning status and actions needed for progress develop student skills for self-monitoring and knowing when they need help. (4) Teachers must break down major learning goals into smaller learning progression components to locate students on the skill set continuum required for mastering learning standards.

Diagnostic assessment

Whereas formative assessment is conducted during instruction and summative assessment is conducted after instruction, diagnostic assessment is conducted before instruction. Also called pre-assessments, these frequently focus upon one domain or area. Administering diagnostic assessments can give educators information about previous knowledge each student has about a subject. This informs teachers where to begin their instruction for all students in the same class to access it without experiencing either significant knowledge gaps or significant repetition of things they already know. Pre-assessments also inform teachers of existing student misconceptions to correct during instruction. And they establish student knowledge baselines to compare knowledge following instruction to assess learning and instructional effectiveness. Teachers can use diagnostic assessment results to inform their development of lesson plans, and also differentiated instruction for individual students within classes to meet their specific needs best. Pre-assessments also gauge student preparation during sequential learning, e.g., after teaching the Coriolis effect, teachers might determine student concept retention through diagnostic pre-assessment; and refresh or reteach as needed, before they proceed to begin teaching a unit about ocean currents.

Multiple-choice tests and oral questioning

Multiple-choice tests have stems—usually questions, sometimes statements—and several answer choices. One answer is correct, others incorrect; in some formats, there is more than one correct answer. These are efficiently, easily administered to large classes. They can be scored by teaching assistants, machines, or computer programs. These are effective to measure memory, knowledge, convergent thinking, and problem-solving in convergent subjects; but not when "correct" answers are equivocal, ambiguous, or disputable. Writing wrong answers reflecting common misconceptions or errors enables diagnostic value from wrong-answer pattern analyses. However, students cannot elaborate on topics. High-quality tests are harder to write than some teachers realize. Overuse can lead students to memorize separate pieces of information instead of developing overall subject understanding. Oral questioning is the most common classroom assessment. Teachers can use hypotheticals ("What would you have done if...?"), get explanations and reasons for specific student practices, challenge practices, and check understanding of underlying concepts or principles not directly observed. Not requiring reading and writing is often more inclusive and less discriminatory. It applies highly to assessing spoken, not written language. It is more valid than reliable, and time-intensive, indicating standard questions for summative assessments or multiple assessors. Recording is required for permanent documentation, which has its own considerations. Experts advise asking students' opinions of lessons and activities before questioning, for highest information quantity and quality.

Different assessment formats

For making preschool and kindergarten placement decisions, developmental scales are useful for assessing their developmental levels in various domains. These tests are also helpful in comparing developmental levels to age norms for diagnosing developmental delays. Developmental scale results then also become useful for designing instructional objectives whereby teachers can help children with developmental delays to reach or approximate normal development. When assessing students with significant disabilities, it is important to assess their adaptive well as intellectual functioning, as these sometimes differ widely. This also informs the levels, types, and weights of instruction for each. When older students are new to a school, diagnostic pre-assessments help educators evaluate their prior knowledge to determine classroom placement and where to begin instruction. When educational records are incomplete or unavailable, new assessments help determine intelligence, literacy levels, strengths and difficulties in specific academic subjects, etc. Standardized tests like ACT and SAT differentiate student verbal vs. quantitative abilities. For example, when a student more verbally than numerically gifted used a 166-point gap between verbal and quantitative SAT scores to justify her math struggles, her guidance counselor responded that her quantitative score nevertheless indicated she should be performing better in math.

Student self-assessment

Self-assessment promotes student reflective and metacognitive skills development, critical thinking in analyzing and judging effectiveness of teacher instructional practices and student learning strategies, and helps teachers identify and understand individual student differences to make their instruction more responsive to student needs. Having students create or contribute to rubrics defining success in group discussions, multimodal presentations, reading response tasks, etc. augments learning levels. Having students create and agree to learning contracts when beginning units engages students in defining learning goals, agreed activities, and products as evidence of learning. Teachers have students revisit contracts frequently during units to document new learning, identify points needing clarification, and obtain teacher or classmate feedback. Teachers can designate a classroom area for "muddy points," questions, or topics that students want the class to revisit. Teachers can build student learning ownership by periodically asking students to choose an item from this board. In the "nameless voice" method, teachers have students submit work samples anonymously for class sharing and discussion of similarities and differences with their understandings. Having students write end-of-unit letters to future students explaining what they learned, tips for learning, working with difficult texts, etc. This promotes both reflection and feedback on student thinking and learning.

Because student needs vary widely, educators must differentiate content, processes, and products of learning for individual student readiness, learning styles, and interests. Also, because of this student diversity, more than one record and voice are needed to recognize and report student growth, development, and learning needs. Moreover, research finds both conducting ongoing assessment and engaging students as partners in their learning and assessment vital. When students must analyze their own thinking and learning critically, they become more motivated to learn; they develop metacognitive skills, enhancing their engagement across subject areas and supporting lifelong learning motivation. When ongoing assessment is used to inform and adjust ongoing instruction, both students and teachers reap benefits of additional knowledge about what students do and do not understand from student feedback. However, students commonly lack the experience, training, and expertise to conduct assessments as teachers can. They obviously are less objective than others when assessing themselves. Individual student differences cause corresponding self-assessment differences, whereas one teacher's assessments of all students may be more uniform. Teacher assessments must accompany self-assessments, to standardize evaluation across students and mitigate self-interested, self-destructive, or overly subjective results.

Peer assessment

Constructivist and active learning theories provide foundations and support for peer assessment. By assigning peer assessment, teachers can empower students to take responsibility for and manage their own learning. They can help students learn assessment techniques and develop lifelong assessment skills. Peer assessment leads to exchanges of ideas and diffusion of knowledge among students, enhancing all individual students' learning. Teachers can also motivate students to engage in more depth with course materials by having them assess one another's learning. Teachers can incorporate peer assessment by identifying activities and assignments wherein peer feedback could benefit students. They can include peer assessment opportunities at different stages of larger assignments, e.g., an outline, first draft, second draft, etc. of a paper. Teachers should create rubrics or guidelines defining tasks clearly for students conducting peer reviews; and use learning exercises to introduce rubrics to assure student abilities for effective rubric applications. Peer reviews can be in-class, homework, online, etc.; teachers should determine these. Teachers must also model constructive criticism, appropriateness, and descriptive feedback in their own responses to inform peer assessment. Including small-group feedback sessions enables recipients to question, and peer reviewers to explain, written comments to recipients.

Before assigning peer assessment, teachers should explain to students the benefits and expectations of the peer review process. One disadvantage is that student relationships and interactions can influence peer review to be personal or subjective. Teachers can keep student work anonymous for peer review, making feedback more objective. Students inexperienced with peer assessment may not know what kinds of feedback are or are not useful and why or why not. Teachers can address this by giving students feedback on their feedback to classmates. They can also give examples to students of feedback with different levels of quality, and discuss with students which are more or less useful and the reasons why. To impart structure, norms, and appropriateness, teachers should provide time limits and clear direction for in-class peer review, and define deadlines for homework peer review assignments. Peer assessments are more valid when students are more familiar with and take more ownership of criteria, so teachers should engage students in discussing designated criteria. Teachers should offer necessary input and guidance during group feedback discussions. Peer assessment is better assigned for academic tasks that students have experience with, not professional tasks. To encourage more individual responsibility, avoid letting multiple students assess identical tasks.

Interpreting student assessment scores

In general, a student's raw score on a statewide assessment equals the number of items that a student answered correctly. Raw scores can only be meaningfully interpreted relative to both the total number of items on the assessment and the raw scores of other students in the same grade. Raw scores must not be compared among different test administrations since minor variations in the test can result in widely varying average performances. With the limitations of the raw score, many assessments use a horizontal scale score allowing score comparison by adjusting for varying test form difficulty in different administrations. Using the horizontal scale score, educators can compare student cohorts (age and grade groups) taking the same subject or grade assessment in different years, compare individual students taking the same subject or grade assessment, and identify satisfactory or advanced performance. A vertical scale score, meanwhile, allows educators to measure student progress across subjects or grades.

Communicating assessment results to students and parents

Experts recommend two steps in reporting assessment results to students: an initial briefing for the whole class or group tested; and then follow-up meetings with individual students, focusing on how teachers will meet their needs. Briefings should include an overview of the assessment program and instruments; how teachers, school, and districts use test results; the process for reviewing results with individual students; which results students receive; and any plans for recognizing outstanding assessment performance. Follow-up meetings should include assessed student strengths and needs, how these relate to other student information from other tests and/or teacher observations, and the plan of action recommended for addressing individual student needs. Teachers and school administrators should jointly report results to parents to build active partnerships for student learning. Individual parent-teacher conferences are ideal for explaining individual student results, reporting school-wide performance, answering parent questions, and explaining instructional improvement initiatives. If these are impossible, teachers can provide written reports carefully describing assessment processes and procedures, explaining how to interpret results, and including contact information for questions. Parent group meetings are alternatives if individual meetings are impossible. Parent newsletter articles describing assessment, scoring, overall school placement, improvement initiatives, FAQs, etc. are additional communication options.

Getting students engaged in class activities and increasing their on-task times

Seating arrangements appropriate to the specific activity enhance engagement and on-task time. Choosing course materials relevant to students, and emphasizing how they can apply the learning in real life, enables students to connect activities with prior knowledge and their lives. Students view schoolwork meaningful to them as more valuable, important, and worth the effort. Giving students some control and choice in learning, e.g., self-monitoring and self-evaluating progress or choice of paired or individual work, increases sense of autonomy, hence engagement. Assigning achievable yet challenging tasks for all students, including those with disabilities, at-risk, remedial, etc. enable students to feel successful, and to believe that they earned their success. Repetitive, rote tasks and seemingly impossible ones both discourage engagement. "Mystery" approaches give students partial or contradictory information and require they develop hypotheses based on available evidence, piquing their curiosity. This also fulfills needs for autonomy, competence, self-directed inquiry, and independent discovery. Assignments only teachers will read are unilateral: teachers typically do not need the information that students submit. Contrastingly, designing cooperative learning and other projects enabling students to share new knowledge with peers promotes reciprocal relationships, making learning activities more engaging.

Unanticipated learning opportunities

According to some experts, effective early childhood development programs combine adult-guided and child-guided educational activities. Adult-guided activities include active, significant roles for children; child-guided activities include intentional adult roles in which adults take advantage of both learning experiences they planned, and unexpected opportunities for learning. For example, consider the preschool teacher whose class collected acorns outdoors and brought them back into the classroom. The teacher observes two children playing with the acorns. One child divides the acorns into two halves. She spreads her half out into a long row and clusters the other child's half into a pile. The second child becomes upset that she has more acorns than he has. The teacher asks the children how they could find out whether they each have the same number of acorns. Prompted by this intentional question, the second child gets the idea of counting both groups of acorns. The teacher observes, gives supportive comments, and asks thoughtful questions. The children discover they have the same number of acorns despite their arrangements and appearances. This teacher used an unexpected opportunity, helping two children normally in Piaget's preoperational stage of cognitive development to achieve an insight associated with Piaget's later concrete operations stage.

Progress maps

When teachers find traditional test results do not give students the feedback they need to understand and correct their errors, they can design classroom assessments to help students organize their learning goals. This involves establishing benchmarks to use as criteria in rubrics; identifying transfer levels as referents for rubric expertise levels; making individual student progress maps, plotting their scores over time, and giving them feedback customized according to their developmental or expertise levels; plotting collective student scores on aggregate progress maps, and planning future learning opportunities in response to score clusters and deviations; and informing student self-reflection and personal goal-setting by embedding these progress maps into students' electronic portfolios. Progress maps describe knowledge, skills, and understandings in their typical developmental sequence, depicting longitudinal improvement in specific subjects and domains by organizing longitudinal assessment data according to subject knowledge and skill continua. They include initial baseline assessment data, e.g., at the beginning of a school year, relative to associated standards; and subsequent formative assessments throughout the year according to developmental benchmark criteria. Their visual nature enables quick, easy appraisal of student progress toward subject content standards. Technology makes data collection, organization, and storage most efficient.

Integrating technology

Examining patterns of teacher and student use of technology can show whether and/or to what degree technology is integrated into their teaching and learning environment. For example, an indication related to teacher activity is use patterns, e.g., the percentage of teachers using computer technologies for a variety of instructional and instruction-related tasks, including locating instructional resources; accessing resources and libraries online; downloading curriculum materials; communicating and networking with colleagues and other professionals; using computers to create instructional tasks, visuals, and/or materials; collaborating with remote teachers and classrooms on projects; communicating with parents; and publishing instructional materials online. Student use patterns, e.g., the percentage of students using computer technologies for various learning and instruction-related tasks, is another indicator of technology integration in the learning environment. Student instruction-related tasks include performing calculations; gathering information from varied sources; information organization and storage; collecting experimental or investigational data; making measurements; analyzing, interpreting, or manipulating data and information to draw conclusions, generate questions, discover relationships; reporting or communicating results, information, or conclusions; creating visual information or data displays; interacting or communicating with classmates, schoolmates, and others outside school; producing audiovisual presentations; composing, editing, and publishing text; creating original art, music, or graphics; publishing materials or projects remotely; and developing understanding of abstract or complex concepts and materials.

Rubrics and analytical checklists

A rubric defines in advance a specific behavior(s), skill(s), or task(s) to perform. It supplies basic guidelines for performing task components and criteria for successful performance of each component. Rubrics also typically define general performance ranges and levels, e.g., unsatisfactory, satisfactory, or excellent, briefly describing each level's characteristics. Teachers and/or students can create rubrics or select from existing ones. The teacher should first go over the rubric with students, explaining what each part means, demonstrating when necessary. Then the teacher directs students to follow the rubric as a guide in performing the task. Finally, the teacher uses the rubric's criteria to assess student work. Advantages include combining learning objectives, associated tasks, performance guidance, and task evaluation criteria; and brevity, conciseness, and clarity. Disadvantages include assigning performance levels, not more precise grades or percentages; and perhaps not lending themselves to more detailed assignments. Analytical checklists pre-define certain behaviors, skills, and tasks; teachers check observation of their presence or absence. Advantages include saving time and effort by pre-listing tasks, behaviors, and skills, enabling quick and easy assessment; and making assessment uniform across students in terms of tasks and components. Disadvantages include not identifying additional valuable accomplishments observed (without additional notes); and sometimes limiting assessment to Yes/No formats, though some checklists do incorporate performance levels like rubrics.

Scoring guides, anecdotal notes, and continua

Scoring guides are typically issued by authors of specific standardized assessment instruments to help teachers and testers score their tests. An obvious advantage of such a scoring guide is that it instructs scorers to follow procedures and interpretations designed by the authors, minimizing chances that scoring will be inaccurate, inappropriate, or interpreted incorrectly. Also, scoring guides do not force assigning specific responses specific scores, but allow some flexibility to use judgment according to individual student responses and test conditions within a reasonable range. Disadvantages include guideline misinterpretation or misapplication by users lacking experience or good judgment. Anecdotal notes have advantages of recording teacher observations of individual student behaviors often not included in standard checklists or test instruments; and collecting information outside of as well as during assessment, which can contribute to valuable insights. Disadvantages include lack of standardization, norms, or criteria for comparison unless a recording teacher includes these; and often, lack of supporting context. Continua offer the advantages of avoiding the limitations of discrete grades, percentages, and numbers, enabling more precise and individualized evaluative description; and more realistic, accurate performance ranges than exact numbers or cutoff scores. Disadvantages include difficulty comparing scores within or among students, classes, and schools without exact numbers, making continua more applicable to individualized than standardized assessment.

Standardized tests of ability and of achievement

Some standardized tests measure abilities, such as intelligence quotient (IQ) tests, which are the most prominent examples; tests of creativity, of divergent thinking (considered a key element of creativity); and more domain-specific abilities, e.g., verbal, numerical, quantitative, spatial abilities, memory, etc., which are often included as subscales on standardized IQ tests. Ability tests do not indicate or necessarily even predict student school grades. They only indicate what a student is capable of, i.e., they gauge competence, not performance. In addition to abilities, some tests measure levels of mental health constructs, e.g., Beck's Depression Inventory and Anxiety Inventory. In contrast to ability and competence or mental and emotional states, standardized achievement tests measure what students actually achieve rather than what they are capable of achieving. Standardized achievement tests are summative evaluations typically given at the ends of school years, not formative evaluations made during instruction. They test what students have learned and can demonstrate knowing and doing. This allows educators to compare individual student progress across years, compare students to peers, and compare their school to others.

Standardized aptitude tests

One thing that most standardized aptitude tests share in common with most standardized ability tests is that both types of instruments measure potential rather than accomplishment. For example, IQ tests measure intellectual ability in various cognitive domains, but not how students perform academically—i.e., what grades they actually get in school. Similarly, aptitude tests measure student interest and ability for certain subject areas and domains—not specifically IQ or cognitive levels, but how inclined a student is toward certain activities or areas of interest. Some tests evaluate broader domain aptitudes, e.g., for numerical or mathematical thinking and activities, verbal or literary thinking and activities, etc. Others evaluate interest and ability for more specific activities, e.g., preference tests often used in career counseling with high school students. While these identify discrete interest areas, when some tests combine responses, they may produce strange results not accurately reflecting the whole person or even applicable career directions, e.g., a student whose responses indicated liking books and nature received results recommending careers of librarian or forest ranger—neither was appropriate. Aptitude and preference tests, like

- 122 -

IQ tests, differ from achievement tests by testing competence, ability, and interests; achievement tests evaluate learning a student has achieved and can demonstrate.

Norm-referenced tests

Norm-referenced tests are standardized tests that provide pre-established norms for student scores on given tests. Before publishing or marketing standardized tests, e.g., national or statewide achievement tests, test authors typically administer their test to groups of students they have selected as samples representative of the larger intended test-taking student population. They then conduct and publish statistical analyses of the scores received by students in the sample groups. These show what the average score or range of scores is, the proportion of students receiving this average, and the distribution of all other scores on the test. Once a test is statistically proven valid and reliable and is published, educators who administer it can compare their students' scores to the established norms supplied with the instrument. This enables school administrators and teachers to compare their students' average and individual performance on the achievement test to the performance of the students in the norm samples. Because the sample students were selected as representative of the national or statewide student population, their scores provide norms against which educators can compare their students' performance. Such comparisons are typically used to satisfy federal and state legal accountability requirements for all schools receiving federal funds to educate their students adequately.

Criterion-referenced tests

Whereas norm-referenced tests provide established norms in the form of average scores, all scores, and score distribution of students selected as samples representative of the larger student population, to which educators can compare their own students' scores, criterion-referenced tests do not compare student results to norms or other students. Instead, they compare student results to some pre-established criterion or criteria. Test authors have selected criteria to indicate successful student performance on each item tested. Criteria can include minimum percentage or number out of a total of correct items; minimum number of attributes included in responses; descriptions of required detail, clarity, and/or other features which responses must match or approximate; in some tests, rates of speed, e.g., assessments of oral reading or speaking fluency; or other criteria specific to the skills or learning being evaluated. Student result data from criterion-referenced tests can be used for formative assessment to monitor student progress, evaluate instructional effectiveness and adjust instruction; and/or as parts of summative assessment to demonstrate students have achieved pre-defined learning objectives, in addition to norm-referenced measures.

Validity, reliability, raw scores, and scaled scores

Validity in testing means that a test instrument measures what it intends and/or claims to measure. For example, a test validated for educational diagnosis and/or placement could be completely invalid for determining high school graduation. However, the same test might be used for both purposes on the condition that the test has been validated for both. Reliability is consistency, i.e., whether a test yields similar results over repeated administrations. Internal consistency is reliability determined by administering two forms of the same test concurrently and finding they correlate. If one such form is given to students and the other form to the same students a month later—eliminating practice and memory effects from giving the same form both times—and they achieve similar scores in both administrations, this establishes test-retest reliability. Tests can be valid but not reliable, or reliable but not valid. Raw scores are students' actual scores on test scales, e.g., number or percentage correct. Scaled scores convert raw scores to common scales permitting

- 123 -

numerical comparison, of individual student progress across semesters and years, among students in subject areas, etc. Scaled scores typically vary within tests among different content-area subscales.

Standard deviation, mean, median, mode, grade-equivalent scores, and age-equivalent score

Percentile is a statistical ranking method indicating a score or value below which a specified percentage of scores falls within a group. For example, if a student's test score is in the 90th percentile, this means s/he scored higher than 90 percent of other students in the group tested. Standard deviation (SD or σ) is the "mean of the mean," measuring score, data dispersion, variance, or spread. Numerically, SD equals the square root of variance. SDs nearer to 0 indicate all data points clustered close to the average; higher SDs indicate wider distribution. The mean is the average of a data set or score distribution. The median is the middle score in a distribution. The mode is the value or number occurring most frequently in a distribution. Grade-equivalent (GE) scores indicate where on a continuum a student's test score falls. For example, if a 9th-grade student scores a 10.5 GE, this represents the raw score typical of a student in the fifth month of 10th grade. Age-equivalent (AE) scores are based on student age, not grade. For example, for a student aged 7.5 years, a 6 AE score indicates performance typical of a 6-year-old. GE and AE scores should only be used as comparative or relative, not absolute assessment measures.

Analytic scoring

Analytic scoring separately evaluates and scores discrete writing features, e.g., concise concept expression, creativity, grammar, punctuation, etc. Teachers may average these scores, but more often weigh them by relative importance. Analytic scoring helps teachers consider all writing elements, preventing them from, for example, giving too low a grade because of poor mechanics to an essay with excellent concept expression or problem analysis. By enabling final score breakdowns and teacher comments, it diagnoses areas needing improvement to guide further student efforts. Disadvantages include being time-intensive for teachers, not all students reading their teacher comments, and not using those teacher comments to benefit future assignments. Also, negative feedback, particularly combined with unclear or confrontational comments, can be counterproductive to student development. Written analytic scales define grading criteria and expectations for students. Teachers should weigh criteria by importance, e.g., if an assignment's goal is learning course information, then ideas, organization, and/or logic outweigh grammar and mechanics. Comments should balance challenge with support. Teachers should avoid confrontational practices like sarcastic comments; crossing, scribbling, or blocking out student work; etc.

Holistic scoring

When teachers have many essays to grade, holistic scoring is less time-consuming than analytic scoring, which divides writing into various components to score separately, deriving the composite score by weighing components according to assignment goals and purposes. Holistic scoring also enables multi-grader scoring. The original teacher chooses at least three student essays which, according to the teacher's criteria based on the learning objectives for the assignment, represent average, high, or low achievement. Using these as models, the teacher and other graders assess many essays written by a class (or classes) of students. Holistic scoring is found highly reliable and consistent as a method of scoring student writing. Because it takes so much less time than analytic scoring, holistic scoring is more efficient. Disadvantages include that, although scores are reliable, individual students are not necessarily informed of specific reasons for their grades. Most teachers write some final comment to give students some idea why their essays were worse, better, or similar to model essays. However, detailed comments throughout as formative feedback for student improvement are not provided as with analytic scoring. Holistic scoring is also most useful for two or more graders and can be impracticable for single instructors.

Explaining tests and results to parents and students

A common parental question is why their children were tested. Educators can explain to parents that standardized tests can identify their child's school strengths as well as areas where their child may need to improve. They can also evaluate and improve their child's school and the entire school district to provide better education. Educators should also tell parents their children are never evaluated based on a single test, and any assessment program is one among multiple tools evaluating student performance. Some parents are bewildered by scores like percentiles, stanines, grade-equivalent scores, etc. Teachers can help clarify these. For example, "stanine" refers to "standard nine," meaning that on a scale from 1-9, a score of 1-3 is below average, 4-6 is average, and 7-9 is above average. Percentiles tell what percentage of students scored below that percentile. Teachers should explain to parents that a score in the 75th percentile does not mean their child got 75 percent of test items correct; rather, it means their child scored higher than 75 percent of other students in the test group. If a student gets an 8th-grade-equivalent score on a 5th-grade reading achievement test, parents may think their child is ready for 8th-grade material; however, teachers should explain this means their child reads 5th-grade material as well as a typical 8th-grader.

When educators explain the meanings of scores like stanines, percentiles, and grade-level equivalents to parents, they should also explain that these are derived by comparing their child's scores with those of a comparison group, which may be a sample of students representative of the national population or the other students in the school district who took the test at the same time. Discussing a student's test scores relative to other students' scores makes test results most meaningful for parents: teachers can tell them how their child is different and/or similar to others in the group. Parents most often want to know what test scores mean. Teachers should compare student test scores with daily classwork before parent conferences to ensure scores match. Differences can be attributable to subscale scores. For example, a student's overall reading test score may seem adequate in the 75th percentile; but the student's subscale score in comprehension might be in the 85th percentile but in the 65th percentile for vocabulary, indicating need for vocabulary improvement. To track progress, teachers should compare students' present to past scores with parents whenever possible.

When explaining test results to younger students, teachers should avoid technical terms that the students will not understand. They can simplify while preserving general accuracy. For example, rather than telling a young child s/he scored in the 95th percentile, a teacher can say s/he did better than most of the other students. Even among parents, audiences vary, influencing how teachers should communicate test results. For example, if a parent is an educator and/or psychometrist, the teacher can likely give percentiles, stanines, grade-level and age-level equivalents without having to explain them. Such knowledgeable parents may only want to know which comparison group was used; or how their child's score compares to a larger, national comparison group, etc. However, for parents with completely unrelated backgrounds, occupations, or little formal schooling, teachers may omit technical terms entirely or give parents concise, clear definitions of them; either way, be prepared to offer a common-sense equivalent, e.g., their child is doing similarly, better, much better, or worse than most other students in the class, group, or school.

Some parents' cultures and/or countries view education as more unilateral and authoritarian than in America. They may punish children for low test scores; and/or avoid helping children with homework, studying, or getting involved in school, viewing these as inappropriately challenging school and teacher authority. In some cultures, students typically receive few years of formal education; parents from these cultures may have lower expectations for children's educational achievement. Regarding English language proficiency test results, some immigrant families want to abandon their native languages as soon as possible to acquire English, discouraging children from using L1s. When these children are still too young for verbal fluency, this can hinder their proficiency in either language. Educators can explain how L1 proficiency contributes to L2 acquisition. Some parental attitudes positively influence English learning. Parents in communities lacking opportunities for independent English learning have positive attitudes toward English acquisition. Most immigrants, viewing literacy positively as key to succeeding in America, want to learn how to help their children in school. While preserving native cultures and languages, many parents also want to participate in mainstream US culture. Many cultural family structures are stronger and more involved than in America; collective commitment to family exceeds individual motivations.

ABCTE Practice Test

1. Which of these is NOT one of the major personality structures proposed by Sigmund Freud in his psychoanalytic theory of development?

    a. Id
    b. Ego
    c. Libido
    d. Superego

2. Among the developmental stages Freud identified in his theory of psychosexual development, which ones occur during infancy and early childhood through elementary ages?

    a. Oral, Anal, and Phallic
    b. Anal, Phallic, and Genital
    c. Phallic, Genital, and Latency
    d. Phallic, Latency, and Genital

3. According to Freud's theory of psychosexual development, which stage is typical of adolescence?

    a. Oral
    b. Anal
    c. Phallic
    d. Genital

4. In Erikson's theory of psychosocial development, which stage(s) and nuclear conflict(s) is/are typically encountered during the teenage years?

    a. Identity vs. Role Confusion
    b. Intimacy vs. Isolation
    c. Both of these
    d. Neither one

5. Which of the following learning processes produces the result of reconstructing or repositioning a belief system or value system?

    a. Cueing and/or retrieving previously acquired knowledge
    b. Integrating new learning into currently existing systems
    c. Self-regulated learning for testing instructional efficacy
    d. Creating cognitive dissonance with an existing position

6. Among these ways in which students acquire skills, which is most common during early childhood?

    a. Independent reading
    b. Learning by playing
    c. Learning by doing
    d. Direct instruction

7. If a high school student is interested in a subject but the school does not offer any classes in it, what is true about other ways the student can acquire skills in this subject?

a. Independently reading books about the subject will not enable the student to acquire desired skills.

b. An internship or apprenticeship will provide instruction, modeling, and hands-on learning by doing.

c. Internet searches can find YouTube videos teaching the skills but not further reading/study matter.

d. Since the student is already enrolled in high school, s/he cannot enroll in an outside course to learn.

8. What is the *first* way in which teachers can apply processes of acquiring and integrating new knowledge to help ELL students access meaningful learning?

a. Activate prior knowledge

b. Activate accommodation

c. Activate assimilation

d. Activate all at once

9. Which of the following reflects a general principle for teachers to apply in responding to student diversity in their classrooms?

a. Ask students to speak for their minorities.

b. Ask students more open-ended questions.

c. Ask students questions with shorter wait time.

d. Ask students to follow differing rules and norms.

10. To address diversity among students within classrooms, which of these is a recommended teacher practice?

a. Substituting American nicknames for more difficult foreign names

b. Varying instructional methods for different student learning styles

c. Establishing boundaries by not talking to students except in classes

d. Not challenging dominant students/putting quiet ones on the spot

11. What is one valid guideline for teachers to avoid problems with classroom diversity?

a. Avoid using idioms; translate or explain any they do use.

b. Avoid linguistic redundancy to prevent student boredom.

c. Avoid using any examples not familiar to all the students.

d. Avoid confusing students by presenting in multiple forms.

12. Which of the following categories of cognitive disabilities most consistently includes the characteristic of a marked gap between intellectual ability and school performance?

a. Autism spectrum disorders (ASDs)

b. Intellectual disabilities (ID aka MR)

c. None of these includes such a gap

d. Specific learning disabilities (SLDs)

13. Among the following auditory disabilities, which one does not involve any part of the hearing mechanism?

    a. Only sensorineural-type hearing loss
    b. The conductive form of hearing loss
    c. Central auditory processing disorder
    d. The condition of complete deafness

14. Legal blindness is defined as which of the following visual acuity measures on an eye test?

    a. 20/200
    b. 20/70
    c. 10/200
    d. 5/200

15. Relative to assessment, what is a definition of statistical reliability?

    a. Consistency in a test's results across repeated administrations
    b. Veracity in a test's measuring what it is purported to measure
    c. Dependability of administering a test the same way each time
    d. Consistency between two tests when comparing their results

16. Which type of reliability indicates whether an assessment gets reliable results across its individual items?

    a. Inter-rater reliability
    b. Test-retest reliability
    c. Parallel-forms reliability
    d. Internal consistency reliability

17. What defines validity in terms of assessment?

    a. Whether a test is consistent over repeated measures
    b. Whether a test measures what it is meant to measure
    c. Whether a test measures a construct using objectivity
    d. Whether a test is scored the same by different people

18. Which of these is/are a subtype(s) of criterion validity?

    a. Concurrent validity
    b. Predictive validity
    c. (a) and (b), not (d)
    d. Construct validity

19. What kind of validity indicates how representative a test is of every part or detail of a construct?

    a. Content validity
    b. Criterion validity
    c. Construct validity
    d. Concurrent validity

20. Which of the following defines discriminant validity in assessment?

    a. Constructs are not combined or confounded in what a test measures.
    b. Constructs expected to be related when tested are found to be related.
    c. Constructs expected to be unrelated are tested and are found unrelated.
    d. Constructs measured by tests can be generalized to the larger population.

21. An educational researcher gives the same test to two groups of students, then delivers an instructional intervention to one group, and then gives both groups the same test again. The intervention/treatment group scores much higher this time; the control (non-treatment) group scores essentially the same as the first time. The researcher concludes that barring other factors, the intervention was what raised one group's scores. What type of validity does this illustrate?

    a. Internal validity
    b. External validity
    c. Ecological validity
    d. Population validity

22. Which of the following accurately describes rubrics as assessment tools?

    a. They typically define specific tasks, skills, or behaviors after performance.
    b. They typically guide task performance but do not give criteria for success.
    c. They typically should be explained to students by teachers after assessing.
    d. They typically define and describe general ranges or levels of performance.

23. What is a disadvantage of using rubrics as assessment tools?

    a. Learning objectives, tasks, guidance, and criteria are combined.
    b. Performance levels are not as precise as grades or percentages.
    c. They afford greater brevity in definition, guidance, assessment.
    d. Rubrics are more concise yet offer more clarity than other tools.

24. Of the following, which is an advantage of using analytical checklists for assessment?

    a. They allow for differences in assessing individual tasks across students.
    b. They require additional notes to identify other notable feats observed.
    c. They save time and effort by listing tasks, skills, or behaviors in advance.
    d. They sometimes constrain assessment to Yes/No without quality levels.

25. Among these, what is a disadvantage of using scoring guides in assessment?

    a. Scoring guides are published by different authors than the tests they accompany.
    b. Scoring guides force teachers to give specific scores to specific student responses.
    c. Scoring guides can be misinterpreted/misapplied by inexperienced/unwise users.
    d. Scoring guides give teachers flexibility to use judgment with responses/conditions.

26. Which of the following is an advantage of using anecdotal notes to assess student work?

    a. Teachers can use these to collect information both during assessment and outside of it.
    b. Unless a teacher adds norms or criteria for comparison, these notes lack standardization.
    c. Teachers cannot record observations of individual student behaviors as with most tools.
    d. Writing anecdotal notes can yield valuable insights but often lack any supporting context.

27. When teachers assess student performance using continua, which is a disadvantage?

    a. More precise evaluative descriptions of student performance instead of discrete grades
    b. Greater difficulty in comparing student, class, and school scores without exact numbers
    c. Performance ranges are more realistic and accurate than exact numbers or cutoff scores
    d. Greater compatibility with individualized student assessment than standardized testing

28. Which of these do standardized ability tests measure in students?

    a. Student competence
    b. Student performance
    c. Student school grades
    d. Student mental health

29. According to Piaget's cognitive theory, how are schemata best defined?

    a. Mental maps
    b. Mental plans
    c. Mental processes
    d. Mental constructs

30. According to cognitive information processing theory, in which of these do people receive input from the environment?

    a. Sensory memory
    b. Working memory
    c. Short-term memory
    d. Long-term memory

31. In his social learning theory, what does Bandura mean by reciprocal determinism?

    a. Learning mutually involves both the learner and the instructor.
    b. Learning mutually involves both the behavior and environment.
    c. Learning mutually involves both the individual and environment.
    d. Learning mutually involves individual, behavior, and environment.

32. Piaget described children as "little scientists" interacting and experimenting with the environment to learn about it and actively build their own knowledge. This reflects which type of philosophy and psychology?

    a. Scaffolding
    b. Cognitivism
    c. Constructivism
    d. Zone of Proximal Development

33. Which type of behaviorist conditioning changes voluntary behaviors through manipulating environmental variables?

    a. Classical conditioning
    b. Operant conditioning
    c. No type of conditioning
    d. Respondent conditioning

34. What is the correct behaviorist term for strengthening a behavior by taking away something?

    a. Positive punishment
    b. Negative punishment
    c. Positive reinforcement
    d. Negative reinforcement

35. In curriculum design, what is/are included in the definition of scope?

    a. All these plus teacher expectations of student performance
    b. Breadth and depth of subject content covered in instruction
    c. Curricular coherence through longitudinal instruction in content
    d. Learning objectives reflecting national, state, and local standards

36. Which of the following represents effective curriculum design in terms of sequence?

    a. Reading before writing
    b. Writing before reading
    c. Speaking before listening
    d. Listening following writing

37. Mapping curriculum scope is a way for teachers to do which of the following?

    a. Ensure curriculum progresses in complexity and abstraction
    b. Respond to relative student interest through the curriculum
    c. Integrate state and district learning standards into curriculum
    d. Assure prerequisite knowledge and logical delivery of content

38. How do state education departments and school districts address curriculum scope and sequence?

    a. Sequencing via developmental strands
    b. (a) and (c) are common, but (d) varies
    c. Organizing scope via key learning areas
    d. States delegate them to school districts

39. When a student is able to consider whether an information source is reputable, has been proven objectively, and is accepted by experts in its discipline, which element of critical thinking does the student demonstrate?

    a. Evaluating supporting evidence
    b. Judging the quality of material
    c. Distinguishing fact from opinion
    d. Finding evidence/no evidence

40. Which of the following describes the process of inductive reasoning?

    a. Top-down and general to specific
    b. Bottom-up and general to specific
    c. Bottom-up and specific to general
    d. Top-down and specific to general

41. As a cognitive element of the learning process, what is a characteristic of planning?

    a. Planning requires concrete thinking, not abstract thinking.
    b. Planning requires both abstract thinking and imagination.
    c. Planning requires organizational, not imaginative abilities.
    d. Planning is on a lower level of higher-order thinking skills.

42. When a student must remember something (e.g., on a test), which cognitive memory process is the most challenging?

    a. Recall
    b. Retrieval
    c. Rehearsal
    d. Recognition

43. Which of the following is a characteristic of indirect instruction?

    a. It is delivered explicitly.
    b. It has uniform lesson plans.
    c. It is more structured by nature.
    d. It involves exploratory activities.

44. What is correct about the definition of independent study as an instructional strategy?

    a. It involves only an individual student working alone.
    b. It can include individuals, partners, or small groups.
    c. It can involve paired students but not small groups.
    d. It can involve small groups but not paired students.

45. Which of the following is an example of experiential learning?

    a. Watching a video, taking notes
    b. Reading a textbook, taking notes
    c. Testing a hypothesis, taking notes
    d. Listening to a lecture, taking notes

46. In the development step of direct instruction procedures, what should teachers do?

    a. Tell rather than show students what behavior they must demonstrate.
    b. In addition to explaining material clearly, give sufficient examples of it.
    c. To assess understanding, do not ask but elicit questions from students.
    d. To help students process information, avoid distracting multimedia aids.

47. When teachers giving direct instruction assign guided practice, which procedure should they follow for students who have not mastered the material?

    a. They should never revert to an earlier step in the process.
    b. They should have these students do more guided practice.
    c. They should have these students do independent practice.
    d. They should offer them further direct instruction and help.

48. Which of the following correctly sequences the steps in a direct instruction procedure?

    a. Development; Introduction/Review; Independent Practice; Guided Practice; Evaluation; Closure
    b. Introduction/Review; Development; Guided Practice; Closure; Independent Practice; Evaluation
    c. Guided Practice; Introduction/Review; Independent Practice; Development; Evaluation; Closure
    d. Independent Practice; Development; Guided Practice; Introduction/Review; Closure; Evaluation

49. What is a characteristic of indirect instruction?

    a. It is teacher facilitated rather than teacher directed.
    b. It is teacher centered rather than student centered.
    c. It is teacher directed rather than teacher facilitated.
    d. It is receptive rather than active knowledge building.

50. Which of these teaching/learning strategies associated with indirect instruction most promotes student visualization, organization, and application of ideas they have learned?

    a. Reading for meaning
    b. Concept mapping
    c. Cloze procedures
    d. Case studies

51. Of the following, which do Cloze procedures involve on the part of the student?

    a. Changing closed sentences into open-ended sentences
    b. Changing open-ended sentences into closed sentences
    c. Connecting phrases or clauses into complete sentences
    d. Changing incomplete sentences to complete sentences

52. Which of these represents a caveat concerning independent instruction?

    a. Students can pursue individual interests with their own paces and styles.
    b. Students develop autonomy, initiative, self-confidence, and self-esteem.
    c. Students benefit from the high flexibility and adaptability of applications.
    d. Students must first have developed skills needed to work independently.

53. After a class unit on environmental education, one student wants to study this topic in greater depth, develop specific expertise in sustainable practices' and research various environmental jobs to consider future career paths. Which kind of learning center(s) would help accomplish all these goals?

    a. Any or all of these
    b. An enrichment center
    c. A skill development center
    d. An interest/exploratory center

54. According to research into achievement motivation, what is the role of student self-determination?

    a. It weakens student motivation by lowering student compliance.
    b. It strengthens student motivation for learning and performance.
    c. It causes qualitative but not quantitative differences in learning.
    d. It is associated with student performance for external motives.

55. Some students find their successes due to their talent and/or hard work and their failures due to their lack of ability and/or not studying; others find their successes due to good luck or help from others and their failures due to bad luck or interference from others. What is motivation theory's term for this?

    a. Attribution
    b. Affirmation
    c. Assignment
    d. Ascription

56. What is the correct meaning of cognitive dissonance?

    a. A cognitive processing disorder affecting understanding
    b. A disruption of cognition caused by a sensory overload
    c. A feeling of discomfort due to contradictory information
    d. A lack of compatibility between instruction and learning

57. A teacher tells a class that anybody who gets 100 percent on the next quiz will be excused from doing homework for that day. According to behaviorist terminology relative to motivation theory, this incentive is an example of what technique?

    a. Positive reinforcement
    b. Primary reinforcement
    c. Negative reinforcement
    d. Secondary reinforcement

58. Which of the following factors is/are NOT a component of intrinsic motivation to learn?

    a. Fascination for the content
    b. Rewards and punishments
    c. Relevance to one's real life
    d. Enhancement of cognition

59. Among characteristics of intrinsic student motivation, which is an advantage?

    a. The length of time that it lasts
    b. The length of time that it takes
    c. The differentiation that it needs
    d. The length of time that it works

60. What is an effective interaction technique related to individual student age differences for teachers to accomplish communication goals?

    a. Give students equally abstract concepts, examples, and materials at every age level.
    b. Give students when younger more abstract content; when older, add the concrete.
    c. Give students content slightly below their current levels so they experience success.
    d. Give students concepts and vocabulary slightly above their current levels at all ages.

61. What is an accurate finding about how gender and race differences can influence teacher and student communication?

    a. Gender and race can influence teacher expectations, but not perceptions of behaviors.
    b. Gender and race can influence teacher perceptions of behaviors by different students.
    c. Gender and race can influence teacher communication but not student communication.
    d. Gender and race can influence teachers, but neither their communication nor students'.

62. What do research findings show about ELL/LEP student communication in classrooms?

    a. When ELL/LEP students avoid answering questions, it is always because they do not know the material.
    b. When ELL/LEP students avoid answering questions, they always know the answers but lack the English.
    c. When ELL/LEP students avoid answering questions, they know content and English but feel discomfort.
    d. When ELL/LEP students avoid answering questions, it may be because of any one, several, or all these.

63. How can teachers interact with diverse students to clarify class goals and purposes for attaining communication goals?

    a. Cover all details thoroughly rather than only emphasizing major points.

    b. Avoid confusing students by comparing and contrasting main concepts.

    c. Support student comprehension by providing analogies and metaphors.

    d. Connect content topics to students' prior knowledge, interests, and values.

64. Which teacher practice is an element of logically structuring classes for effective communication and interaction with classes of individually differing students?

    a. Presenting problems to students without developing solutions

    b. Recounting processes or events out of chronological sequence

    c. Showing students how connected ideas relate to main themes

    d. Clarifying topics with literal presentations rather than as stories

65. To communicate effectively with all students in diverse classrooms, which of these is NOT a recommended teacher technique for transitions between topics?

    a. Implicit transitions requiring student inferences

    b. Verbal signals to the students about transitions

    c. Making mini-summaries of the preceding topics

    d. Establishing some connections between topics

66. How do experts advocate that teachers communicate with their students' parents?

    a. Always using electronic communications, which take less time and parents prefer

    b. Applying the same method universally with all parents to be the most consistent

    c. Utilizing multiple methods, hoping some will be effective for some of the parents

    d. Asking each student's parents which forms of communication work best for them

67. To recruit parents as allies to reinforce school expectations at home, teachers should establish and communicate high standards and expectations at the beginning of the school year. Why?

    a. Because research finds parental expectations strongly predict student achievement

    b. Because research finds teacher expectations more influential than those of parents

    c. Because communications later in the year will get more subjective parent responses

    d. Because communications later in the year will be less supportive but more objective

68. Among strategies that the U.S. Department of Education (ED) includes in its model for parent involvement, which is described accurately?

    a. Communicating not about teacher qualifications, but rather about data for accountability

    b. Training parents to help children achieve academically rather than influence school policy

    c. Emphasizing parental involvement opportunities over supplemental educational services

    d. Communicating with parents only in English, always using uniform, standardized formats

69. According to experts, how should teachers distribute the cognitive levels of the questions they ask relative to student grade levels?

    a. All elementary and secondary grades should be asked half higher- and half lower-level questions.

    b. More than half the questions should be at higher cognitive levels for all student grades.

    c. More than half at higher levels for secondary grades, below half in elementary grades.

    d. More than half the questions should be at lower cognitive levels for all student grades.

Copyright © Mometrix Media. You have been licensed one copy of this document for personal use only. Any other reproduction or redistribution is strictly prohibited. All rights reserved.

70. Regarding open-ended teacher questions that require students to apply, analyze, evaluate, and synthesize/create information vs. questions that require students to remember and understand information, what have research studies found?

    a. Combining these two types of questions is more effective than either one alone.
    b. Asking the first type of questions is always more effective than the second type.
    c. Asking the second type of questions more often than the first type works better.
    d. Using either one or the other kind exclusively works better than combining them.

71. For which kinds of students is it effective for teachers to ask pre-reading questions?

    a. Older and/or high-ability students
    b. Students who are more motivated
    c. Younger students and poor readers
    d. For both (a) and (b), but not for (c)

72. What have research studies discovered about teacher use of wait time in questioning?

    a. Teachers give less wait time to students they perceive as better learners.
    b. Teachers give less wait time to students they perceive as slower learners.
    c. Teachers further student achievement by using slightly shorter wait times.
    d. Teachers produce no effects on student achievement through wait times.

73. What kinds of teacher questions will get students actively involved in lesson content?

    a. Only cognitively lower-level questions requiring students to remember and understand
    b. Only higher-level questions requiring students to apply, analyze, evaluate, and synthesize
    c. Cognitively lower-level and higher-level questions can elicit active student involvement
    d. Cognitively lower-level or higher-level questions will not get students actively involved

74. How do teachers help students by making classrooms *intellectually* safe?

    a. They enable students to take risks.
    b. They enable students to collaborate.
    c. They enable every student to participate.
    d. They enable effective, challenging activity.

75. To make a classroom emotionally safe, what can teachers include among rules for both their students and themselves to follow?

    a. It is never okay for any of us to insult any others.
    b. It is okay to laugh at others if it is in a friendly way.
    c. It is okay to tell others to shut up if they are being rude.
    d. It is only okay to put down people who really deserve it.

76. Which of the following do experts advise for managing productive learning environments in the classroom?

    a. For independence, do not arrange signals to start work.
    b. Sequence tasks on a continuum from easiest to hardest.
    c. Avoid informing students about upcoming task challenges.
    d. Keep tasks simple and uncomplicated for students to excel.

77. To assess whether their classrooms are active learning environments, what should teachers measure?

   a. How many students are working on-task
   b. How much time students are working on-task
   c. How strongly students are attending and engaged
   d. How deeply students are engaged, plus (a), (b), (c)

78. Research finds which of these is true regarding classroom conflicts?

   a. Violent actions reflect a lack of values.
   b. Violent actions share retribution goals.
   c. Violent actions begin as major incidents.
   d. Violent actions are from slow escalation.

79. Based on research findings, how does role-playing contribute to effective conflict resolution in the classroom?

   a. Role-playing makes conflicts appear less humorous.
   b. Role-playing focuses students on their own feelings.
   c. Role-playing teaches perspective-taking and empathy.
   d. Role-playing promotes subjective reactions to conflict.

80. Which of these most accurately reflects expert recommendations of effective strategies for resolving classroom conflicts?

   a. De-emphasize conflicts by not letting students record them.
   b. Have students record observations, identifying participants.
   c. Discuss student reactions without judging them good or bad.
   d. Have students track conflicts over time and discuss reactions.

81. Informed by research results, experts on conflict resolution recommend which of the following as good listening behaviors for teachers to impart to students?

   a. Asking questions as needed, but not interrupting others
   b. Avoiding embarrassing others by not making eye contact
   c. Giving others suggestions or advice about what they said
   d. Staying objective by not nodding/smiling as others speak

82. When students have been involved in classroom conflicts, what does it accomplish for teachers to have them write about these?

   a. It makes them ruminate about and extend conflicts.
   b. It gives them time out for cooling off and reflecting.
   c. It helps them review their feelings, not alternatives.
   d. It keeps them from learning anything from conflicts.

83. What is most true about the relationship of teaching and classroom management?

   a. Teacher management decisions are more complex when instruction is more demanding.
   b. Encouraging student responsibility changes student behavior without affecting content.
   c. When students solve novel problems and create products, teacher decisions are simpler.
   d. Teachers focus on helping students meet academic demands instead of social demands.

84. Effective teacher strategies for organizing and managing learning environments that result in high student engagement and low misbehavior include which of these?

    a. Alerting student attention through a focus on the entire class
    b. Concealing teacher awareness of student behavior from them
    c. Designing and implementing activities without any overlapping
    d. Having instruction proceed steadily without adding momentum

85. How do teachers inform classroom behavior management with understanding of group dynamics, specifically individual students' group roles?

    a. They develop friendly relationships with student leaders, instigators, and consciences.
    b. They develop friendly relationships with student enforcers, procurers, and negotiators.
    c. They develop strategies for keeping student leaders, procurers, and negotiators on-task.
    d. They develop friendly relationships and on-task strategies for students in all these roles.

86. Which of these is NOT a pair of low-impact teacher interventions that prevent undesirable student behaviors from escalating?

    a. Showing interest in student work and encouraging students in their endeavors
    b. Showing awareness of student behaviors through physical proximity and touch
    c. Embarrassing and punishing students in front of classmates to prevent rebellion
    d. Reminding students of successful instances and modifying lesson presentations

87. How can teachers establish positive, productive learning environments for students whose developmental levels vary within the same classroom?

    a. Observe levels/types of children's play and provide only activities matching these.
    b. Give older elementary and middle school students high school-type collaboration.
    c. Do not expect new preschoolers' sharing, but do model, encourage, and reward it.
    d. Confine productive learning environments in high school classes to the classrooms.

88. A teacher observes young children playing in the classroom to inform the kinds of play activities to offer them. To promote development, which students should the teacher offer opportunities for full cooperative play with others?

    a. Students who are playing by themselves
    b. Students playing associatively with peers
    c. Students who are watching others playing
    d. Students playing near but not with others

89. How should teachers arrange classroom furnishings and materials to create supportive climates?

    a. Arrangements should not let students feel too comfortable.
    b. Arrangements should discourage dialogue among students.
    c. Arrangements should keep students from owning the room.
    d. Arrangements should support collaboration among students.

90. To communicate high expectations to all students, what should teachers do?

    a. Identify which students they expect less from as early as they can.
    b. Avoid identifying student similarities that influence expectations.
    c. Realize teacher expectations have more influence than behaviors.
    d. Treat students differently according to what they expect of them.

91. Research studies have identified which teacher behaviors are based on different expectations of students?

    a. Teachers ask equally challenging questions of low-expectancy students.
    b. Teachers call on low-expectancy and high-expectancy students equally.
    c. Teachers go into less depth exploring low-expectancy student answers.
    d. Teachers reward less rigorous answers from low-expectancy students.

92. Which of the following is a right of teachers under the First Amendment?

    a. The right to academic freedom of expression
    b. The right to protection against discrimination
    c. The right to due process in termination notice
    d. The right to establish student behavioral rules

93. The IDEA guarantees due process rights to parents for which of the following?

    a. To advance notice, but not refusal, of special education placement
    b. To refuse special education services but not to get advance notice
    c. To advance notice and refusal of identification and evaluation only
    d. To advance notice and refusal of all these special education stages

94. Among legal rights and responsibilities of students, which of these is federal rather than varying by state or district?

    a. Free, appropriate public education
    b. Reporting dangerous behaviors
    c. Advocating for policy changes
    d. Peaceful dispute resolution

95. According to the U.S. Department of Education (ED), at which of these levels is a teacher not a student teacher, but paid, and not a teacher of record, but completing a supervised practicum?

    a. Novice Teacher
    b. Leader Teacher
    c. Master Teacher
    d. Resident Teacher

96. A tenured teacher who coaches and advocates academically, serves as an example of lifelong learning, and often may stay at this level throughout the teaching career is identified by which U.S. Department of Education (ED) term?

    a. Professional Teacher
    b. Resident Teacher
    c. Master Teacher
    d. Teacher Leader

97. Among the following ED designations for teacher levels, which are *most* likely to become school principals, given proper professional development?

    a. Teacher Leaders are
    b. Master Teachers are
    c. (a) and (b) more than (d)
    d. Professional Teachers are

98. In today's public schools, who are most often responsible for instructing special education students?

   a. Educational specialists
   b. Special education teachers
   c. The most applicable therapists
   d. The regular classroom teachers

99. How are teachers required to ensure educational equity?

   a. By delivering uniform instruction to all students
   b. By offering different opportunities to students
   c. By treating students less fairly if they deserve it
   d. By using materials reflecting multicultural views

100. Legal and ethical requirements of classroom teachers include which of these?

   a. Teachers are required to keep student records confidential, but not other information.
   b. Teachers are required to protect the privacy of any or all student personal information.
   c. Teachers are required to seek, but not get permission, to utilize copyrighted materials.
   d. Teachers are required to ask only authors for permission to use copyrighted materials.

Answers and Explanations

1. C: The libido is part of the id according to Freud. It represents psychic energy as well as sex drive. Freud's three major personality structures are the id (a), which generates unconscious impulses; the ego (b), which realistically regulates acting on id impulses; and the superego (c), which morally regulates the id and ego.

2. A: The Oral stage is associated with infancy; the Anal stage with toddlerhood; and the Phallic with preschool ages. The Latency stage is associated with elementary school ages, and the Genital stage is associated with adolescence.

3. D: Freud associated his Oral (a) stage with infancy; the stage he named Anal (b) with toddlerhood; the Phallic (c) stage with preschool ages; the Latency stage with elementary school ages; and the Genital (d) stage with adolescence.

4. C: Erikson described the stage and nuclear conflict of Identity vs. Role Confusion (a) as typical of adolescence, when young people seek to form individual personal identities and social relationships are the focus. Teens successfully resolving this conflict feel true to themselves; those failing have weak/poorly defined self-images and are confused about their roles in life. By their late teens, young adults experience Erikson's stage and nuclear conflict of Intimacy vs. Isolation (b), when they seek to form intimate relationships with others and relationships are the focus. Those successfully resolving the conflict develop loving relationships; those failing become isolated and lonely. Since (c) is correct, (d) is incorrect.

5. D: Four learning processes related to constructing knowledge (Timperley et al., 2007) are cueing or retrieving previously acquired knowledge (a), which produces the result of examining and/or consolidating it; integrating new learning into currently existing systems (b) of beliefs or values, which produces the result of adopting and/or adapting new knowledge; creating cognitive dissonance with an existing position (d), belief, or value, which produces the result of reconstructing or repositioning the current belief or value system; and developing self-regulated learning related to instructional efficacy (c), which produces the results of monitoring student progress and adjusting instruction to be most effective.

6. B: Learning through playing is the most common way of acquiring motor, cognitive, linguistic, emotional, social, and other skills during early childhood. Students are typically older than early childhood when they read on their own to acquire skills (a) in subjects that interest them. While young children also acquire many skills by doing (c), so do students of all ages. While young children acquire skills through direct instruction (d) in preschool and from their parents, students of all ages also acquire skills through direct instruction from educators.

7. B: High school students have multiple options for acquiring skills in subjects not taught by their schools. Some students *can* acquire the skills desired in some subjects by reading books on them on their own (a), particularly books with how-to instructions, photos, and diagrams as well as theory and principles (e.g., photography). Through internship or apprenticeship, students can get instruction, modeling, and hands-on learning and practice (b). Students can search online, not only for countless YouTube video tutorials, but also for further reading matter and study materials (c). Other than practical considerations like lack of time, there is no reason a high school student cannot enroll in an outside course (d) to acquire skills not taught in the high school.

8. A: The first learning process ELL high school students engage in when encountering new information/experiences is activating prior knowledge. Relating new to existing knowledge makes new information meaningful. The second process, assimilation (c), is fitting new information into existing knowledge. The third, accommodation (b), resolves cognitive dissonance when new information challenges existing beliefs/understandings by changing existing knowledge/beliefs or rejecting the new input. The first way teachers can apply these processes to help high school ELLs access meaningful learning is activating their prior knowledge by relating new ideas they teach in English to students' native languages: pairing unfamiliar with familiar language and experience helps students understand and acquire concepts. Since these processes are sequential and (a) is first, (d) is incorrect.

9. B: Asking more open-ended questions invites diverse students to share their experiences and observations. Teachers should NOT ask students to be spokespersons for their minority groups (a), but treat them as individuals. Teachers should extend their wait time (c) when asking questions. This gives ELL students more time to translate questions into their L1s, process questions, formulate answers, and translate them into English, and includes students with disabilities and those who are more reflective and/or less assertive due to their cultural backgrounds or individual personalities. To promote respect, teachers should apply norms and rules that treat all students equally, not differently (d).

10. B: Since students have different learning styles, teachers are advised to address diversity by varying their instructional methods to accommodate more variation. Teachers should also make the effort to learn and pronounce ALL students' names correctly, including foreign names they find difficult, rather than substituting American nicknames (a), which is disrespectful. Teachers should talk with and encourage students outside of classes (c) to show their interest and increase student comfort with student-teacher interactions. Teachers should take advantage of small-group settings to ask questions that challenge the most dominant students and draw out the quietest ones, which is not putting them on the spot (d) when done gently and tactfully, but encouraging them to express themselves and participate.

11. A: Idiomatic expressions do not have literal meanings, so they confuse ELL students. Teachers should avoid using idioms, and if/when they do, translate and/or explain them. Linguistic redundancy is valuable not only for ELLs but all students. Teachers should use it, e.g., speaking information aloud while students also see it in print, as it will help students learn rather than bore them (b). While some examples are regionally, culturally, historically, or politically unfamiliar to some students, teachers cannot always give universally understood examples (c); instead, they should offer a diverse variety, obtaining some of the background from students. Presenting information in multiple forms reinforces it rather than confusing students (d).

12. D: Students with specific learning disabilities (SLDs) do not have intellectual impairments; they have impairments in processing information. Therefore it is most typical of students with SLDs to show a marked gap between intellectual ability and school performance. Students with ASDs (a) can have any degree of intellectual impairment or none. Those with high IQs may excel academically but have difficulty with social interactions, transitions, and sensory input, and/or demonstrate rigid routines and schedules, restricted interests, and repetitive behaviors. Students with ID/MR (b) typically learn the same ways as others, but more slowly. Generally their intellectual ability and school performance are less disparate than those of students with SLDs. Hence (c) is incorrect.

13. C: Central auditory processing disorder is categorized as an auditory disability because it impairs the ability to understand spoken language received through the auditory sense (hearing).

- 143 -

But it does not involve the outer, middle, or inner ear or auditory nerves. It involves a deficit in the brain's ability to interpret the meanings and structures of speech sounds. Sensorineural hearing loss (a) involves the cochlea in the inner ear and/or auditory nerves leading to the brain. Conductive hearing loss (b) involves the outer and/or middle ear, where something obstructs conduction of sound, e.g., a deformed pinna/auricle, wax buildup, a closed or malformed or ear canal, fluid/pus buildup in the middle ear due to otitis media (middle ear infection), otosclerosis immobilizing the ossicles in the middle ear, etc. Complete deafness (d) most typically involves total sensorineural hearing loss.

14. A: Legal blindness is defined as 20/200, i.e., reading at 20' on a Snellen eye chart what one should be able to read at 200'. Seeing at from 20/200 to 20/70 (b) after correction in the better eye is labeled as low vision. Seeing at from 5/200 to 10/200 (c) is the definition of travel vision. Seeing at from 3/200 to 5/200 (d), which typically involves seeing moving objects, is called motion perception. Seeing at lower than 3/200, and seeing bright light at 3' but not movement, is called light perception.

15. A: Relative to assessment, statistical reliability is how consistent a test's results are across repeated administrations. Choice (b) is a definition of statistical validity. Choice (c) describes being able to replicate the test administration itself, not results across administrations. Choice (d) describes consistency between two tests, not consistency within one test across administrations.

16. D: Internal consistency reliability measures how consistent individual items within the same test are with each other in assessing the same construct. Inter-rater reliability (a) measures how consistent the ratings, observations, or scoring of different human beings are with one another. Test-retest reliability (b) determines how consistent a test's results are across administrations at different times. Parallel-forms reliability (c) determines how consistent two different versions of the same test are at measuring the same construct.

17. B: The definition of statistical validity regarding assessment is whether a test measures what it is meant (or claimed) to measure. A test may measure very accurately, yet measure a different construct than expected or more than one construct—e.g., if a test is identified as measuring anxiety but it measures depression also or instead, it is not valid. Consistency over repeated uses (a) defines reliability. Measuring objectively (c) defines a lack of bias. Consistency among different people's scoring (d) or observations defines inter-rater reliability.

18. C: Criterion validity is whether a test reflects a particular set of skills. It includes both concurrent validity (a), which compares the test to an established "benchmark" test used as a criterion, and predictive validity (b), which measures how well a test predicts abilities in a certain construct by testing people in that construct and comparing results with later results to see if the earlier results predicted the later ones. Construct validity (d) is how well a test measures what it is supposed to measure and is not a subtype of criterion validity.

19. A: Content validity is how representative a test is of every single component of the construct it measures. Criterion validity (b) is how representative a test is of a certain skill set. Construct validity (c) is how representative a test is of a certain construct it is designed to measure (e.g., if it is meant to measure depression, it should not measure anxiety). Concurrent validity (d) is a subtype of criterion validity and indicates how well a test correlates with an established benchmark test.

20. C: Discriminant validity, also called divergent validity, confirms that constructs we expect to be unrelated are in fact unrelated. When constructs are not combined or confused in a test's measurement (a) as they should not be, this indicates the test has construct validity. When

- 144 -

constructs we expect to be related are confirmed to be related (b), this indicates convergent validity. When a construct measured by a test given to a sample group can be generalized to a larger population (d), it has external validity.

21. A: When a test (or an experimental research design) shows cause and effect, it has internal validity. External validity (b) is whether or how much a test's results (or research effect) can be generalized to larger populations, other settings, measurement variables, and/or treatment variables. External validity includes ecological validity (c), i.e., how impervious a test or effect is to environmental influences, and population validity (d), i.e., how representative of the population the sample tested is and whether the sampling method used is acceptable.

22. D: As assessment tools, rubrics typically define general ranges or levels of performance (e.g., excellent, satisfactory, or unsatisfactory) and briefly describe characteristics of each. They define specific tasks, skills, or behaviors *before* they are performed (a) to guide students, as well as provide referents afterward for evaluating performance. In addition to guiding task execution, they *do* provide criteria for performing tasks successfully (b). Teachers should explain rubrics to students so they can follow them in performing tasks, *before* using them to assess student task performance, not after (c).

23. B: The fact that rubrics combine learning objectives, tasks, guidance to students for performing those tasks, and criteria (a) for evaluating student task performance is an advantage they have as assessment tools. The fact that the performance levels they assign are not as precise as number or letter grades or percentages (b) is a disadvantage. The fact that they are brief in nature (c) is an advantage for both students and teachers. The fact that they are both more concise and clearer than many other assessment tools (d) is another advantage.

24. C: Using analytical checklists as assessment tools has the advantage of saving time and effort by listing the tasks, skills, or behaviors to be performed and assessed in advance. They also have the advantage of making assessment uniform across students relative to tasks and/or their components (a). They do require additional notes for teachers to identify other notable feats that teachers observe students accomplishing beyond the designated tasks (b), but this is a disadvantage. Although some checklists include performance levels similarly to rubrics, others constrain assessment to Yes/No responses (d), another disadvantage.

25. C: Scoring guides typically are published by the authors of the tests they accompany, not different authors (a); this is an advantage in minimizing inaccurate or inappropriate scoring or incorrect score interpretation, as the authors direct teachers/other scorers to follow procedures they designed for their tests. They do not force teachers to give specific scores to specific student responses (b); rather, they allow teachers reasonable flexibility to use their own best judgment with individual student responses and/or test conditions (d), an advantage. The possibility that scoring guides can be misinterpreted or misapplied by inexperienced users or those with poor judgment (c) is a disadvantage.

26. A: One advantage of writing anecdotal notes as an assessment tool is that teachers can collect information about student skills and behaviors outside of assessment activities as well as during them; this can help teachers realize valuable insights into student learning and behavior. The fact that such notes are not standardized unless the teacher incorporates norms or criteria for comparison (b) is a disadvantage. An advantage of anecdotal notes is that teachers *can* record observations of individual student behaviors, which standard test instruments, checklists, and most other tools do *not* allow (c). The fact that anecdotal notes often lack any supporting context (d) is a disadvantage.

27. B: When teachers use performance continua for assessment, they can describe student performance evaluatively with more precision than when they assign separate grades (a), an advantage. However, for comparing assessment scores among students, classes, and/or schools, the lack of exact numbers on a continuum is a disadvantage (b). On the other hand, the performance ranges provided by continua are more realistic and accurate than assigning exact numerical scores or referring to cutoff scores (c), an advantage. Except for comparisons (b)—in which case standardized tests are better—the superiority of continua for individualized assessment (d) is an advantage.

28. A: Standardized tests of ability, like IQ, creativity, verbal, numerical, spatial, memory, and other abilities measure student competence, i.e., their capacity rather than what they actually do, which is performance (b). Ability tests do not indicate and do not necessarily predict student school grades (c), which are also what they do rather than what they are capable of doing. Student mental health (d) is measured by some standardized tests, but not by standardized ability tests.

29. D: According to Piaget, schemata are his term for mental constructs people use to construct knowledge and understand the environment. For example, infants might form schemata for "things that taste good," "things that taste bad," "people I recognize," etc. Schemata are not mental maps (a), plans (b), or processes (c).

30. A: Sensory memory, also known as sensory register, is cognitive information processing theory's term for the capacity wherein we receive sensory input from the environment (i.e., anything we see, hear, feel, smell, and/or taste). Working memory (b) is the capacity that we use for temporarily rehearsing input/information, sometimes dividing it into "chunks" to make it more manageable, and encoding it, all of which are done in short-term memory (c). Encoding is done to enable transferring input/information from short-term to long-term memory (d) for storage.

31. D: By his term reciprocal determinism, Bandura means that learning involves the individual, the behavior, and the environment, all of which influence and are influenced by one another. This term does not specifically refer only to student and teacher (a), to behavior and environment only (b), or to individual and environment only (c).

32. C: The philosophy and psychology of actively constructing one's own knowledge of the world is known as constructivism. Scaffolding (a) is temporary needed support teachers provide for student learning and gradually withdraw as students acquire higher skill levels. Cognitivism (b) is the type of psychology Piaget's theory involves as a theory of cognitive development; however, the description of actively building one's own knowledge refers specifically to constructivism. The Zone of Proximal Development (d) was Vygotsky's term for the distance between what a learner can do independently and what that learner can do with help or guidance.

33. B: Classical conditioning (a) changes involuntary behaviors through manipulating environmental variables. Operant conditioning (b) changes voluntary behaviors through manipulating environmental variables. Respondent conditioning (d) is another name, coined by operant conditioning pioneer B.F. Skinner, for classical conditioning (a). Since (b) is correct, (c) is incorrect.

34. D: In behaviorism, reinforcement is anything strengthening the probability of repeating a behavior. Punishment is anything weakening that probability. In behaviorism, "positive" means presenting a stimulus; "negative" means removing one. Hence positive punishment (a) is presenting a stimulus that makes a given behavior less likely. Negative punishment (b) is removing a stimulus that makes a given behavior less likely. Positive reinforcement (c) is presenting a

stimulus that makes a given behavior more likely. Negative reinforcement (d) is removing a stimulus to make the behavior more likely.

35. A: In curriculum design, the scope of curriculum is defined as how much subject content the teacher covers in instruction, by both breadth and depth (b); how coherent curriculum teachers make the curriculum through teaching basic concepts in subject content over several years (c); learning objectives, clearly defined, that reflect national, state, and local standards (d); and teacher expectations of student accomplishment (a) resulting from instruction as well as how much subject content teachers must cover.

36. A: Curriculum design should sequence instruction logically to match developmental sequences. Receptive language develops before expressive language, so reading should be taught before writing (a), not vice versa (b), and listening before speaking, not vice versa (c). Also, oral language develops before written/printed language, so listening and speaking should precede reading and writing; hence listening should not follow writing (d).

37. C: Mapping curriculum *scope* is a way for teachers to integrate state and school district learning standards. A way for teachers to ensure that the curriculum progresses from simpler to more complex and from more concrete to more abstract (a) is mapping curriculum *sequence*. They can also respond to degrees of student interest in subject content (b), make sure students learn prerequisite knowledge first for certain content, and deliver content in a logical progression (e.g., from local to global environment in social studies) (d) by mapping curriculum *sequence*.

38. B: Common curriculum planning devices used by both state and district curriculum departments are to divide curriculum sequence according to designated developmental strands (a), and to organize curriculum scope according to designated key learning areas (c). While some states delegate curriculum scope and sequence to individual school districts (d) for certain subjects, they define these for other subjects.

39. A: Elements of critical thinking include distinguishing fact from opinion (c) in text or speech by looking for objectivity, facts, and proof vs. subjectivity, non-factual information, and absence of proof; finding evidence or no evidence (d) to support the writer or speaker's arguments by examining the text or speech; evaluating evidence used to support (a) arguments or statements by considering whether its source is reputable, proven, and accepted by authorities in the field; and judging the quality of material (b) or information by comparing it to other material/information, consulting one's own previous experience, and listening to one's own intuition.

40. C: Inductive reasoning is bottom-up and specific to general. It begins with accumulating specific observations, clues, or information; then identifies patterns or commonalities among these; and finally, based on the preponderance of evidence, draws conclusions about a general principle/theory. Deductive reasoning is top-down and general to specific (a). It begins with a general principle/theory/field of information; then, through deducting elements, narrows down to more a specific hypothesis; tests it through observations/data confirming or refuting it; and finally, based on the most specific evidence, draws conclusions about a specific effect/relationship. Choices (b) and (d) pair contradictory concepts.

41. B: Planning requires abstract thinking (a), as it involves mentally representing actions before actually performing them, and imagination (b) to envision doing things not done yet. Planning both requires and promotes organization as well as imagination (c). Planning is identified as being on a higher level among higher-order thinking skills, not lower (d).

42. A: Recall accesses information from long-term memory, e.g., when a student must write an essay or answer a question without the aid of contextual/other clues, it is more challenging. Retrieval (b) is simply a general term for accessing stored memories; it includes both recall (a) and recognition (d). Rehearsal (c) temporarily repeats information in short-term memory using working memory until it can be transferred, also using working memory, into long-term memory. Recognition (d) accesses memory with the aid of contextual clues, e.g., identifying the correct answer among incorrect ones on a multiple-choice test; it is less challenging than recall.

43. D: Indirect instruction promotes student exploration, inquiry, discovery learning, problem solving, and learning abstract concepts and patterns. It is delivered implicitly, whereas direct instruction is delivered explicitly (a). Lesson plans vary, whereas direct instruction uses uniform lesson plans (b). It is less structured, whereas direct instruction is more structured (c). Direct instruction promotes piquing initial student interest; learning facts, rules, and sequences; and analyzing text/workbook material. Whereas indirect instruction is student-centered, direct instruction is teacher-centered.

44. B: The definition of independent study encompasses not only the individual student working alone (a), but also two students working as partners (c) or small groups of students (d) working together. In fact, teachers can even use independent study as an instructional strategy with the whole class. Regardless of the number of students, independent study is less teacher-centered/teacher-directed; the teacher functions as a facilitator and guide. Provided they have developed the required skills, students have more autonomy and choices with independent study.

45. C: Testing a hypothesis requires conducting research, e.g., doing an experiment, making field observations, or administering a survey and analyzing the results. Watching videos (a), reading textbooks (b), and listening to lectures (d)—even while taking notes—are not experiential learning activities because they do not involve hands-on learning activities in which students participate directly. Rather than passively absorbing information, students learn by doing in experiential activities.

46. B: After introducing new information or reviewing, the development step of direct instruction includes modeling the behavior(s) students must demonstrate (a) to show skills and/or knowledge; explaining material to be learned clearly and moreover giving students sufficient examples (b); both asking questions of students and also eliciting questions from them to assess their understanding (c); and using multimedia and visual aids, which help students process information rather than distracting them (d).

47. D: It is not true that teachers should never go back to an earlier step in direct instruction procedures (a). In fact, included in offering further direct instruction is repeating the development step that precedes guided practice (d) as well as other help, rather than simply having them continue in guided practice (b) if it has not already worked. Teachers should not assign independent practice (c), which is a more advanced step than guided practice.

48. B: To follow direct instruction principles, the steps in a teaching procedure begin with (1) introduction of new material or review of learned material and proceed to (2) development of material to be learned; (3) guided student practice of knowledge/skills to be learned; (4) closure to conclude the lesson, recap what it covered, remind students of the learning goal, and prepare them for the next step; (5) independent student practice of knowledge/skills through assigned tasks/activities; and (6) evaluation of student learning.

49. A: Indirect instruction is facilitated by the teacher, who assigns students to select activities and guides them in doing so and supervises and supports their work, rather than more controlled and directed by the teacher (c). As such, it is student-centered, not teacher-centered (b). Rather than involving receptive or passive learning, it has students actively construct their knowledge (d).

50. B: Concept mapping helps students to visualize, organize, and apply the concepts they have learned. Reading for meaning (a) helps students read actively, including predicting, identifying main ideas/themes, inferring, analysis, comparison, evaluation, etc. Cloze procedures (c) help students develop sequencing awareness and linguistic relationships; search, predict, and reconstruct; and determine meaning from context. Case studies (d) help students apply content knowledge and skills through case analysis and explanation.

51. D: Cloze procedures supply students with incomplete sentences wherein blanks are substituted for some key words; they must fill in these blanks with the correct words to make complete sentences. This teaches syntax, sequence, searching, prediction, reconstruction, linguistic relationships, and ascertaining meaning from context. Cloze procedures do not involve changing closed to open-ended (a) or open-ended to closed sentences (b), or connecting phrases or clauses into sentences (c).

52. D: One caveat concerning independent instruction is that for students to participate, they must first have developed the skills required for working independently. The ability of students to pursue individual interests in their own styles at their own paces (a); student development of autonomy, initiative, self-confidence, self-esteem (b), etc.; and the benefits to students of how flexibly and adaptably independent instruction can be applied (c) are all advantages of independent instruction rather than caveats.

53. A: Self-contained classroom learning centers supply varied, easily accessed learning materials for self-directed student learning activity. Students can independently study class topics in greater depth in enrichment centers (b), learn specific expertise related to such topics in skill development centers (c), and find out more information, like researching various careers related to these topics, in interest and/or exploratory centers (d).

54. B: Research into achievement motivation finds student self-determination strengthens motivation. Self-determination involves independently initiating activities rather than only complying with teacher direction; this does not weaken motivation (a). Stronger motivation to learn produces greater learning, not just learning in different ways (c). Self-determination is associated with student performance for internal, not external motives (d).

55. A: Attribution is the term in motivation theory for the way people assign causes or reasons for their successes and failures. Affirmation (b) means stating that something is true. Assignment (c) and ascription (d) are synonyms for the word attribution, but are not the term used in motivation theory for how and to what people attribute cause for their outcomes.

56. C: Cognitive dissonance is a term coined by psychologist Leon Festinger to describe the discomfort we feel when considering contradictory information. We resolve this discomfort by rejecting certain information, or forming new schemata or changing existing ones to accommodate some information. This term is not related to a disorder (a), sensory overload (b), or incompatible instructional and learning (d) processes.

57. C: Positive reinforcement (a) motivates the individual(s) by presenting something that increases the probability of a behavior's occurrence and/or recurrence. Primary reinforcement (b) is unconditioned, i.e., it naturally reinforces or increases a behavior's probability (e.g., food, water,

sleep). Negative reinforcement (c) motivates the individual(s) by removing something whose removal reinforces or increases a behavior's probability. Secondary reinforcement (d) is conditioned, i.e., it did not originally reinforce the behavior but has been made to do so by pairing it with a primary reinforcement.

58. B: Rewards and punishments given by teachers foster extrinsic motivation rather than intrinsic motivation. Components of intrinsic student motivation to learn include fascination with the subject matter (a); relevance of learning to real life (c); and recognition that learning enhances one's cognitive skills (d).

59. A: An advantage of intrinsic student motivation is that it has greater longevity than extrinsic student motivation via external rewards; it is also self-sustaining, unlike extrinsic motivation. The length of time it takes (b) for teacher preparation to develop it; the amount of individual differentiation it needs (c) for teachers to give different students; and the length of time it takes to work (d) for changing student behavior are all disadvantages.

60. D: Teachers should give concepts and vocabulary slightly above students' current levels at every age to provide challenge and stimulate growth rather than material slightly below current levels, which will not do these things and ultimately will make them experience more boredom than success (c). Younger students need concrete concepts, terms, examples, and materials; older students can manage more abstract ones (a), (b).

61. B: Gender and race are found to influence how teachers perceive identical behaviors from different students. For example, teachers can perceive volunteering answers as aggressive in African-American students but enthusiastic in white students. Depending on whether they are male or female, teachers may perceive the same responses as assertive vs. disruptive. Hence gender and race differences influence not only teacher expectations of students, but also teacher perceptions of student behaviors (a). These factors can influence both teacher and student communication (c), (d).

62. D: When ELL/LEP students are reticent to respond to teacher questions, some of them may sometimes not know the content, but this is not always the reason (a). Some may know the material but lack the English (b) to express it. They may know the content and also the English to express it, yet still feel uncomfortable (c) with their LEP levels. Any one, several, or all of these factors may influence how these students respond (d).

63. C: For attaining communication goals, teachers can interact with diverse students for clarifying class goals and purposes by concentrating on major points and letting students find additional details through other activities (a); they can also achieve these goals by comparing and contrasting concepts, which clarifies them rather than confuses students (b). Connecting content topics to students' prior knowledge, interests, and values (d) as well as to student experience and the topics' utility for students is a way teachers can interact with students to stimulate their curiosity and interest rather than to clarify class goals and purposes.

64. C: Elements of structuring classes logically to enhance communication with all students include presenting them with problems and then developing solutions (a); recounting processes or events in chronological sequence (b); showing them how interconnected ideas in content are related to its main, overarching themes (c); providing outlines; and presenting topics as stories (d) to help students relate to them through narrative structure instead of viewing them as collections of unrelated or irrelevant information.

65. A: Experts recommend that for effective communication, teachers make *explicit* transitions between topics by signaling them verbally (b), making mini-summaries of each topic before moving to the next topic (c), and/or establishing the connections between one topic and the next (d). They do NOT recommend leaving transitions between topics implicit for students to infer (a).

66. D: Although electronic communications take less time and many parents prefer them, some still want phone calls or traditional handwritten notes (a). (Also, even within e-communications, parents may prefer text messages, emails, Facebook, Twitter, classroom blogs, classroom videos, class websites, etc.) Experts do not recommend using the same method universally (b), which will only suit some parents but not others, or utilizing multiple methods without knowing individual parental preferences (c). They advise that teachers ask parents which forms of communication work best for them, and use these accordingly.

67. A: Research studies identify parental expectations as among the strongest predictors of student achievement. They also identify teacher expectations as influential, but not more so than those of parents (b). Another reason to establish and communicate high standards and expectations at the beginning of the school year is because communications later in the year will then receive responses from parents that are less subjective (c), more objective, and also more supportive (d).

68. B: In its model for involving parents via parent-educator partnership for enhancing student achievement, ED includes both communicating accountability data in a timely way and communicating teacher qualifications (a) in core subjects; training parents both to help their children achieve academically and to influence school policy (b) through participation in school advisory councils and other groups; equally emphasizing both opportunities for home and school involvement and also supplemental education services (c) available; and communicating in whichever languages and formats are appropriate (d) for individual parents.

69. C: Teachers should ask more than half of their questions at higher cognitive levels (i.e., requiring students to apply, analyze, evaluate, and synthesize or create information) for students in secondary grades, and include smaller proportions at this level for students in elementary grades, rather than by dividing question types equally for all grades (a), giving more high-level questions to all grades (b), or giving more low-level questions (i.e., requiring students only to remember and understand information) to all grades (d).

70. A: Research studies have found that combining questions at higher cognitive levels (i.e., those requiring students to apply, analyze, evaluate, and synthesize/create information) with those at lower cognitive levels (i.e., those requiring students to remember and understand information) is more effective than only asking the first kind (b), only asking the second kind (c), or using either one exclusively (d).

71. D: It is found effective for teachers to ask pre-reading questions of older students, high-ability students (a), and students who are genuinely interested (b) in the subject matter. However, younger students and those who read poorly (c) do not benefit from pre-reading questions because these students focus only on the material they need for answering them rather than on otherwise important content.

72. B: Research studies have discovered that although it seems contradictory, teachers tend to allow *less* wait time for students they perceive as slower learners to answer questions rather than waiting less for students they perceive as better learners (a). Studies also have found that slightly *increasing* wait time rather than decreasing it (c) furthers student achievement; therefore, (d) is incorrect.

73. C: Teachers can stimulate active student involvement in subject content by asking both cognitively lower-level questions requiring students to remember and understand information, and cognitively higher-level questions requiring students to apply, analyze, evaluate, and/or synthesize information rather than only the former (a) or only the latter (b). Even simple factual questions engage students by requiring them to think about and respond to them. Therefore, it is not true that questions will not promote active student involvement (d).

74. C: Teachers enable every individual student to participate by making classrooms *intellectually* safe. They enable students to take risks (a), to collaborate (b), and to engage effectively in challenging activities (d) by making classrooms *emotionally* safe.

75. A: A good rule for teachers to establish for both their students and themselves to make the classroom emotionally safe is never to insult others. More good rules include never laughing at others in any way (b), never telling others to shut up regardless of what they are saying or doing (c), and never putting others down, even when we think they deserve it (d).

76. B: Experts advise teachers to present tasks in a sequence from easiest to most challenging. They also advise that when beginning with the easiest tasks, teachers make sure students know that later tasks will be more challenging rather than not informing them (c). They advise teachers to establish a consistent signal for students to start work (a), e.g., "Please begin," to habituate students to respond whenever they hear it. Additional advice is to assign complex and rich tasks that offer diverse students opportunities to excel (d) and assist classmates.

77. D: To assess whether they have established active learning environments in their classrooms, teachers should measure not only quantity, i.e., how many students are thinking and speaking on-task (a) and how much time students are spending on-task (b), but also quantity, i.e., how strongly students are attending and engaged (c) and how deeply they are engaged (d) in the subject matter.

78. B: Research finds that violent actions in classrooms do not reflect a lack of values (a), but rather reflect value systems that condone violence; that they commonly share goals of retribution (b) against others; that most begin as minor, not major incidents (c); and that despite interactions' not being initially predatory, conflicts escalate rapidly, not slowly (d).

79. C: Based on findings of research into conflict resolution in schools, experts recommend role-playing as an effective strategy because it can introduce humor into the conflict resolution process (a); helps students consider the feelings of others (b); teaches them to view behaviors from others' perspectives and empathize with others (c); and promotes more objective examination of conflicts (d) to gain insights about their origins.

80. D: Among strategies for effective classroom conflict resolution, experts recommend that teachers have students track conflicts they partake of and/or witness over time; record their observations in journals (a), but keep the identities of participants anonymous (b); and then discuss various student reactions to these conflicts that they have observed, including the advantages and disadvantages of each (c).

81. A: Conflict resolution experts advise teachers, based on research results, to instruct students in good listening behaviors, including asking questions as needed but not interrupting others; making eye contact (b) with others while listening to them; avoiding giving others suggestions or advice about what they shared (c); and providing speakers with positive reinforcement by nodding and smiling (d) while listening when appropriate.

82. B: Assigning students to write about conflicts they have been involved in gives them time-out periods wherein they can cool off and reflect about events and their roles in them. Writing does not force students to ruminate over conflicts or extend them further (a); it enables them to analyze what happened, review their feelings, retrospectively consider alternatives (c) they might have chosen instead, and use the conflicts as learning opportunities (d).

83. A: When instruction is more demanding—e.g., when students are asked to solve novel problems and create products—teacher decisions are not simpler (c) but more complex. When teachers encourage student responsibility, both teachers and students approach and understand instructional content differently (b). Teachers must not only help students meet academic demands for comprehension and manipulation of subject content, but also help them meet social demands (d) for effective demonstration of their content knowledge in interactions with others.

84.A: According to research findings, teacher learning environment strategies that produce high student engagement and low student misbehavior include focusing on the whole class when alerting student attention (a); communicating teacher awareness of student behaviors to students (b); designing and implementing overlapping activities (c); and lesson planning and delivery that enable instructional momentum (d).

85. A: Teachers who are aware of individual students' group roles as a part of group dynamics apply their understanding to manage their classrooms by developing friendly relationships with students who play roles in groups of leaders, instigators, and consciences; they also do this by developing strategies for keeping students who play group roles of procurers and negotiators on-task (c) rather than developing friendly relationships with them (b), and rather than by applying both strategies equally with students in all roles (d).

86. C: Embarrassing students in front of classmates and/or punishing them do NOT prevent, but actually incite, individual and group student rebellion. Showing interest in student work and encouraging students (a), alerting students to change their behaviors through physical proximity and touch (b), reminding students of times when they succeeded and modifying lesson presentations (d) to be more interesting than any distractors are all low-impact teacher interventions that prevent undesirable student behaviors from escalating.

87. C: Considering developmental levels for positive classroom environments, teachers can observe children's levels/types of play (unoccupied, independent, onlooker, parallel, associative, cooperative) and offer them not only matching activities (a), but also experiences at the next higher levels/types. Teachers must remember that older elementary and middle school students have not developed the social interaction skills of high school students, and accordingly guide them in peer collaboration (b). They should not expect new preschoolers to share, but instead should model, encourage, and reward sharing (c). For high school students, teachers can extend learning environments beyond classrooms (d) to surrounding communities, including service projects.

88. B: According to Mildred Parten (1932), play indicated social maturity from least to most as unoccupied behavior; independent or solitary play (a); watching others playing (c); playing near but not directly with others (d); playing with others but without structure or rules (b); and playing cooperatively with others, including interest in both the activity and the players as well as structure, rules, and interpersonal interaction. To stimulate growth, the teacher should offer students opportunities to play at the next higher level, i.e., offer those playing associatively (b) opportunities for full cooperative play.

89. D: To create supportive classroom climates, teachers should arrange the furniture and materials to promote student comfort (a), dialogue (b), ownership (c), and collaboration (d).

- 153 -

90. A: To communicate high expectations to all students, teachers should identify students they expect less from as soon as possible, because it is hard to accept or modify negative expectations already formed. Research finds student similarities influence teacher expectations, though teachers resist admitting this; therefore, experts advise teachers to identify similarities (b) for actively preventing biases from controlling their thoughts and/or behaviors. Since teacher behaviors have more influence than teacher expectations, not vice versa (c), teachers must identify their different behaviors toward low-expectancy students. They must also consciously treat high- and low-expectancy students the same, not differently (d).

91. D: Research studies have identified that teachers ask students they expect less from less challenging questions (a) than they ask others; call on them less often (b) than on others; explore their answers in less depth (c) than others' answers; and reward less rigorous responses from them (d) than the responses they reward from other students.

92. A: The right to academic freedom of expression is a right of teachers under the First Amendment. The rights to protection against discrimination (b), due process in termination notice (c), and establishing student behavior rules (d) are all rights of teachers under the Fourteenth Amendment.

93. D: The IDEA legislation guarantees parents due process rights to advance notice (a), and also to refuse (b), not only identification and evaluation (c) of their children for, but also placement of their children in, special education and related services.

94. A: A free, appropriate public education (in the least restrictive environment possible) is a federal right guaranteed to students with qualifying disabilities under the IDEA. Reporting dangerous behaviors (b) to school staff is a student responsibility that varies by state or school district. Student rights to advocate for changes in policy (c) or law and to peaceful dispute resolution (d) also vary by state or district.

95. D: A Resident Teacher is one who is not a student teacher, not yet a teacher of record but being paid, and completing a practicum or residency supervised by a Master Teacher (c). A Novice Teacher (a) has certification but is still developing with a Master Teacher's partnership, and does not have but is eligible for tenure. A Teacher Leader (b), the highest level, works partly with administrators/leadership teams and partly in classrooms. A Master Teacher (c) is a key leadership team member, leading school teams and also sometimes working in both classrooms and faculty support.

96. A: ED identifies Professional Teachers as tenured teachers who coach and advocate academically, serve as examples of lifelong learning, and often stay at this level throughout their teaching careers. ED identifies Resident Teachers (b) as paid teachers, but not teachers of record and not student teachers, who are completing their supervised residency or practicum required for certification. ED identifies Master Teachers (c) as school team leaders, classroom teachers, faculty support providers, and professional team teaching resources and models, and further identifies Teacher Leaders (d) as combining leadership and teaching, designing review/evaluation systems, and developing practice communities.

97. C: Teacher Leaders (a) and Master Teachers (b) are at the ED levels most likely to become school principals if they have the necessary development. Professional Teachers (d) have tenure, set examples for students and colleagues for lifelong learning, and provide academic coaching and advocacy as well as effective instruction; however, according to ED, they often spend their whole careers at the Professional Teacher level rather than moving into administrator positions.

98. D: Because inclusive education is a federal legal mandate and mainstreaming is the commonest means of compliance today, regular classroom teachers most often have the responsibility for the instruction of special-needs students—even if these students are also assigned educational specialists (a), special education teachers (b), and whichever therapists are most applicable (c) to an individual student's needs. Classroom teachers collaborate with these personnel, but still usually have the main responsibility for instruction.

99. D: Because of diverse student needs, teachers are required to ensure educational equity by differentiating their instruction accordingly with student abilities (a), offering equal opportunities to all students (b), treating all students fairly (c), and choosing and/or adapting instructional materials to reflect multicultural perspectives (d) to which multicultural students can relate.

100. B: Teachers are legally and ethically required to keep student records confidential (a) and also to protect the privacy of any or all student personal information. By copyright law, teachers are legally required both to seek and get permission (c) from either authors or publishers (d) to utilize copyrighted materials as teaching resources.

How to Overcome Test Anxiety

Just the thought of taking a test is enough to make most people a little nervous. A test is an important event that can have a long-term impact on your future, so it's important to take it seriously and it's natural to feel anxious about performing well. But just because anxiety is normal, that doesn't mean that it's helpful in test taking, or that you should simply accept it as part of your life. Anxiety can have a variety of effects. These effects can be mild, like making you feel slightly nervous, or severe, like blocking your ability to focus or remember even a simple detail.

If you experience test anxiety—whether severe or mild—it's important to know how to beat it. To discover this, first you need to understand what causes test anxiety.

Causes of Test Anxiety

While we often think of anxiety as an uncontrollable emotional state, it can actually be caused by simple, practical things. One of the most common causes of test anxiety is that a person does not feel adequately prepared for their test. This feeling can be the result of many different issues such as poor study habits or lack of organization, but the most common culprit is time management. Starting to study too late, failing to organize your study time to cover all of the material, or being distracted while you study will mean that you're not well prepared for the test. This may lead to cramming the night before, which will cause you to be physically and mentally exhausted for the test. Poor time management also contributes to feelings of stress, fear, and hopelessness as you realize you are not well prepared but don't know what to do about it.

Other times, test anxiety is not related to your preparation for the test but comes from unresolved fear. This may be a past failure on a test, or poor performance on tests in general. It may come from comparing yourself to others who seem to be performing better or from the stress of living up to expectations. Anxiety may be driven by fears of the future—how failure on this test would affect your educational and career goals. These fears are often completely irrational, but they can still negatively impact your test performance.

> **Review Video: 3 Reasons You Have Test Anxiety**
> Visit mometrix.com/academy and enter code: 428468

Elements of Test Anxiety

As mentioned earlier, test anxiety is considered to be an emotional state, but it has physical and mental components as well. Sometimes you may not even realize that you are suffering from test anxiety until you notice the physical symptoms. These can include trembling hands, rapid heartbeat, sweating, nausea, and tense muscles. Extreme anxiety may lead to fainting or vomiting. Obviously, any of these symptoms can have a negative impact on testing. It is important to recognize them as soon as they begin to occur so that you can address the problem before it damages your performance.

> **Review Video:** 3 Ways to Tell You Have Test Anxiety
> Visit mometrix.com/academy and enter code: 927847

The mental components of test anxiety include trouble focusing and inability to remember learned information. During a test, your mind is on high alert, which can help you recall information and stay focused for an extended period of time. However, anxiety interferes with your mind's natural processes, causing you to blank out, even on the questions you know well. The strain of testing during anxiety makes it difficult to stay focused, especially on a test that may take several hours. Extreme anxiety can take a huge mental toll, making it difficult not only to recall test information but even to understand the test questions or pull your thoughts together.

> **Review Video:** How Test Anxiety Affects Memory
> Visit mometrix.com/academy and enter code: 609003

Effects of Test Anxiety

Test anxiety is like a disease—if left untreated, it will get progressively worse. Anxiety leads to poor performance, and this reinforces the feelings of fear and failure, which in turn lead to poor performances on subsequent tests. It can grow from a mild nervousness to a crippling condition. If allowed to progress, test anxiety can have a big impact on your schooling, and consequently on your future.

Test anxiety can spread to other parts of your life. Anxiety on tests can become anxiety in any stressful situation, and blanking on a test can turn into panicking in a job situation. But fortunately, you don't have to let anxiety rule your testing and determine your grades. There are a number of relatively simple steps you can take to move past anxiety and function normally on a test and in the rest of life.

> **Review Video:** How Test Anxiety Impacts Your Grades
> Visit mometrix.com/academy and enter code: 939819

Physical Steps for Beating Test Anxiety

While test anxiety is a serious problem, the good news is that it can be overcome. It doesn't have to control your ability to think and remember information. While it may take time, you can begin taking steps today to beat anxiety.

Just as your first hint that you may be struggling with anxiety comes from the physical symptoms, the first step to treating it is also physical. Rest is crucial for having a clear, strong mind. If you are tired, it is much easier to give in to anxiety. But if you establish good sleep habits, your body and mind will be ready to perform optimally, without the strain of exhaustion. Additionally, sleeping well helps you to retain information better, so you're more likely to recall the answers when you see the test questions.

Getting good sleep means more than going to bed on time. It's important to allow your brain time to relax. Take study breaks from time to time so it doesn't get overworked, and don't study right before bed. Take time to rest your mind before trying to rest your body, or you may find it difficult to fall asleep.

> **Review Video: The Importance of Sleep for Your Brain**
> Visit mometrix.com/academy and enter code: 319338

Along with sleep, other aspects of physical health are important in preparing for a test. Good nutrition is vital for good brain function. Sugary foods and drinks may give a burst of energy but this burst is followed by a crash, both physically and emotionally. Instead, fuel your body with protein and vitamin-rich foods.

Also, drink plenty of water. Dehydration can lead to headaches and exhaustion, especially if your brain is already under stress from the rigors of the test. Particularly if your test is a long one, drink water during the breaks. And if possible, take an energy-boosting snack to eat between sections.

> **Review Video: How Diet Can Affect your Mood**
> Visit mometrix.com/academy and enter code: 624317

Along with sleep and diet, a third important part of physical health is exercise. Maintaining a steady workout schedule is helpful, but even taking 5-minute study breaks to walk can help get your blood pumping faster and clear your head. Exercise also releases endorphins, which contribute to a positive feeling and can help combat test anxiety.

When you nurture your physical health, you are also contributing to your mental health. If your body is healthy, your mind is much more likely to be healthy as well. So take time to rest, nourish your body with healthy food and water, and get moving as much as possible. Taking these physical steps will make you stronger and more able to take the mental steps necessary to overcome test anxiety.

> **Review Video: How to Stay Healthy and Prevent Test Anxiety**
> Visit mometrix.com/academy and enter code: 877894

Mental Steps for Beating Test Anxiety

Working on the mental side of test anxiety can be more challenging, but as with the physical side, there are clear steps you can take to overcome it. As mentioned earlier, test anxiety often stems from lack of preparation, so the obvious solution is to prepare for the test. Effective studying may be the most important weapon you have for beating test anxiety, but you can and should employ several other mental tools to combat fear.

First, boost your confidence by reminding yourself of past success—tests or projects that you aced. If you're putting as much effort into preparing for this test as you did for those, there's no reason you should expect to fail here. Work hard to prepare; then trust your preparation.

Second, surround yourself with encouraging people. It can be helpful to find a study group, but be sure that the people you're around will encourage a positive attitude. If you spend time with others who are anxious or cynical, this will only contribute to your own anxiety. Look for others who are motivated to study hard from a desire to succeed, not from a fear of failure.

Third, reward yourself. A test is physically and mentally tiring, even without anxiety, and it can be helpful to have something to look forward to. Plan an activity following the test, regardless of the outcome, such as going to a movie or getting ice cream.

When you are taking the test, if you find yourself beginning to feel anxious, remind yourself that you know the material. Visualize successfully completing the test. Then take a few deep, relaxing breaths and return to it. Work through the questions carefully but with confidence, knowing that you are capable of succeeding.

Developing a healthy mental approach to test taking will also aid in other areas of life. Test anxiety affects more than just the actual test—it can be damaging to your mental health and even contribute to depression. It's important to beat test anxiety before it becomes a problem for more than testing.

> **Review Video: Test Anxiety and Depression**
> Visit mometrix.com/academy and enter code: 904704

Study Strategy

Being prepared for the test is necessary to combat anxiety, but what does being prepared look like? You may study for hours on end and still not feel prepared. What you need is a strategy for test prep. The next few pages outline our recommended steps to help you plan out and conquer the challenge of preparation.

Step 1: Scope Out the Test

Learn everything you can about the format (multiple choice, essay, etc.) and what will be on the test. Gather any study materials, course outlines, or sample exams that may be available. Not only will this help you to prepare, but knowing what to expect can help to alleviate test anxiety.

Step 2: Map Out the Material

Look through the textbook or study guide and make note of how many chapters or sections it has. Then divide these over the time you have. For example, if a book has 15 chapters and you have five days to study, you need to cover three chapters each day. Even better, if you have the time, leave an extra day at the end for overall review after you have gone through the material in depth.

If time is limited, you may need to prioritize the material. Look through it and make note of which sections you think you already have a good grasp on, and which need review. While you are studying, skim quickly through the familiar sections and take more time on the challenging parts. Write out your plan so you don't get lost as you go. Having a written plan also helps you feel more in control of the study, so anxiety is less likely to arise from feeling overwhelmed at the amount to cover.

Step 3: Gather Your Tools

Decide what study method works best for you. Do you prefer to highlight in the book as you study and then go back over the highlighted portions? Or do you type out notes of the important information? Or is it helpful to make flashcards that you can carry with you? Assemble the pens, index cards, highlighters, post-it notes, and any other materials you may need so you won't be distracted by getting up to find things while you study.

If you're having a hard time retaining the information or organizing your notes, experiment with different methods. For example, try color-coding by subject with colored pens, highlighters, or post-it notes. If you learn better by hearing, try recording yourself reading your notes so you can listen while in the car, working out, or simply sitting at your desk. Ask a friend to quiz you from your flashcards, or try teaching someone the material to solidify it in your mind.

Step 4: Create Your Environment

It's important to avoid distractions while you study. This includes both the obvious distractions like visitors and the subtle distractions like an uncomfortable chair (or a too-comfortable couch that makes you want to fall asleep). Set up the best study environment possible: good lighting and a comfortable work area. If background music helps you focus, you may want to turn it on, but otherwise keep the room quiet. If you are using a computer to take notes, be sure you don't have any other windows open, especially applications like social media, games, or anything else that could distract you. Silence your phone and turn off notifications. Be sure to keep water close by so you stay hydrated while you study (but avoid unhealthy drinks and snacks).

Also, take into account the best time of day to study. Are you freshest first thing in the morning? Try to set aside some time then to work through the material. Is your mind clearer in the afternoon or evening? Schedule your study session then. Another method is to study at the same time of day that you will take the test, so that your brain gets used to working on the material at that time and will be ready to focus at test time.

Step 5: Study!

Once you have done all the study preparation, it's time to settle into the actual studying. Sit down, take a few moments to settle your mind so you can focus, and begin to follow your study plan. Don't give in to distractions or let yourself procrastinate. This is your time to prepare so you'll be ready to fearlessly approach the test. Make the most of the time and stay focused.

Of course, you don't want to burn out. If you study too long you may find that you're not retaining the information very well. Take regular study breaks. For example, taking five minutes out of every hour to walk briskly, breathing deeply and swinging your arms, can help your mind stay fresh.

As you get to the end of each chapter or section, it's a good idea to do a quick review. Remind yourself of what you learned and work on any difficult parts. When you feel that you've mastered the material, move on to the next part. At the end of your study session, briefly skim through your notes again.

But while review is helpful, cramming last minute is NOT. If at all possible, work ahead so that you won't need to fit all your study into the last day. Cramming overloads your brain with more information than it can process and retain, and your tired mind may struggle to recall even previously learned information when it is overwhelmed with last-minute study. Also, the urgent nature of cramming and the stress placed on your brain contribute to anxiety. You'll be more likely to go to the test feeling unprepared and having trouble thinking clearly.

So don't cram, and don't stay up late before the test, even just to review your notes at a leisurely pace. Your brain needs rest more than it needs to go over the information again. In fact, plan to finish your studies by noon or early afternoon the day before the test. Give your brain the rest of the day to relax or focus on other things, and get a good night's sleep. Then you will be fresh for the test and better able to recall what you've studied.

Step 6: Take a practice test

Many courses offer sample tests, either online or in the study materials. This is an excellent resource to check whether you have mastered the material, as well as to prepare for the test format and environment.

Check the test format ahead of time: the number of questions, the type (multiple choice, free response, etc.), and the time limit. Then create a plan for working through them. For example, if you have 30 minutes to take a 60-question test, your limit is 30 seconds per question. Spend less time on the questions you know well so that you can take more time on the difficult ones.

If you have time to take several practice tests, take the first one open book, with no time limit. Work through the questions at your own pace and make sure you fully understand them. Gradually work up to taking a test under test conditions: sit at a desk with all study materials put away and set a timer. Pace yourself to make sure you finish the test with time to spare and go back to check your answers if you have time.

After each test, check your answers. On the questions you missed, be sure you understand why you missed them. Did you misread the question (tests can use tricky wording)? Did you forget the information? Or was it something you hadn't learned? Go back and study any shaky areas that the practice tests reveal.

Taking these tests not only helps with your grade, but also aids in combating test anxiety. If you're already used to the test conditions, you're less likely to worry about it, and working through tests until you're scoring well gives you a confidence boost. Go through the practice tests until you feel comfortable, and then you can go into the test knowing that you're ready for it.

Test Tips

On test day, you should be confident, knowing that you've prepared well and are ready to answer the questions. But aside from preparation, there are several test day strategies you can employ to maximize your performance.

First, as stated before, get a good night's sleep the night before the test (and for several nights before that, if possible). Go into the test with a fresh, alert mind rather than staying up late to study.

Try not to change too much about your normal routine on the day of the test. It's important to eat a nutritious breakfast, but if you normally don't eat breakfast at all, consider eating just a protein bar. If you're a coffee drinker, go ahead and have your normal coffee. Just make sure you time it so that the caffeine doesn't wear off right in the middle of your test. Avoid sugary beverages, and drink enough water to stay hydrated but not so much that you need a restroom break 10 minutes into the test. If your test isn't first thing in the morning, consider going for a walk or doing a light workout before the test to get your blood flowing.

Allow yourself enough time to get ready, and leave for the test with plenty of time to spare so you won't have the anxiety of scrambling to arrive in time. Another reason to be early is to select a good seat. It's helpful to sit away from doors and windows, which can be distracting. Find a good seat, get out your supplies, and settle your mind before the test begins.

When the test begins, start by going over the instructions carefully, even if you already know what to expect. Make sure you avoid any careless mistakes by following the directions.

Then begin working through the questions, pacing yourself as you've practiced. If you're not sure on an answer, don't spend too much time on it, and don't let it shake your confidence. Either skip it and come back later, or eliminate as many wrong answers as possible and guess among the remaining ones. Don't dwell on these questions as you continue—put them out of your mind and focus on what lies ahead.

Be sure to read all of the answer choices, even if you're sure the first one is the right answer. Sometimes you'll find a better one if you keep reading. But don't second-guess yourself if you do immediately know the answer. Your gut instinct is usually right. Don't let test anxiety rob you of the information you know.

If you have time at the end of the test (and if the test format allows), go back and review your answers. Be cautious about changing any, since your first instinct tends to be correct, but make sure you didn't misread any of the questions or accidentally mark the wrong answer choice. Look over any you skipped and make an educated guess.

At the end, leave the test feeling confident. You've done your best, so don't waste time worrying about your performance or wishing you could change anything. Instead, celebrate the successful completion of this test. And finally, use this test to learn how to deal with anxiety even better next time.

> **Review Video:** 5 Tips to Beat Test Anxiety
> Visit mometrix.com/academy and enter code: 570656

Important Qualification

Not all anxiety is created equal. If your test anxiety is causing major issues in your life beyond the classroom or testing center, or if you are experiencing troubling physical symptoms related to your anxiety, it may be a sign of a serious physiological or psychological condition. If this sounds like your situation, we strongly encourage you to seek professional help.

Thank You

We at Mometrix would like to extend our heartfelt thanks to you, our friend and patron, for allowing us to play a part in your journey. It is a privilege to serve people from all walks of life who are unified in their commitment to building the best future they can for themselves.

The preparation you devote to these important testing milestones may be the most valuable educational opportunity you have for making a real difference in your life. We encourage you to put your heart into it—that feeling of succeeding, overcoming, and yes, conquering will be well worth the hours you've invested.

We want to hear your story, your struggles and your successes, and if you see any opportunities for us to improve our materials so we can help others even more effectively in the future, please share that with us as well. **The team at Mometrix would be absolutely thrilled to hear from you!** So please, send us an email (support@mometrix.com) and let's stay in touch.

If you'd like some additional help, check out these other resources we offer for your exam:

http://MometrixFlashcards.com/ABCTE

Additional Bonus Material

Due to our efforts to try to keep this book to a manageable length, we've created a link that will give you access to all of your additional bonus material.

Please visit http://www.mometrix.com/bonus948/abcteprotk to access the information.